ENCYCLOPEDIA
OF
WORLD
GEOGRAPHY

SECOND EDITION

ENCYCLOPEDIA
OF
WORLD
GEOGRAPHY

SECOND EDITION

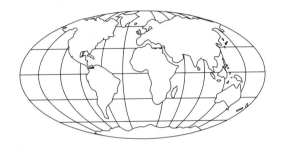

VOLUME TWENTY-ONE
Southeast Asia

Marshall Cavendish
New York · Toronto · Sydney

2002 Reference Edition

Marshall Cavendish Corporation
99 White Plains Road
Tarrytown, New York 10591-9001

www.marshallcavendish.com

AN ANDROMEDA BOOK

Planned and produced by
Andromeda Oxford Ltd
11–13 The Vineyard, Abingdon,
Oxfordshire OX14 3PX, England

www.andromeda.co.uk

Copyright © Andromeda Oxford Ltd
2002

**Library of Congress
Cataloging-in-Publication Data**

Encyclopedia of world geography /
[general advisory editor, Peter
Haggett].-- 2nd ed.
        p. cm.
    Includes bibliographical references
and index.
    ISBN 0-7614-7289-4 (set)
    ISBN 0-7614-7310-6 (v. 21)
    1. Geography--Encyclopedias.
I. Haggett, Peter.
    G133 .E48 2001
    910--dc21

                                    2001028437

Printed by: L.E.G.O. S.p.A., Vicenza,
Italy

06 05 04 03 02 01   6 5 4 3 2 1

This page: *Elaborate handcarving using
local hardwood*
Title page: *The Orangutan,* Pongo
pygmaeus, *one of the region's
endangered species*

CONTENTS

INTRODUCTION

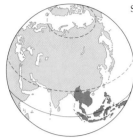

Southeast Asia

SOUTHEAST ASIA COMPRISES A MAINLAND PENINSULA (containing Myanmar, Thailand, Laos, Cambodia, Vietnam and Malaysia) and some 20,000 or more islands that lie on either side of the Equator. The region straddles the boundaries of the Eurasian, Pacific and Indo-Australian tectonic plates, and the movements of these plates have shaped much of the physical landscape. They created the mountain chains that curve from Myanmar to Indonesia, formed Sulawesi's strange contorted shape and molded the innumerable volcanoes scattered around the region. Krakatau, an island off Java, was the scene of the world's greatest modern volcanic eruption in 1883. The hypothetical boundary known as Wallace's Line runs through Southeast Asia separating the Indomalayan and Australasian biogeographical regions, each of which have quite distinctive plants and animals. They include the Javanese rhino, the dipterocarp trees, the *Rafflesia* (producing the largest flower in the world), the Komodo dragon and families of flying mammals adapted to the dense rainforests. Many of these, including the Balinese tiger and the Sumatran elephant are threatened by extinction as the growing population searches for land.

The region is one of the world's great crossroads. In ancient times it was strategically located on the trade routes between the great trading civilizations of China and India. Today it is ideally placed between international trading blocs, and Singapore is still one of the world's major commercial centers. In the 18th century China, the Netherlands and several other nations sent traders to the region in search of spices, tropical fruits and minerals. They brought their own religions, including Islam, Hinduism, Christianity and Buddhism. Many, particularly the Chinese, settled in the region, creating a blend of faiths and cultures that accounts for both the dynamic forces in the region and its political tensions. In the 20th century, the region was caught up in the ideological rivalries between capitalism and communism, leading to prolonged war and civil conflict on the mainland, which persisted longest in Cambodia.

The region's 531.6 million people, a high percentage of whom are under 15 years old, represent a massive resource that is driving rapid economic growth, even in formerly communist countries. Today Thailand, Malaysia and Indonesia are the world's emerging industrial economies; all three are within the Japanese economic orbit. However, they are also beginning to pay the price of success, as economic growth has begun to endanger the region's tropical forests and coral reefs.

North America

Central and South America

A	ALBANIA
AU	AUSTRIA
B	BELGIUM
BO	BOSNIA HERZEGOVINA
C	CROATIA
CZ	CZECH REPUBLIC
HUN	HUNGARY
M	MACEDONIA (FORMER YUGOSLAV REPUBLIC OF)
N	NETHERLANDS
R	RUSSIA
S	SLOVAKIA
SL	SLOVENIA
SW	SWITZERLAND
YU	YUGOSLAVIA

Europe

Asia

GREENLAND
(Denmark)

SVALBARD
(Norway)

ICELAND

NORWAY
SWEDEN
FINLAND
ESTONIA
LATVIA
LITHUANIA

UNITED
KINGDOM
DENMARK
BELARUS

IRELAND

RUSSIA

N
GERMANY POLAND
B
LUXEMBOURG CZ
FRANCE SW AU HUN UKRAINE
SL S MOLDOVA
C BO ROMANIA
ANDORRA YU
ITALY A M BULGARIA
PORTUGAL SPAIN GREECE ARMENIA
GIBRALTAR TURKEY
(UK)
MALTA
TUNISIA CYPRUS SYRIA
LEBANON
MOROCCO IRAQ IRAN

KAZAKHSTAN
MONGOLIA

AZERBAIJAN
GEORGIA
TURKMENISTAN UZBEKISTAN
KYRGYZSTAN
TAJIKISTAN

CHINA

NORTH
KOREA
SOUTH
KOREA
JAPAN

WESTERN
SAHARA
(Morocco)

ALGERIA LIBYA
EGYPT
ISRAEL
JORDAN
BAHRAIN
SAUDI
ARABIA
OMAN
QATAR
KUWAIT
AFGHANISTAN
PAKISTAN
NEPAL
BHUTAN

BANGLADESH
MYANMAR LAOS

TAIWAN

NORTHERN
MARIANA
ISLANDS
(United States)

MAURITANIA
MALI NIGER CHAD
SUDAN
ERITREA
YEMEN
DJIBOUTI

INDIA
THAILAND VIETNAM
CAMBODIA

PHILIPPINES

GUAM
(United States)

CAPE
VERDE
SENEGAL
MBIA
INEA-
SSAU GUINEA
SIERRA LEONE
LIBERIA
CÔTE
D'IVOIRE
BURKINA
FASO
BENIN
NIGERIA
TOGO
GHANA
CENTRAL
AFRICAN
REPUBLIC
ETHIOPIA
SOMALIA

UNITED ARAB
EMIRATES

SRI LANKA

BRUNEI

PALAU

FEDERATED STATES
OF MICRONESIA

EQUATORIAL GUINEA
CAMEROON
SAO TOME
& PRINCIPE
GABON
REPUBLIC OF CONGO
CABINDA
(Angola)
DEMOCRATIC
REPUBLIC
OF
CONGO
RWANDA
BURUNDI
UGANDA
KENYA
TANZANIA

MALDIVES

MALAYSIA

SINGAPORE

INDONESIA

PAPUA
NEW GUINEA

NAURU

SOLOMON
ISLANDS

SEYCHELLES

COMOROS

ANGOLA
ZAMBIA
MALAWI
ZIMBABWE
NAMIBIA
BOTSWANA
MOZAMBIQUE
MADAGASCAR
MAURITIUS
REUNION
(France)

VANUATU

NEW
CALEDONIA
(France)

SWAZILAND
SOUTH
AFRICA
LESOTHO

AUSTRALIA

NEW
ZEALAND

Africa

Australasia, Oceania and Antarctica

Antarctica

2888

Southeast Asia

COUNTRIES IN THE REGION

MYANMAR · LAOS · THAILAND · CAMBODIA
VIETNAM · MALAYSIA · SINGAPORE · BRUNEI
INDONESIA · PHILIPPINES

A trio of monks in Myanmar (*left*) stroll back to their Buddhist monastery. The mainland peninsula and roughly 20,000 tropical islands of Southeast Asia present a vibrant mosaic of different faiths and cultures, the mystical often jostling with the secular.

capital city ■
major town ●

height of land (meters)

3000
2000
1000
500
200
0

▲ mountain peak

Myanmar (Burma)

UNION OF MYANMAR

Myanmar (Burma) is the westernmost of the southeast Asian countries, with Bangladesh and India to the northwest, China to the northeast, and Laos and Thailand to the east. In 1989 the military government changed the official name of the country to Union of Myanmar, which is gradually obtaining international acceptance.

ENVIRONMENT

Myanmar consists, broadly, of a central lowland area enclosed by parallel ranges of forbidding mountains to the east and west. To the north a complex knot of mountains – part of the great Himalayas range – radiates out into branches.

The westernmost branch runs southwest along the Indian frontier, forming a series of densely forested ridges. The central ranges in the north dwindle rapidly, while the higher eastern branches run southeastward into China. From here, the Irrawaddy river flows south for some 2,100 km (1,300 mi), passing the ancient city of Mandalay and the modern capital, Rangoon, and ending in a broad flat delta where it enters the Andaman Sea.

To the east the land rises sharply, the broad uplands of the Shan Plateau adjoining further mountain ranges along the Laotian and Thai borders. Along the long neck of land in the southeast, which Myanmar shares with Thailand, are further mountainous ridges, notably the Tenasserim range.

Myanmar has a tropical monsoon climate moderated to a certain extent by altitude; only the coastal areas are consistently hot throughout the year. The mountains in the far north are subject to freezing winter temperatures, but act as a barrier to cold air from the north. Between May and October the southwest monsoon brings high humidity and torrential rains; up to 95 percent of the average annual rainfall of 2.5 m (15 ft) occurs during this period. A cooler dry period from October to February gives way to a hot season from March to mid-May when temperatures can soar to over 46°C (115°F) in Pagan, in central Myanmar. Rainfall is heaviest on the coastal ranges, and lightest in the central lowlands around Mandalay. About half the land area is still forested. Forests range from evergreen hardwoods in the wettest areas to hardier monsoon forest where the rainfall is less torrential. Scrubland is characteristic of the driest areas, and mangroves flourish around the deltas. Above 900 m (3,000 ft), pine and evergreen oak predominate, giving way to rhododendrons in the northern mountains.

Myanmar is rich in wildlife. Large mammals include elephants, tigers, leopards and bears, as well as small populations of rhinoceroses, wild water buffaloes and gaurs (Indian bison). The forests teem with gibbons and several kinds of monkeys. Reptiles include endangered crocodiles and gharials in the rivers, turtles along the coasts, and many species of snake, some of them highly venomous.

SOCIETY

Myanmar's two earliest civilizations were the Mon culture, founded in the south in about the 3rd century BC by the Buddhist Mon people from Thailand and Cambodia; and the Pyus people from the north, who established themselves in the Irrawaddy lowlands near Prome in central Myanmar. In the 9th century AD the Pyu lands were conquered by their northern

Coils of brass (*above*) twisted around her neck from the age of five give this Karenni woman the elongated neck considered elegant by her people. The weighty loops do not stretch the neck, but make it appear long by forcing the collarbones downward.

Ruined by time and earthquake (*left*) the great Buddhist temples of Pagan (the capital of Burma 1044–1287) testify to its ancient splendor. The city, sprawling for 16 sq km (6 sq miles), was founded in 849 AD but declined after being sacked by the Mongols.

neighbors and former subjects, the Burmans. In the 11th century a Burman king, Anawrahta (reigned 1044–77), united the whole country under his rule, with the city of Pagan its capital and heart of a Buddhist kingdom that flourished for 250 years. Pagan was eventually destroyed by the Mongols in 1287.

The Chinese invaded in the middle of the 17th century, once more plunging the whole area into war. Subsequently, the Burman leader Alaungpaya (ruled 1752–60) and his successors emerged as rulers. They began to extend their territory along the coast and westward into the Indian state of Assam, where they confronted the British in the first Anglo-Burmese war of

Basic technology A worker in a Myanmar lacquer factory uses an elementary machine to apply a coat of lacquer to a drum. Although its economy is improving, Myanmar remains technologically backward due to a longterm self-sufficiency that rejected Western aid.

NATIONAL DATA – MYANMAR

Land area 676,577 sq km (261,228 sq mi)

Climate	Altitude m (ft)	Temperatures		Annual precipitation mm (in)
		January °C (°F)	July °C (°F)	
Rangoon	23 (75)	25 (77)	27 (81)	2,618 (103.1)

Major physical features highest point: Hkakabo Razi 5,881 m (19,296 ft); longest river: Irrawaddy 1,092 km (1,300 mi)

Population (2000 est.) 41,734,853

Form of government military republic

Armed forces army 265,000; navy 12,000; air force 9,000

Largest cities Rangoon (capital – 3,938,900); Mandalay (1,037,300); Moulmein (360,400); Pegu (223,700)

Official language Burmese

Ethnic composition Burman 68%; Shan 9%; Karen 7%; Rakhine 4%; Chinese 3%; Mon 2%; Indian 2%; others 5%

Religious affiliations Buddhist 89%; Christian 4%; Muslim 4%; animist beliefs 1%; others 2%

Currency 1 kyat (K) = 100 pyas

Gross domestic product (1999) US $59.4 billion

Gross domestic product per capita (1999) US $1,200

Life expectancy at birth male 53.2 yr; female 56.3 yr

Major resources tin, petroleum, natural gas, lead, silver, tin, precious stones, copper, tungsten, rice, pulses, timber, opium

1824–26. As a result, the British acquired Assam, together with the Burmese states of Arakan and Tenasserim along the coast. A second war (1852–53) led to further losses; the British took Rangoon, and annexed Lower Burma. After the third Anglo-Burmese war (1885–86), the British made the entire Kingdom of Burma a province of India, a decision that greatly angered the Burmese. In 1937 Britain separated Burma from India, making it a crown colony, but independence was not granted until 1948, three years after the end of Japanese occupation (1942–45) in World War II.

In 1962 the country's civilian government was overthrown in a military coup led by General Ne Win (b. 1911). Over the next 12 years Ne Win and his Revolutionary Council nationalized banks and businesses and isolated the country from foreign contacts. In 1989 the country was renamed Myanmar. Following a further military coup, a multiparty election in May 1990 brought victory to the opposition parties. However, the military rulers refused to give up power, and imprisoned the party leaders. In April 1992 there was a mass expulsion of Indian Muslims.

Opposition leader, Aung San Suu Kyi, was released from house arrest in 1995 but restrictions on political freedom remain. The name of the government was changed to the State Peace and Development Council (SPDC) in November 1997. The military regime has made no commitment to a return to democracy in the near future.

Of the country's 41.7 million people the Burmans make up about 69 percent. They live mainly in the central lowlands and coastal districts. Among the many ethnic minority groups, the Karens of the far southeast, and the Chins and Kachins of the west and north, have close affinities with the Burmans. The ancient Mon people are now confined to central coastal districts. Altogether 100 or more different languages are spoken.

Myanmar has a long literary tradition, based on a writing system adapted from that of the Mon, who in turn inherited an even older Indian script. Buddhism is the dominant religion among most ethnic groups, and its beliefs have inspired Myanmar's artistic culture.

ECONOMY

Rice has been Myanmar's major crop and its principal export for well over a century. Other significant crops include cereals, cotton, peanuts and various pulses.

Traders at an inland floating market on Lake Inle, central Myanmar, sell to customers as they float by lakeside villages built on stilts. A relatively small percentage of the land in Myanmar is farmed for fruit and tree crops; bananas are sent to this area in bulk.

Forest hardwoods earn valuable foreign currency, as does the flourishing opium crop. Cattle are the main livestock, and fish, mostly caught at sea, are a vital part of the local diet.

Myanmar's rich mineral resources include sufficient natural gas and petroleum to meet domestic needs, as well as various metal ores, notably copper, tungsten and silver, and jade from the northern mountains. The country is also one of the world's chief sources of rubies and sapphires. Electricity is produced by both oil-fired and hydroelectric power plants.

Since independence there has been heavy investment in industry, especially petroleum and metal refining. The food and timber processing industries have also received new investment, and cottage industries have been subsidized.

Myanmar's roads and railroads are largely in the central and southern coastal lowlands. Few roads are surfaced, and most goods are carried by water. The Irrawaddy forms the main artery of a system of waterways that can bring small boats to any paddy that has surplus rice to sell; Rangoon is the chief port and trading center. The national airline operates domestic flights from Rangoon to other major cities, as well as international routes to Southeast Asian and Indian destinations. All the news media are owned and operated by the government.

Healthcare is free, but there is a serious shortage of medical supplies and modern drugs. Most of the population are still at the mercy of diseases such as malaria, cholera, hepatitis, tuberculosis and polio, and malnutrition is common among children. Primary education is free and compulsory, and some secondary education is available. There are six universities as well as vocational medical and technical higher education.

Laos

LAO PEOPLE'S DEMOCRATIC REPUBLIC

L AOS, BETWEEN THAILAND AND VIETNAM, IS the only landlocked state in Southeast Asia. The population, about 5.5 million, is one of the lowest in the region.

ENVIRONMENT

Northwestern Laos rises from the Mekong valley lowlands to the Xieng Khouang Plateau. North and east of the plateau the landscape becomes extremely mountainous. In the southwest the Mekong river forms the frontier with Thailand. The monsoon season between May and October is generally hot and humid with heavy rainfall. In the cooler dry season from November to late April

The thatch-roofed village of Nong Het, in northeastern Laos, suggests a rural idyll. In fact, life is basic for the majority of Laotian peasants who derive much of their income from rice – the country's principal crop – which they grow on small, irrigated holdings.

humidity and rainfall are low. More than half the land is forested.

SOCIETY

The first Lao peoples arrived from southwestern China in about the 8th century AD. In the following centuries Laos was invaded by the Burmese, Vietnamese and Thais before it was established as a French protectorate starting in 1893 and completed by treaties in 1904 and 1907.

Laos achieved independence in 1953 but the constitutional monarchy was opposed by the Communist Pathet Lao movement, which controlled the north. The conflict escalated in the 1960s, with the war in Vietnam. A ceasefire was signed in 1973, and in 1975 the Pathet Lao gained power. In 1991, a new constitution provided for a president to be elected five yearly by the national assembly but political parties are banned.

Four ethnic groups are officially recognized in Laos. The official Lao language is spoken primarily by the Lao-Lu, or valley Lao. The majority of Laotians are Theravada Buddhists.

ECONOMY

Agriculture accounts for more than three-quarters of the workforce. The largest single crop is rice. Opium, grown in northern Laos, has become an important (unofficial) cash crop; others are coffee, tobacco and cotton. The forests yield hardwood, spices and oils. There are reserves of coal, metal ores and precious

stones, but the manufacturing sector is limited to processing raw materials.

Most of the roads are unsurfaced, and there are no railroads in the interior. River traffic is the country's lifeline, linked to railroad terminals on the Thai bank. Health conditions are poor and life expectancy is short. Primary, secondary and some further education are available, but literacy levels are generally low.

NATIONAL DATA – LAOS

Land area	236,800 sq km (91,400 sq mi)			
Climate		**Temperatures**		**Annual**
	Altitude m (ft)	January °C (°F)	July °C (°F)	precipitation mm (in)
Vientiane	162 (531)	21 (70)	27 (81)	1,715 (67.5)

Major physical features highest point: Phou Bia 2,820 m (9,251 ft); longest river: Mekong (part) 4,180 km (2,600 mi)

Population (2000 est.) 5,497,459

Form of government one-party (Communist) republic with one legislative house

Armed forces army 33,000; navy 500; air force 3,500

Capital city Vientiane (632,200)

Official language Lao

Ethnic composition Lao 67.1%; Palaung-Wa 11.9%; Tai 7.9%; Miao/Yao 5.2%; Mon-Khmer 4.6%; others 3.3%

Religious affiliations Buddhist 57.8%; traditional beliefs 33.6%; nonreligious 4.8%; Christian 1.8%; Muslim 1.0%; others 1.0%

Currency 1 new kip (NK) = 100 at

Gross domestic product (1999) US $7 billion

Gross domestic product per capita (1999) US $1,300

Life expectancy at birth male 52.6 yr; female 55.9 yr

Major resources coal, tin, gold, gemstones, rice, coffee, opium, tobacco, timber, cotton, hydroelectric power

Thailand

KINGDOM OF THAILAND

THAILAND, KNOWN AS SIAM UNTIL 1939, IS AT the heart of the Indochinese peninsula in Southeast Asia. An independent kingdom for many centuries and one that has never known colonial rule – Thailand maintains strong ties with the West and with neighboring countries, and is renowned for both the beauty of its traditional culture and its graceful people.

ENVIRONMENT

Thailand is bordered by Myanmar to the west, Laos to the northeast and east, and Cambodia to the southeast. To the south it faces the Gulf of Thailand. The southwestern part of the country forms a long isthmus between the Andaman Sea and the Gulf of Thailand, meeting the border with Malaysia in the far south.

The land

Thailand is a tropical country of high mountains and rainforests, broad floodplains and sandy beaches. The highest land is in the far north, where a series of fold-mountain ranges are the last bastion of the great Himalayan chain. The deep, forested valleys form a picturesque backdrop to ancient temple sites, notably that of Wat Prathat, perched high on the slopes of the mountain Doi Suthep above the former royal city of Chiang Mai.

A range of mountains continues southward along the Myanmanese border and runs the full length of the southwestern isthmus. These mountains, lower than those farther north, drop steeply on the western side toward the Andaman Sea. The east coast, on the Gulf of Thailand, is gentler but equally indented, with hundreds of sandy bays along its length. Both coasts are fringed with beautiful islands, including Phuket, one of the largest.

The fertile central plains of the Chao Phraya river delta are the most densely populated part of the country, where most of its agricultural and commercial activities are concentrated. The capital, Bangkok, is in the south near the coast. This area in particular suffers regular and often severe seasonal flooding.

Eastern Thailand is occupied by the Khorat Plateau, a tilted platform made up of rolling sandstone hills. This forms a steep escarpment to the west overlooking the central plains and (to the south) the Cambodian border. A further range of hills in the far southeast of the country forms the continuation of the Cardamom Mountains of southern Cambodia.

Climate

Thailand has a tropical monsoon climate, with most of the annual rainfall occurring between May and September. In general,

Animal power An elephant, guided by its rider, uses intelligence and strength to lift a log higher onto the pile in Thailand's northern mountains. Several thousand elephants continue to be used in the lumber industry, being more suited than machines to the rough terrain.

Sewing to survive (*right*) A woman belonging to the Meo hill tribe near Chiang Mai, in northern Thailand, sits at her sewing machine as she makes clothes for the local townspeople. Such work, which brings in much-needed money, helps to complement the traditional (but illegal) earnings from the harvest of opium poppies.

White sands, clear water (*left*) The beach at Krabi Ao Pranang, on Thailand's rugged southwest coast beside the Andaman Sea, offers the kind of coastal beauty that lures tourists from around the world. Thailand receives several million foreign visitors every year, making tourism the country's largest source of foreign exchange

rainfall is lightest in the northeast and heaviest in the south and over the mountains, but this can vary greatly because of exposure to prevailing winds. Some parts of the west coast, especially along the isthmus, often receive at least four times as much rain as the east.

The climate is generally hot and humid throughout the year, with March and April the hottest months. It is rainy from June to October, and coolest between October and February when there are occasional frosts in the northern mountains. There are two separate monsoon seasons in the southwest.

Plants and animals

With much of the natural forest cover cleared for agriculture, less than one-third of the land is now forested, and most of this is in the more inaccessible northern areas. There, hardwoods predominate, particularly teak and resin-producing trees. Elsewhere the forests are tropical evergreens, with bamboos and palms.

Game hunting has reduced the wildlife considerably. Leopards and tigers are now rare, and rhinoceroses and tapirs nearly extinct. There are still a few elephants in the wild, but most of them have now been domesticated for use in agriculture and forestry. All kinds of reptiles are found, particularly lizards and snakes, and turtles are common along the sandy coasts of the south.

SOCIETY

Thailand, or "land of the free", though never colonized has not escaped foreign cultural and political influences, both from its neighbors and from the West.

History

The Thai people are believed to have arrived from southwestern China about a thousand years ago. In the 13th century the Sukhothai empire – with its own highly developed culture – was established in the north of the central plain. This was later absorbed by the Buddhist kingdom of Ayutthaya, which emerged farther south in about 1350. Ayutthaya itself was exposed to both cultural influence and the threat of invasion by neighboring Khmer (Cambodian) and Burmese kingdoms. The Khmers were defeated in the 1400s, but in 1767 a Burmese victory and occupation ended Ayutthaya rule.

The Burmese were soon ousted, however, and the Chakkri dynasty of monarchs was established in 1782 at the new capital of Bangkok; their succession has continued to the present day. By the middle of the 19th century the borders of Siam, as the country was then called, had expanded considerably and there was a huge influx of immigrants from China, who gradually came to dominate commercial life. Under the scholar-king Mongkut (reigned 1851–68) and his son Chulalongkorn (1868–1910) Thailand was ushered into the modern age: treaties of friendship and commerce were signed with the West, slavery was abolished and study abroad encouraged. It was Chulalongkorn who adroitly managed to preserve Thailand's independence in the face of the colonial powers; nevertheless, links with the West were strong – so much so that Thailand entered World War I in 1917 on the side of the Allies. (A token force of Thai troops was sent to fight in France.)

In 1932 a bloodless coup established a constitutional monarchy. This was the

NATIONAL DATA – THAILAND				
Land area 513,115 sq km (198,115 sq mi)				

Climate		**Temperatures**		**Annual**
	Altitude m (ft)	January °C (°F)	July °C (°F)	precipitation mm (in)
Bangkok	2 (7)	26 (78)	28 (83)	1,400 (55.1)

Major physical features highest point: Doi Inthanon 2,595 m (8,514 ft); longest river: Mekong (part) 4,180 km (2,600 mi)

Population (2000 est.) 61,230,874

Form of government multiparty constitutional monarchy

Armed forces army 150,000; navy 56,000; air force 43,000

Largest cities Bangkok (capital – 6,416,300); Nonthaburi (296,500) (243,000); Khorat (184,200); Chiang Mai (173,700)

Official language Thai

Ethnic composition Thai 75.0%; Chinese 14.0%; others 11.0%

Official religion Buddhism

Religious affiliations Buddhist 94.4%; Muslim 4.0%; Christian 0.5%; others 1.1%

Currency 1 baht (B) = 100 satang

Gross domestic product (1999) US $388.7 billion

Gross domestic product per capita (1999) US $6,400

Life expectancy at birth male 65.8 yr; female 72.0 yr

Major resources tin, tungsten, iron ore, lead, gypsum, tantalite, natural gas, oil, lignite, rice, maize, soybeans, sugar cane, cassava, sorghum, rubber, jute, livestock, timber, fisheries, tourism

first of a series of coups, with alternating periods of democratic and military rule. In 1939, Siam was renamed Thailand. During World War II, the country was forced into an alliance with Japan, but afterward, Thailand received massive economic and military support from the United States, which later used it as a base during their involvement in the Vietnam War (1965–73). Political instability was increased by wars in neighboring countries, guerrilla activity in border areas and a steady influx of refugees. In 1991 the government was toppled by a military coup led by General Suchinda Kraprayoon. He was prime minister for a month in 1992 when he was forced to resign after brutally crushing demonstrations calling for democratic reform. After the 1996 election a new constitution limited the power of the military and separated the executive, legislative and judicial branches of government.

Government

The monarchy is hereditary and there is a bicameral National Assembly. The head of government is the prime minister, who is required by a 1992 constitutional amendment to be an elected member of the House of Representatives. Under the 1996 constitution the Senate will consist of a 200-member elected body with members serving six-year terms and the House of Representatives, with 392 members, will become a 500-member body elected for four-year terms after 2000.

People

Most of the population (about 61 million) are ethnic Thais, including some 27 percent of Laotian origin. The large Chinese population (about 12 percent) lives mainly in urban areas, whereas people of Malay ancestry – who practice Islam – are concentrated mainly in the south. The northern hills and forests are inhabited by half a million non-Thai peoples, such as the Karen, Meo (or Mong, from their Mongolian looks), Lahu and Akha. Other non-Thais include Vietnamese and Khmer refugees, concentrated along the eastern border. The official language is Thai, but Chinese, Malay and English are widely spoken.

The vast majority of the population are Buddhist, and Thai culture reflects this, not only in its ornamental temples and religious art (sculptures – many of the Buddha – and mural paintings), but also in the popular festivals that accompany the many religious and royal ceremonies. The festivals are usually joyous occasions

Bangkok's Grand Palace (*left*), with its imposing buildings and ornate temples decorated with gilt, glass mosaic and Chinese ceramics, was begun in the late 18th century when the city was made the capital of Siam (Thailand's former name). Originally it was the center of the royal court, and entry was forbidden to lower-ranking citizens. Today, however, the complex is a major tourist draw for people from all over the world.

Rice terraces (*right*) hug the contours of a hillside near Mae Sariang in the northwest. Intensive cultivation has made the country the region's biggest rice exporter.

Metal finger-cones (*below right*) lend spiky grace to a Thai dancer's hands. Traditional Thai court dances have a rich repertoire of expressive movements that particularly emphasize the hands.

that may feature folk dancing, beauty contests, Thai boxing and fireworks. One of the most distinctive and the most obvious Thai architectural features of the temples are the roofs, which are steep, many-tiered and covered with colorful, glazed tiles. Classical dance in Thailand is modeled on Indian temple dancing, while classical Thai music is extremely percussive.

ECONOMY

Thailand's economy was largely agriculture-based until the 1990s. Services are now providing 49 percent of GDP, industry 39 percent and agriculture 12 percent. Strong growth rates encouraged foreign investment and speculation on Thailand's currency in 1997 led to an economic crisis that threatened to spread to other stock markets and to Western economies. A loan from the International Monetary Fund (IMF) and the implementation of an austerity program encouraged a return to modest economic growth by late 1999.

Agriculture and fisheries

Around one-half of the labor force are in agriculture, most of them working in the country's extensive paddy fields. Rice is the nation's primary staple and principal export; other major crops include maize, tapioca, sugar cane and soybeans. The hill peoples of northern Thailand have traditionally grown poppies for opium, but there have been recent efforts to introduce alternative cash crops, such as tea and tobacco. Cattle and buffalo are used mainly as draft animals, while pigs and poultry are raised for meat. Fish from the sea and freshwater varieties form a

major part of the Thai diet. Forestry contributes to the export trade, large eucalyptus plantations replacing the depleted teak, yang and rubber forests in the north of the country.

Industry and commerce

Thailand is one of the largest producers of tin. It also has other mineral resources such as iron ore, gypsum and tantalite (from which the rare, acid-resistant metal tantalum is extracted). The main source of power is offshore natural gas, reserves of oil, and brown coal (lignite). Manufacturing is smallscale and industrial activity is concentrated on the production of clothing, electrical goods, beer, cement, chemicals and motorcycles.

Since 1982 tourism has been Thailand's largest revenue earner, but the spread of AIDS is a cause of concern to the industry. More than 7 million tourists a year come to sample the night-life of Bangkok, to visit the religious sites, or to relax in one of the many coastal and island resorts.

Transportation and communications

Bangkok, with a population of over six million, is the center from which all transportation systems radiate. Railroads are well developed, whereas roads are often inadequate, especially in the more remote areas and in the rainy season. Rivers and canals, the traditional mode of transportation, are now less significant than the railroads. There are over 20 ports besides Bangkok, but most international trade is carried out through the capital, whose international airport is at the center of an extensive internal flight network.

Broadcasting is state-controlled and several radio and television stations are owned by the military. There are over 30 daily newspapers, several in Chinese.

Welfare and education

Social welfare systems are generally inadequate, but some help is given to those in most need. The government has tried to provide primary healthcare throughout the country, but there are still major health problems; infant mortality is high, and there is a serious shortage of trained medical staff and resources.

Education is free and compulsory for children aged from 7 to 15, and literacy levels are high. Several universities and institutions including colleges in the private sector offer higher education.

Cambodia

STATE OF CAMBODIA

CAMBODIA IS THE HOMELAND OF THE KHMER peoples of southern Indochina (the country is known by its own people as Kampuchea). One of the poorest states in the region, Cambodia suffered severely from involvement in the Vietnam War, and faces an uncertain future after three decades of internal and external conflict.

Riverside bustle (*above*) The shores of the Mekong river in Phnom Penh, capital of Cambodia, throng with people as fresh produce is unloaded from wooden barges, and a passenger boat, carrying cargo and bicycles on the top deck, docks at the pier.

Cleared for agriculture (*below*) Well-watered paddyfields in central Cambodia glint in the sun. The lowland forests have been cut down and replaced by fields of rice, the staple crop, which rely on seasonal flooding by the Mekong and Tonle Sap (Great Lake).

ENVIRONMENT

Cambodia is a mainly lowland country bordering Thailand to the northwest, Laos to the northeast, and Vietnam to the east and southeast; to the southwest it faces the Gulf of Thailand. Tonle Sap (the Great Lake) at the heart of Cambodia lies to the west of a wide alluvial plain fed by the waters of the Mekong river and its tributaries. Southwest of Tonle Sap, the Cardamom and Elephant Mountains overlook a narrow coastal plain.

The climate is generally hot, with high humidity and heavy rainfall between mid May and early October – the time of the southwest monsoon. From early November to mid March the dry season brings low humidity, sparse rainfall and gentle northeasterly winds.

Some 70 percent of Cambodia is covered by forest, ranging from broadleaf evergreens and deciduous woodlands in the north to dense tropical rainforests on the mountains overlooking the sea. Lowland areas support open forest and savanna grassland, with paddies, reeds and bamboo forest in the wetter floodplains of the rivers. Animal life includes elephants, tigers, leopards and bears, as well as many water birds along the rivers.

SOCIETY

About the 6th century AD the emerging Chenla empire took control of the area that is present-day Cambodia. Gradually, Khmer peoples arrived from the north, and after the breakup of Chenla in the 8th century a powerful Khmer dynasty emerged. Known as the Angkorian dynasty, it lasted until the 15th century. In 1863 Cambodia, by then little more than a puppet of Siam (modern Thailand) and Vietnam, was obliged to become a French protectorate, retaining its monarchy.

The Japanese occupied Cambodia in 1941, but French rule was reimposed after World War II. In 1955 the French granted independence, and in 1960 Prince Sihanouk (b. 1922), on the death of his father, became head of state. For the next 10 years, during the Vietnam War, Cambodia remained officially neutral, but Sihanouk allowed the communist North Vietnamese to operate against United States' forces from secret bases within the country. In 1970 Sihanouk was overthrown in a rightwing, pro-United States' coup led by General Lon Nol. The government tried to eradicate the Vietnamese presence but it was unsuccessful. The United States' Air Force took over the job, subjecting the country to an intense and often indiscriminate aerial bombardment that lasted until 1973. This drove many Cambodians to join the Khmer Rouge ("Red Cambodians") – a leftwing movement led by Pol Pot that soon took power in the countryside. In 1975 the capital Phnom Penh fell to the Khmer Rouge, and the government was ousted.

With Pol Pot as premier, the Khmer Rouge began to transform the entire society in the most brutal way. Whole

urban populations were moved onto the land and forced to work on vast irrigation and agricultural projects. Anyone regarded as in any way hostile to the regime was killed. By 1979, when Vietnamese troops and Cambodian rebels captured Phnom Penh, more than 2 million people had died through disease, starvation and mass execution. Although the Cambodian people were relieved to see the Khmer Rouge overthrown, the West and China did not welcome the establishment of a Vietnamese-backed regime at Phnom Penh. When, in 1982, the Khmer Rouge formed an alliance with other opposition groups, it won the overt diplomatic, and covert military, support of the West and China. Under pressure from the United States the Vietnamese withdrew in 1989. The long and bloody civil war came to an end in 1991, when Prince Sihanouk won an agreement to introduce power-sharing among all of the major factions, including the hated and feared Khmer Rouge. The first free elections were held in June 1993 under United Nations' supervision, with a coalition led by Sihanouk winning a majority. Under a new constitution in 1993 Sihanouk was elected king and appointed a new government. The Khmer Rouge was outlawed in 1994. Pol Pot was captured by Khmer Rouge dissidents in late 1997. He evaded being tried by an international court by committing suicide in 1998.

The great majority of Cambodia's people are Khmers, who speak their own language. Many are Buddhists, despite the suppression of all religion under the Pol Pot regime (1975– 79). The significant ethnic minorities are the Chinese and the Chams, said to be of Indonesian origin, and who are traditionally Muslims. Some 350,000 Cambodians live across the Thai border as refugees from the civil war.

ECONOMY

Cambodia lives by its rice crop, rice fields accounting for nearly 90 percent of arable land. Most people live and work as subsistence farmers. Besides rice, they also grow some fruit, and raise livestock; water buffalo are reared as draft animals. Tonle Sap is one of the world's richest sources of freshwater fish. Cambodia's vast forests are threatened by indiscriminate local tree-felling.

The country has limited mineral reserves, and electricity generation relies entirely on imported fuel. Manufacturing is confined to local processing of rubber and wood, and agricultural products.

Cambodia's road network dates from French colonial days. Few roads are surfaced, and many areas have no roads at all. Flooding is a problem in the rainy season, also affecting the country's vital waterway links. There are two railroads connecting Phnom Penh with Bangkok in Thailand and with Kompong Som, the country's only maritime port. Phnom Penh has an international airport. All press and broadcasting media are state-controlled.

Healthcare is gradually improving. However, diseases such as cholera and malaria cannot be controlled and malnutrition is common. Education was severely hit by the wars but children now receive six years of compulsory schooling and literacy is improving.

NATIONAL DATA – CAMBODIA

Land area 181,035 sq km (69,898 sq mi)

Climate	Altitude m (ft)	Temperatures		Annual precipitation mm (in)
		January °C (°F)	July °C (°F)	
Phnom Penh	12 (39)	26 (78)	29 (84)	1,308 (51.5)

Major physical features highest point: Mount Aural 1,813 m (5,948 ft); longest river: Mekong (part) 4,180 km (2,600 mi); largest lake: Tonle Sap 10,000 sq km (3,860 sq mi)

Population (2000 est.) 12,212,306

Form of government limited constitutional monarchy with one legislative house

Armed forces army 36,000; navy 1,000; air force 1,000

Capital city Phnom Penh (1,098,900)

Official language Khmer

Ethnic composition Khmer 90%; Vietnamese 5%; Chinese 1%; others 4%

Official religion Buddhism

Religious affiliations Buddhist 95%; others 5%

Currency 1 riel = 100 sen

Gross domestic product (1999) US $8.2 billion

Gross domestic product per capita (1999) US $710

Life expectancy at birth male 46.8 yr; female 49.7 yr

Major resources rice, fruit, livestock, timber, rubber, gemstones, fisheries

Vietnam

SOCIALIST REPUBLIC OF VIETNAM

Taking ducks to market (*above*) in a bicycle rickshaw in Ho Chi Minh City. Since the 1960s the city has been flooded with rural immigrants fleeing the war-torn countryside and setting up stalls and small businesses in the former open spaces of the old colonial city.

VIETNAM, ON THE EAST COAST OF THE INDO-chinese peninsula, has experienced centuries of foreign occupation, war and strife, and, more recently, partition. Today Vietnam is reunified and striving to rebuild its economy with the help of foreign aid, a strong government and its own considerable natural resources.

ENVIRONMENT

Vietnam is a long, narrow and largely mountainous country sharing a frontier with China to the north and bordered by Laos and Cambodia to the west. Its 2,500 km (1,600 mi) long coastline faces the Gulf of Tonkin to the northeast, the South China Sea to the east and south, and the Gulf of Thailand to the far southwest.

The land

Central Vietnam is dominated by the rugged mountains known as the Annam Highlands, whose crest mostly follows the western border. To the east lies a narrow coastal plain, and at either end sprawling floodplains, formed by the Red river delta in the northeast and the great Mekong river delta in the south. These fertile rice-growing plains are densely populated, even though the rivers often overflow their banks. Flooding is particularly severe in the Red river delta, where protective dikes have been built.

The central section of the Annam Highlands has several high peaks, while the southern part is broader, consisting of a series of dissected plateaus. The highest mountain ranges are in northwestern Vietnam, rising to 3,143 m (10,312 ft) on Fan Si Pan; the ranges extend westward and northward into Laos and China. In the far northeast, beyond the fertile plains of the Red river, the uplands become lower and gentler toward the border with southeastern China.

Climate

Vietnam has a tropical monsoon climate, but with considerable local variation. Summers are hot and humid everywhere; but in winter, only the north is relatively cool, while the south stays hot. Heavy rains fall between May and October, when there are also frequent typhoons. The winter months are drier, sunny and much less humid.

Plants and animals

The varied climate has helped produce a rich mix of vegetation, including tropical evergreen and subtropical deciduous

forests. Among the wide variety of trees are pine, teak and ebony. Mangrove forests grow along parts of the coast. The tropical forests cover two-fifths of the country, but deforestation has been remorseless – hardwoods are felled and exported for much-needed hard currency – and this has led to serious flooding and erosion. Government reforestation has not kept pace with the loss of forests. In addition the vegetation was severely damaged by the United States' military action (1965–73) in the Vietnam War, when the southern forests were sprayed with defoliant chemicals, in particular Agent Orange.

Vietnam's wildlife is rich and varied. The forests are home to a number of big cats – including tigers and leopards – as well as elephants, civets, bears and various species of monkeys and deer. Smaller mammals include mongooses, flying squirrels and porcupines. There are crocodiles along the river banks, 180 species of reptiles and 273 bird species. Sadly, uncontrolled and illegal hunting, as well as destruction of habitats has led to the extinction of many local animal populations. The tapir and Sumatran rhinoceros are already extinct, and the decline is set to continue.

SOCIETY

Throughout their history, the Vietnamese people have had to struggle for survival in the face of invasion and colonization by more powerful nations.

History

By 200 BC a Vietnamese nation had already been established on the delta plain of the Red river. However, for more than a thousand years the people were under the domination of China. It was not until 900 AD that the Vietnamese achieved independence. In the following centuries they repulsed Mongol and Chinese invasions, extended their borders southward along the coast, and consolidated their power. Later, it proved more difficult to sustain, and there were periods of civil war and division.

French missionaries began to arrive in the 17th century, but as their influence grew they attracted hostility, and many were expelled or executed. The French government intervened, at first on behalf of the missionaries, but later – in the mid 19th century – to further its own colonial ambitions. By 1883 Vietnam was a French colony made up of three territories: Tonkin in the north, Annam in the center, and Cochin China in the far south. French rule was deeply resented by the Vietnamese, and this gave rise to the growth of nationalist movements.

During World War II Vietnam was occupied by Japan. After Japan's defeat, Ho Chi Minh (1892–1969), leader of the communist-dominated League for Vietnamese Independence (Viet Minh), proclaimed an independent republic. But the French would not let go, and for eight years fought to regain their former possessions, until they were finally defeated at Dien Bien Phu in 1954. The international conference that ended the war partitioned the country, giving Ho Chi Minh's Viet Minh government control north of the 17th parallel, while anticommunists backed by the French were granted all the land to the south of the dividing line. It was agreed that elections would be held to reunify the country, but with the Viet Minh the most likely winners, the South Vietnamese prime minister, Ngo Dinh Diem (1901–63), supported by the United States, scuppered the agreement and declared South Vietnam an independent republic.

North Vietnam, backed by the Soviet Union, began a long military campaign to reunite the country. As guerrilla activity intensified, the United States intervened with economic and military aid for South Vietnam. American involvement in the war escalated: in 1965 the United States began bombing North Vietnam, and by 1968 there were more than half a million United States' troops in Vietnam. Eventually a combination of factors – opposition to the war at home, the loss of American lives and the persistence of the North Vietnamese – forced the United States to withdraw from Vietnam in 1973. The fighting continued, however, until the fall of Saigon in 1975 when the whole of Vietnam came under communist

Paddyfields at twilight (*left*) reflect the dying rays of the sun. Paddy rice is overwhelmingly the most important crop throughout the region. Production exceeds 100 million tonnes across Southeast Asia, supplying domestic demand and export markets.

NATIONAL DATA – VIETNAM

Land area 331,653 sq km (128,052 sq mi)

Climate	Altitude m (ft)	Temperatures January °C (°F)	July °C (°F)	Annual precipitation mm (in)
Hanoi	16 (52)	17 (62)	29 (84)	1,830 (72.0)

Major physical features highest point: Fan Si Pan 3,143 m (10,312 ft); longest rivers: Mekong (part) 4,180 km (2,600 mi): Red (part) 805 km (500 mi)

Population (2000 est.) 78,773,873

Form of government one-party communist republic with one legislative house

Armed forces army 500,000; navy 12,000; air force 15,000

Largest cities Ho Chi Minh City (3,380,100); Hanoi (capital – 1,376,100); Haiphong (570,800); Da Nang (446,00)

Official language Vietnamese

Ethnic composition Vietnamese 87.3%; Chinese 1.8%; Tai 1.7%; Thai 1.5%; Khmer 1.4%; Muong 1.3%; Nung 1.1%; others 3.9%

Religious affiliations Buddhist 55.3%; Roman Catholic 7.0%; Muslim 1.0%; others 36.7%

Currency 1 dong (D) = 10 hao = 100 xu

Gross domestic product (1999) US $143.1 billion

Gross domestic product per capita (1999) US $1,850

Life expectancy at birth male 65.7 yr; female 70.6 yr

Major resources coal, oil, natural gas, phosphates, chromite, gold, rice, tea, coffee, rubber, timber, fisheries

Freshly made nests of noodles (*above*) are spread out to dry in the sun before being packaged at a state-run noodle factory in Ho Chi Minh City, where they are made. Most of the wheat used for making the noodles – a staple food in Vietnam – has to be imported.

Cargo containers large and small (*right*) in Ho Chi Minh City's busy harbor (still called Saigon), which lies some 50 km (30 mi) from the south coast on the Mekong river delta. The deepwater port on Khank Ho island handles most of southern Vietnam's trade.

control. Following a series of single-party elections in 1976, the country was renamed the Socialist Republic of Vietnam.

The war had devastated the land and left millions homeless; thousands more refugees fled the country. In 1979 Vietnam invaded neighboring Cambodia to overthrow the Khmer Rouge regime, and China responded by invading Vietnam from the north. The Chinese forces were defeated, but only at the cost of many lives. During the 1980s Vietnam released over 10,000 political prisoners and gradually introduced limited economic liberalization although many "boat people" still fled to Hong Kong. Vietnam finally withdrew from Cambodia in 1989 and in the 1990s continued relations with China and the US and became a full member of the Association of South East Asian Nations (ASEAN). The US had removed its 30-year-old trade embargo against Vietnam in 1994 and in 2000 the two countries signed a landmark trade agreement.

Government

The 1992 constitution affirms the power of the Communist Party to guide the state according to Marxist–Leninist principles. The National Assembly is made up of 450 members, elected for five-year terms. This body elects the president, who appoints the prime minister and cabinet. The president heads a State Council which issues decrees when the Assembly is not sitting.

People

Most of the country's 78.7 million people are ethnic Vietnamese, but there are as many as 60 minority groups. These include members of neighboring nationalities, such as Chinese and Thais, as well as survivors of much older civilizations, such as the Cham and the Khmer. (Khmer form the majority in Cambodia.)

As Vietnam has been strongly influenced by China through the centuries, for a long time their languages were thought to be related. Recent research has shown, however, that Vietnamese is related to Khmer rather than to Chinese. Vietnamese is the official language, but French and the various ethnic minority languages are all in current use.

Religious allegiances reflect both ethnic divisions and past colonial influences. Buddhism is the principal religion, but Chinese Taoism and Confucianism are also important, and have strongly influenced local Buddhist practices. The large Roman Catholic minority (7 percent of the population) is a consequence of the past work of French missionaries.

ECONOMY

Vietnam is one of the poorest countries in the world. It is struggling to develop a

Faded elegance Late 19th-century homes built by the colonial French in Hanoi, the Vietnamese capital, still house Vietnamese families despite the ravages of war and neglect. Hanoi became the capital in 1010, when it was called Thang Long – "City of the Soaring Dragon".

modern economy, but is heavily dependent on foreign aid. Until the late 1980s the Soviet Union was both the chief trading partner and primary source of aid, but changes in international relations have led Vietnam to seek aid from other, formerly hostile, countries such as Australia and the US. In 1986 the Vietnamese implemented a policy aimed at reforming its centralized economic system.

Agriculture and fisheries
Agriculture employs 67 percent of the total labor force and accounts for 27 percent of GDP. Farming is concentrated in the two river delta areas, where rice, the principal staple and export crop, is grown; other crops include cassava and yams. Tea, coffee and rubber plantations have been established on the mountain slopes, and tropical fruit is cultivated throughout the country. Fish is the main staple apart from rice, with shellfish a substantial export commodity. Forestry too is expanding, but modernization has been slow, both in forestry and in fishing.

Industry
Vietnam is rich in natural resources, having large amounts of coal, phosphates and chromites as well as smaller deposits of other minerals, including gold. Crude oil production was nearly 8 million tonnes in 1995 and there are natural gas reserves. Mining and manufacturing account for more than one-fifth of GDP but employ only one-tenth of the labor force. Apart from the manufacture of cement and steel, most industry is light, concentrating on chemicals, food processing, textiles and paper and handicrafts. During the early 1990s Vietnam began to establish strong trading links with Japan, Taiwan, Thailand and Singapore, and also to attract substantial foreign investment such that services had come to contribute 40 percent of GDP by the late 1990s. However, the economy suffered in the Asian financial crisis of 1997–98 and political adherence to central planning continued to slow economic growth.

Transportation and communications
Road and rail transport is inadequately developed. The terrain presents difficulties and the war left a legacy of damage. Most roads are unsurfaced and heavy rains can turn these into quagmires. Rail links with China were reopened in 1996. The extensive waterways system includes a large network of rivers and canals in the delta areas. Various airports operate internal flights, and international air services fly from Hanoi and Ho Chi Minh City.

Press and broadcasting are under direct government control, and there were a number of daily newspapers and 3.2 million television sets in 1995. The telephone network is expanding with foreign aid – there were three mobile phone networks in 1996 with 35,000 subscribers and around 6,000 Internet users.

Welfare and education
Health and welfare provisions have been greatly improved in recent years, and now extend to previously neglected rural areas. Although there is still a shortage of skilled medical professionals, the incidence of disease has been reduced.

The government places an emphasis on education and training, having nationalized all former private schools. All education is free, and literacy rates are well over 90 percent for both sexes. There are seven universities, two distance-learning universities and nine for specialized study.

Malaysia

M ALAYSIA IS A VIBRANT AND ETHNICALLY complex nation. It consists of West Malaysia on a southern limb of the Southeast Asian mainland; and East Malaysia, comprising two states – Sabah and Sarawak – on the island of Borneo.

ENVIRONMENT

Malaysia covers an area of some 330,442 sq km (127,584 sq mi). West Malaysia borders Thailand to the north. Sarawak occupies the northwest of Borneo facing the South China Sea, while neighboring Sabah in the far north of the island lies close to the Philippines.

Northern and central West Malaysia are predominantly mountainous. The southeastern corner of the peninsula is characterized by broad river valleys and extensive coastal plains. In East Malaysia the mountainous backbone of Borneo rises to 4,094 m (13,452 ft) at the summit of Mount Kinabalu in northern Sabah. A complex pattern of secondary mountain ranges descends to foothills and broad plains along the coast.

East and West Malaysia share a similar equatorial climate, with high temperatures and high humidity throughout the year. Annual rainfall levels are high. Between November and March the northeast monsoon blows, followed by the southwest monsoon from April to October. The wettest areas are generally in East Malaysia in January.

The dense rainforests support thousands of plant species, among them the *Rafflesia arnoldii*, found in Sabah, which has the largest flower in the world measuring up to 80 cm (32 in) in diameter. There are mangroves on sheltered coasts. Animal life in West Malaysia includes tigers, tapirs and the now rare Javan and Sumatran rhinoceroses. East Malaysia has yet more species, notably Sun bears, Proboscis monkeys and the endangered orangutan in lowland rainforest.

SOCIETY

Malaysia has a long history of invasion and settlement by different indigenous peoples. The complex ethnic mix has created a rich culture, but also conflict.

The earliest ancestors of the Malays came from southern China in about 3000 BC. By about 100 AD the Malayans had established trade links with China and India, absorbing both Hinduism and Buddhism. Islam was brought by Persian traders about the 7th century.

In 1511 the Portuguese captured and occupied the city-state of Malacca, which soon became a major center for the lucrative spice trade. The Dutch took Malacca in 1641, but by then the spice trade was in decline. Malacca was captured by the British in 1795, and in 1819 they settled Singapore Island. North Borneo (later Sabah) ceded to Britain in 1762, and in

Limestone pinnacles (*right*), eroded by rain into stone daggers, break through the montane forest in Sarawak's Mulu National Park, East Malaysia. The rugged interior of Sarawak is a forbidding frontier between Malaysia and Indonesia's Kalimantan.

Living on the edge (*below*) in Mengkabong, a coastal village in Sabah, East Malaysia, the houses are built on stilts to prevent flooding. Although a tourist attraction, the village has no services, is polluted, and the fishing in nearby waters is poor.

Flighty amphibian (*above*) Wallace's flying frog can glide 12–15 m (40–50 ft) by using the expanded webbing between its fingers and toes. It is one of a multitude of animal species living in Mulu National Park, Sarawak; many more have yet to be discovered.

1841 the British gained Sarawak.

The free port of Singapore prospered, and in 1867 the Strait Settlements (Pinang, Malacca and Singapore) became a British crown colony. Meanwhile the arrival of Chinese migrants on the peninsula in search of tin provoked violent conflicts with Malays. In the early 20th century British investment led to growth in rubber and tin production, encouraging a wave of settlers from India.

During World War II the Japanese

NATIONAL DATA – MALAYSIA				
Land area 330,442 sq km (127,584 sq mi)				

Climate		Temperatures		Annual precipitation
	Altitude m (ft)	January °C(°F)	July °C(°F)	mm (in)
Kuala Lumpur	39 (128)	27 (81)	27 (81)	2,441 (96.1)

Major physical features highest point: Mount Kinabalu 4,094 m (13,452 ft); longest river: Rajang (Borneo) 560 km (350 mi)

Population (2000 est.) 21,793,293

Form of government federal multiparty constitutional monarchy with two legislative houses

Armed forces army 85,000; navy 12,000; air force 12,500

Largest cities Kuala Lumpur (capital – 1,419,400); Johor Baharu (691,000); Ipoh (552,800);

Official language Bahasa Malaysian

Ethnic composition Malay and other indigenous peoples 61.4%; Chinese 30.0%; Indian 8.1%; others 0.5%

Official religion Islam

Religious affiliations Muslim 52.9%; Buddhist 17.3%; Chinese folk religions 11.6%; Hindu 7.0%; Christian 6.4%; others 4.8%

Currency 1 ringgit (M$) = 100 sen

Gross domestic product (1999) US $229.1 billion

Gross domestic product per capita (1999) US $10,700

Life expectancy at birth male 67.6 yr; female 73.9 yr

Major resources tin, bauxite, copper, iron ore, petroleum, rubber, palm oil, timber

Helping hands at the latex (rubber) glove factory on the island of Pinang, off the west coast of the Malaysian Peninsula. Seeds of the rubber tree first reached Malaysia in the 1890s, and the country is one of the world's largest producers of rubber.

Hindus, Muslims and Sikhs, as well as Christians. West Malaysia has a few smaller groups of native non-Malay peoples, most of them living in isolated mountain areas. In East Malaysia there are about 25 such ethnic groups, which account for more than half its population of 2.6 million.

ECONOMY

Malaysia's economy is one of the strongest in Southeast Asia, but there is little trade between the poorer states of East Malaysia and the more prosperous peninsular states.

Farming and forestry form a vital part of the Malaysian economy, employing about one-third of the total labor force. Malaysia's vast rainforests provide ample supplies of roundwood for export, and this important resource is now being replenished through a reforestation program. The main crop is rubber, of which Malaysia is the world's leading supplier. Palm oil is the other major cash crop, and rice the main staple. The recent increase in trawler fishing has led to bigger catches in offshore fishing grounds.

Malaysia is one of the world's leading tin producers. Bauxite, copper and iron ore are mined, and petroleum accounts for more than one-tenth of the country's export earnings.

Despite the great potential for hydroelectric power, most of Malaysia's electricity is generated by oil-fired power stations. Manufacturing includes electronic components for export alongside rubber goods and petroleum products.

On the peninsula broad highways link major population centers. Buses, taxis and trishaws – bicycle rickshaws – are principal means of transportation in the cities and countryside. Railroads are equally well developed. In East Malaysia, rivers provide the best means of communication. The ports along the Strait of Malacca are important to international shipping. Malaysia Airlines offers domestic flights as well as international services. The country's press is privately owned, but subject to government censorship. Broadcasting is all state-run.

Healthcare is free for those living near government clinics or hospitals. In rural areas animal-borne diseases such as. malaria are still common. Welfare programs assist the poor, the disabled and the old. About nine-tenths of the country's children attend primary school; after this they may go on to secondary school. Malaysia also has five universities.

occupied Malaya, Singapore and Borneo. After the war, British efforts to create a single Malay state brought strong opposition. In 1948, when a federation was formed between Pinang and the peninsular states, the Chinese-dominated Malayan Communist Party (MCP) rebelled. An anticommunist, anticolonial coalition of political parties was formed, which in 1955 won all but one of the seats in the federation parliament. Two years later, on 31 August 1957, Malaya achieved total independence. The constitution favored Malays but all ethnic groups were given freedon of worship and basic rights. In 1963 Sarawak and Sabah joined Malaya in the new independent Federation of Malaysia; Singapore left the federation in 1965. During the 1970s the federation recognized the Pan-Malayan Islamic Party and gave it a share in government. The multiparty National Front, headed by Mahathir Mohamed,

remained in power throughout the 1990s after returning to power in 1990.

Malaysia is a federal constitutional monarchy made up of 13 states. Nine of the states have sultans as their titular heads, who elect one of their number to be Malaysia's king for a five-year term. The remaining four heads of state – of Malacca, Pinang, Sabah and Sarawak are elected or appointed by their individual state legislatures.

The two-chamber federal parliament includes a lower house whose 193 members are freely elected by the people, and an upper house whose 69 members are mostly appointed by the king and the prime minister.

Malaysia's population is about 21.8 million. The largest group are the Malays, who form a slight majority in West Malaysia. Most are Muslim, and their language has been adopted as the national standard.

In East Malaysia the Chinese, who make up nearly one-third of the country's total population, are the largest group; most are Taoist or Buddhist. The Indian populations of West Malaysia include

Singapore

REPUBLIC OF SINGAPORE

S INGAPORE IS ONE OF THE SMALLEST, MOST densely populated and most prosperous countries in the world. Most of the population of over 4 million people live on Singapore Island; the rest inhabit 54 neighboring islets.

Singapore Island has a low but undulating landscape with a hillier district in the center. The climate is uniformly hot and humid throughout the year, with high rainfall. Indigenous mammals include the crab-eating macaque (a type of monkey).

Modern Singapore was founded in 1819 by Sir Thomas Stamford Raffles (1781–1826) of the British East India Company, and later became a British crown colony.

In 1963 it was incorporated into the Federation of Malaysia, but two years later left the federation to become an independent republic.

The head of state is a directly-elected president, and most legislative power rests with the 87-member parliament, 81 elected every five years. However, the People's Action Party, is effectively the only political party. The three main ethnic groups – Chinese, Malay and Indian – speak a variety of languages, including English, and practice various religions.

Agriculture and fisheries are relatively unimportant; many staple foods, including fish, have to be imported. The prosperous and expanding manufacturing sector is based on imported raw materials. Major industries include petrochemicals, textiles and shipbuilding. Financial services, banking and tourism are also major money earners.

There are road and rail links to neighboring parts of Malaysia, and a busy international airport. Healthcare, welfare and education are all of a high standard.

Singapore's gracious colonial buildings are dwarfed by huge international hotels, tax-free shopping complexes and office blocks in the commercial heart of the city. Already a busy trading center in the 14th century, modern Singapore is an economic colossus.

NATIONAL DATA – SINGAPORE

Land area   622 sq km (240 sq mi)

Climate	Altitude m (ft)	Temperatures January °C (°F)	July °C (°F)	Annual precipitation mm (in)
Singapore	10 (33)	26 (79)	27 (81)	2,282 (89.8)

Major physical features   largest island: Singapore 572 sq km (221 sq mi); highest point: Bukit Timah 176 m (581 ft)

Population   (2000 est.) 4,151,264

Form of government   multiparty republic with one legislative house

Armed forces   army 45,000; navy 3,000; air force 6,000

Capital city   Singapore (3,637,700)

Official languages   Chinese, Malay, Tamil, English

Ethnic composition   Chinese 76.4%; Malay 14.9%; Indian/Sri Lankan 6.4%; others 2.3%

Religious affiliations   Buddhist 28.3%; Christian 18.7%; nonreligious 17.6%; Muslim 16.0%; Taoist 13.4%; Hindu 4.9%; others 1.1%

Currency   1 Singapore dollar (S$) = 100 cents

Gross domestic product   (1999) US $98 billion

Gross domestic product per capita   (1999) US $27,800

Life expectancy at birth   male 75.8 yr; female 82.1 yr

Major resources   primarily manufacturing, shipbuilding, financial services, tourism

Indonesia

REPUBLIC OF INDONESIA

T HE REPUBLIC OF INDONESIA FORMS A LONG
island bridge between the Asian and
Australian continents. It comprises a vast
archipelago of 13,677 islands extending
5,100 km (3,200 mi) from Sumatra in the
west to Irian Jaya (now West Papua) on
New Guinea in the east, off the north
coast of Australia. Two of the larger
islands are shared with other countries:
the northern coastal section of Borneo
belongs to Malaysia, while the eastern
half of New Guinea forms the main part
of Papua New Guinea. The eastern part of
the smaller southeastern island of Timor
belonged to Portugal until 1975.

NATIONAL DATA – INDONESIA

Land area 1,919,443 sq km (741,101 sq mi)

Climate	Altitude m (ft)	Temperatures January °C (°F)	July °C (°F)	Annual precipitation mm (in)
Jakarta	8 (26)	26 (79)	27 (81)	1,755 (69.1)

Major physical features highest point: Mount Jaya (New Guinea) 5,029 m (16,499 ft); longest river: Barito (Borneo) 885 km (550 mi); largest lake: Lake Toba (Sumatra) 1,775 sq km (685 sq mi)

Population (2000 est.) 224,784,210

Form of government multiparty republic with two legislative houses

Armed forces army 214,000; navy 42,000; air force 20,000

Largest cities Jakarta (capital – 10,226,200); Surabaya (2,954,400); Bandung (2,657,600); Medan (2,143,100); Palembang (1,439,900)

Official language Bahasa Indonesian

Ethnic composition Javanese 45.0%; Sundanese 14.0%; Madurese 7.5%; Coastal Malays 7.5%; others 26.0%

Religious affiliations Muslim 86.9%; Christian 9.6%; Hindu 1.9%; Buddhist 1.0%; others 0.6%

Currency rupiah

Gross domestic product (1999) US $610 billion

Gross domestic product per capita (1999) US $2,800

Life expectancy at birth male 60.7 yr; female 65.3 yr

Major resources copper, tin, nickel, bauxite, gold, silver, phosphates, manganese, petroleum, natural gas, coal, rubber, tea, coffee, spices, vegetable oils, timber

ENVIRONMENT

Indonesia lies at the junction of three
sections of the Earth's crust, and its
animal life is sharply differentiated between Asian and Australian species.

The land

Indonesia's islands are strewn across 8
million sq km (more than 3 million sq mi)
of tropical seas. Geologically, the country
divides into three sections. The western
section includes Borneo in the north and
the whole southern chain of islands, from
Sumatra in the west to Timor in the
southeast; these together form part of the
Sunda shelf, a mostly submerged, southeastward extension of the Asian continent. In the center, Sulawesi (east of
Borneo), and the southern Moluccas to
the east of it, are part of a long, partially
submerged mountain chain that extends
northward to the Philippines. The Sahul
shelf in the east, which includes New
Guinea and the northern Moluccas immediately to the west, forms a northern
extension of Australia.

The Indonesian part of Borneo, known
by its Indonesian name of Kalimantan, is
dominated by mountains in the north
bordering the Malaysian states of Sarawak and Sabah. The thickly forested
central highlands descend to broad, flat
alluvial swamplands.

The island of Sumatra rises from swampy, forest-covered lowlands in the east to
the lofty Barisan Mountains running the
whole length of the southwest-facing
coast; they include 10 active volcanoes
and a number of beautiful crater lakes,
notably Lake Toba in the north, lying
nearly 900 m (3,000 ft) above sea level.

Southeast of Sumatra, across the narrow Sunda Strait, lies the mountainous
but heavily populated island of Java. A
long volcanic range, forming the backbone of the island, includes 50 active
volcanoes and a further 17 that have only
recently become dormant. The fertile valleys and lowlands either side are broader
to the north than to the south. The volcanic arc stretches eastward across the
Lesser Sunda Islands of Bali, Lombok,
Sumbawa and Flores. Sumba and Timor,
lying to the south of the main island
chain, are rugged but not volcanic.

Sulawesi island is roughly K-shaped,
and made up of mountainous peninsulas
radiating from a central highland core.
The long, highly volcanic peninsula of
Minahassa extends to the northeast. The
islands of the Sahul shelf – New Guinea

and the northern Moluccas – are struc-
turally similar to those of the Sunda shelf.
There are mountains on the northern
side, including some active volcanoes,
whereas southern New Guinea has large
areas of low-lying swampland.

Indonesia has as many as 220 active
volcanoes. Ash and debris from their
eruptions enriches the local soils, encouraging settlement and agriculture despite the attendant risks. In August 1883
the small volcanic island of Krakatau, in
the Sunda Strait between Sumatra and
Java, exploded with such force that it
produced tsunamis (sea waves) up to 36
m (120 ft) tall. Some 36,000 people lost
their lives. The eruption of Mount Agung
on Bali in 1963 killed over 1,500 people.

Most of Indonesia receives rainfall throughout the year, but the amount depends on exposure to the prevailing seasonal winds; these are determined by the way that the humid equatorial air interacts with the air masses over the two neighboring continents. The northwest monsoon blows from December through February, while southeasterly winds predominate from June through August. Winds are lighter and more variable during the two transitional periods.

In the southeast, coasts and islands have a dry season during the monsoon, when they receive dry air from Australia's arid interior. Most other areas show less variation, though local geography can make a big difference. The capital, Jakarta, for example, is protected by the Javanese mountains from the weather brought by the southeast monsoon.

Plants and animals

The muddy coastlines bordering lowland areas are lined by mangroves that broaden out into vast mangrove swamps in southern Borneo and eastern Sumatra, where the adjoining seas are unusually shallow. Inland, much of the archipelago is covered in forest.

The Indonesian tropical rain forests are among the richest habitats in the world but they have been devastated in many places through logging and settlement. They contain some 30,000 plant species, of which 4,000 are trees. Among the most useful plants are bamboos, teaks and fruit trees, such as bananas and durians. Above 1,500 m (5,000 ft), oaks, laurels and magnolias predominate.

This region is also home to some of the world's most varied wildlife, including 1,480 bird species (16 percent of the world's total), of which 370 are endemic. Of the 500 mammal species, 100 are unique to the archipelago. Also unique is the Komodo dragon, the world's largest lizard at 3 m (10 ft) long, found on Komodo and neighboring islands. The wildlife is divided between Australian and Asian species by an imaginary boundary, known as the Wallace line, that runs from north to south. To the west of the line are Borneo and Bali (Asian species), to the east of it Sulawesi and Lombok (Australian species). Asian animals include elephants, tigers, leopards, Javan and Sumatran rhinoceroses, tapirs, orangutans and gibbons, but many of these are endangered species. Australian animals include cockatoos, bower birds, birds of paradise, and marsupials such as possums and bandicoots.

The home of the Toradjans (*above*), one-time headhunters thought to be descendants of early Austronesian settlers, is in the interior of the lush Indonesian island of Sulawesi. They now farm the volcanic soils for rice, sugar cane, copra and rattan.

The Sulawesi cuscus (*left*), a marsupial with long claws and a prehensile tail for gripping the tree trunks, is well adapted to life in the rainforest. Sulawesi's unique animal life also includes the babirusa (a species of wild pig) and the anoa, or dwarf buffalo.

Climate

The entire archipelago lies close to or on the Equator. Temperatures are high throughout the year, and are influenced by altitude rather than latitude. Lowland areas can be extremely hot, but the highlands are cooler; only the central mountains of Irian Jaya (now West Papua) rise high enough to receive any snow.

SOCIETY

Indonesia represents the union of many islands and peoples with their own diverse and often conflicting histories. In terms of population – 224.8 million – it is the fifth largest country in the world.

History

The Indonesian archipelago is one of the oldest inhabited areas on Earth. Early human beings called Java man (*Homo erectis*) lived there over 500,000 years ago. The ancestors of most Indonesian peoples probably arrived from Asia from about 1000 BC. Later, Indian traders and exiles came to settle, often marrying into the Indonesian aristocracy. Hinduism spread throughout the area, followed by Buddhism in the 7th century AD.

In the 9th century the region was ruled by the powerful Sailendra princes, the builders of the magnificent Buddhist monument of Borobodur in central Java. The kingdom's decline in the late 12th century was arrested by the rise of the great Majapahit empire of Java, which reached its height in the mid 14th century, but broke up a century later. The decline of the Majapahits was partly due to the influence of the Islamic faith introduced by Arabic traders from the west. At first Islam spread slowly, but was soon assisted by the desire of many local rulers to employ the skills of the Arabs.

In the early 16th century the Portuguese seized the Moluccas, or Spice Islands. Then, in 1608, the Dutch East India Company's fleet forced the Portuguese to capitulate, allowing the Netherlands to establish effective economic control of the Moluccas, Java and Sumatra. The Dutch colonies were taken by Britain in 1811, but were returned to the Netherlands by

A colorful Balinese procession (*above*) Elaborate towers of fruit are carried by local Balinese villagers to a Hindu festival as offerings to the gods. These annual ceremonies often involve a banquet and may be accompanied by a traditional gamelan orchestra.

Authority with an uncertain future (*below*) A chief of the Dani people of Irian Jaya (West Papua) – increasingly exposed to Western influence from tourists – represents one of some 250 ethnic groups on the island.

the Treaty of Vienna in 1814–15. Following an Anglo-Dutch treaty in 1824, the Netherlands took control of the remaining island territories by force and ruled.

As Dutch territorial expansion continued into the 20th century, it gave rise to Western-influenced nationalist movements. In 1927 Ahmed Sukarno (1901–70), an engineering graduate, founded the first of several Indonesian nationalist parties. In 1942, during World War II, the Japanese invaded, but the occupiers promised independence, and installed Sukarno as one of their administrators. When the Japanese surrendered in 1945, Sukarno declared the islands independent as the single country, Indonesia. However, the Dutch retained western New Guinea

(now West Papua) until 1962.

Sukarno's long rule was marked by corruption, economic problems and conflict with Malaysia. Hostile to all Western countries, he espoused a communist-style ideology, assumed increasingly dictatorial powers, and eventually alienated his former allies, the military.

In 1965 the army took control under General Suharto (b. 1921); mass executions of communists took place throughout the country, and Sukarno was put under house arrest until his death in 1970.

Suharto, appointed president in 1968, remained in power until 1998 despite promising a swift return to democracy. He successfully opened up the economy to Western investment but ran an authori-

Symbol of mystery, a silhouetted Hindu temple on an island in a Balinese lake. In the 16th century, when Islam triumphed over Hinduism on neighboring Java, Bali became a haven for exiled Hindus. Today, it is the only bastion of Hinduism in the Indonesian archipelago.

tarian regime with the aid of the military. In 1975 Indonesia invaded East Timor and suppressed a revolt on Irian Jaya. In 1998 riots erupted following serious economic problems and Suharto resigned in favor of vice president Baccharuddin Jusuf Habibie. Habibie promised political and economic reforms and over the next year set in motion an investigation of government corruption, freed the press, granted an amnesty to political prisoners, allowed investigations of human rights abuses and reduced the number of seats allocated to

the military in the legislature. In 1999, Habibie revoked laws banning political parties and announced East Timor would be allowed to hold a referendum on independence. The first free, multiparty elections since 1955 were held in May with the largest bloc of seats won by the Indonesian Democratic Party of Struggle (PDI-P) but following a corruption scandal and international censure over East Timor, Habibie lost the presidential election in October to Abdurrahman Wahid with Megawati, leader of the PDI-P, as vice president. The East Timor referendum took place under UN auspices on August 30 and resulted in a majority vote for independence. However, paramilitary violence immediately erupted requiring

UN intervention. As negotiations over the secession of East Timor continued, Indonesia was faced with demands for independence from the provinces of Aceh in northern Sumatra and Irian Jaya, which became West Papua in 1999.

Government

Executive power lies with the president and vice president who are elected every five years by the People's Consultative Assembly. The president appoints a cabinet and departmental heads. The legislative body, the House of People's Representatives (DPR) is made up of 400 elected and 100 appointed members who serve a term of five years. The People's Consultative Assembly, which meets every five years, is made up of the DPR plus 200 appointed members. Its functions are to elect the president and to determine national policy and the constitution.

People

The Indonesians comprise 200 to 300 ethnic groups, most of which probably have Austronesian (Malayo-Polynesian) ancestry. The exception are the Papuan peoples of New Guinea, who are of Australoid origin, like the Australian Aborigines. Most islands have their own language, and Sumatra has at least 15. But all these languages, apart from some more distantly related groups in New Guinea and the northern Moluccas, derive from Austronesian roots.

Although the Javanese are the dominant ethnic group, the official language, Bahasa Indonesia, is based on an east Sumatran form of Malay that spread to Malaya and coastal areas of Borneo; it is now spoken as a second language by most educated people. The only significant immigrant group are the ethnic Chinese. Indian, Arab and European residents are much fewer in number, but like the Chinese they live mainly in the cities and are prominent in business life.

Most of the population are Muslims, but only a minority are orthodox. The form of Islam generally practiced has been heavily influenced by Buddhism and Hinduism. Hinduism is strongest in Jogjakarta, the cultural heart of Java, and on Bali, where the culture is preserved in many of its ancient forms. Much of it also survives in the performance of the popular Javanese shadow plays, the highly theatrical dance displays and the traditional music of the Javanese royal courts.

ECONOMY

Indonesia's economy was tightly controlled under the Suharto regime with much corruption and a high level of foreign debt. Most development came from foreign aid and investment. Indonesia suffered badly in the 1997 Asian financial crisis; as investors withdrew money from the region, the value of Indonesia's currency fell by 80 percent. An IMF/World Bank rescue package and financial controls brought the situation under control – inflation which had soared to 70 percent in 1998 was brought down to 2 percent in 1999. However, future economic prosperity is closely tied to political stability.

Agriculture and fisheries

Agriculture employs about 40 percent of

Dusty work Masked to prevent themselves inhaling wood-dust, these workers stack plywood at a sawmill in east Kalimantan, Borneo. Because Indonesia has banned the export of raw timber for environmental reasons, plywood has become the country's chief export apart from oil.

the labor force and produces about 20 percent of GDP. Rice is the major crop, other staples such as cassava and soybeans are grown. Cash crops include rubber, of which Indonesia is one of the world's largest suppliers, coffee, tea and spices.

Indonesia's vast forests have until recently supplied an ever-increasing demand for timber and its many associated products. However, international concern has been expressed at the accelerating rate of Indonesia's deforestation – 1 million ha (2.5 million acres) per year between 1950 and 1981 and 5.42 million ha between 1990 and 1995. The government has implemented some controls and reforestation. The fishing industry is still growing with the help of Japanese expertise.

Industry

Indonesia's considerable mineral wealth includes ores of tin, copper, nickel, aluminum (bauxite) and manganese. Petroleum and natural gas from Sumatra, Borneo and the Java Sea provide vital export revenue; and, along with Sumatran coal, fuel for the electricity industry. The chief manufactures are chemicals, agricultural products, electronic components, rubber tires, and textiles made from imported raw materials.

Transportation and communications

Shipping is the most important means of transportation, providing a vital link between Indonesia's far-flung populations. Java and Sumatra both have state-operated railroads, but only Java has an adequate network of roads. The two major international airports are at Jakarta and at Denpasar on Bali, a favorite tourist destination.

Indonesia has a thriving press and communications industry, until the end of the 1990s these were government-controlled. There are good internal telephone as well as cellphone services and satellite links.

Welfare and education

Most communicable diseases in Indonesia – a result of malnutrition and severe housing shortages – are gradually being brought under control.

The majority of Indonesians are literate, following a concerted government education program. Most children go to primary school for six years, and many spend a further six years in secondary education, which includes vocational, technical and agricultural training. There are public universities in every province as well as many private institutions.

Brunei

SULTANATE OF BRUNEI, ABODE OF PEACE

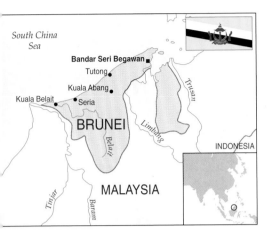

B RUNEI – AN "ABODE OF PEACE" ACCORDING to its unique official title – is an independent sultanate on the northwest coast of Borneo, surrounded and divided in two by the Malaysian state of Sarawak.

ENVIRONMENT

The two parts of Brunei are separated by a few kilometers of coastline where the Limbang river enters Brunei Bay. Both share a landscape of hills and valleys bordering a narrow and often swampy coastal plain. The smaller eastern enclave is more rugged. The humid tropical climate brings heavy monsoon rains between November and March.

Most of Brunei is covered in dense tropical forest, rich in hardwoods. Inaccessibility makes it a haven for wildlife such as monkeys, apes and birds.

SOCIETY

Brunei is known to have had trading links with China since before the 6th century AD. The Portuguese navigator Ferdinand Magellan (1480–1521) was the first European visitor in 1521. At that time the Sultanate of Brunei effectively controlled the whole of Borneo and part of the Sulu Islands and the Philippines to the northeast. In 1839 Sarawak was ceded to the "White Raja" James Brooke (1803–68) and his descendants, while other areas were lost to the British North Borneo Company; Brunei finally became a British protectorate in 1888. In 1929 the first petroleum reserves were discovered.

Following Japanese occupation during World War II Brunei reverted to British rule. In 1959 it adopted a constitutional government and in 1984 achieved full independence within the Commonwealth. Since then, all effective political power has been vested in the sultan.

With around 336,000 people occupying 5,765 sq km (2,226 sq mi), Brunei has the lowest and least dense population of any Southeast Asian country. Malay-descended Muslims make up the majority of the population, followed by Chinese and Indians. The small indigenous population includes Ibans, Dyaks and others.

ECONOMY

Petroleum is the mainstay of the Brunei economy, giving the country one of the highest per-capita incomes in Southeast Asia. There are also natural gas reserves. Other income derives chiefly from small-scale agriculture (pepper and rice), and forestry (cork and rubber).

Main transportation routes are along the coast and rivers, apart from a few roads along the coast. Excellent healthcare is available free of charge, even in isolated locations by means of a "flying doctor" service. Free education also extends to remote areas.

NATIONAL DATA – BRUNEI			
Land area 5,765 sq km (2,226 sq mi)			
Climate	**Temperatures**		**Annual precipitation**
	January °C (°F)	July °C (°F)	mm (in)
Bandar Seri Begawan	27 (80)	28 (82)	3,275 (128.9)
Major physical feature highest point: Pagonprick 1,850 m (6,070 ft)			
Population (2000 est.) 336,376			
Form of government nonparty constitutional monarchy with one advisory body			
Armed forces army 3,400; navy 700; air force 400			
Capital city Bandar Seri Begawan (71,500)			
Official language Malay			
Ethnic composition Malay 68.0%; Chinese 20.0%; others 12.0%			
Official religion Islam			
Religious affiliations Muslim 66.0%; Buddhist 14.0%; Christian 10.0%; others 10.0%			
Currency 1 Brunei dollar (B$) = 100 cents			
Gross domestic product (1999) US $5.6 billion			
Gross domestic product per capita (1999) US $17,400			
Life expectancy at birth male 70.3 yr; female 73.4 yr			
Major resources petroleum, natural gas, pepper, rice, cork, rubber, timber			

Carried in splendor (*right*) Brunei's absolute monarch Hassanal Bolkiah waves to onlookers from his ornamental float during a procession through the streets of the capital. The sultan's wealth is derived from Brunei's petroleum and natural gas resources.

Philippines

REPUBLIC OF THE PHILIPPINES

THE REPUBLIC OF THE PHILIPPINES, LYING some 800 km (500 mi) off the southeast coast of Asia, encompasses an archipelago of 7,107 islands containing an estimated 81 million people. The republic is set on the western edge of the Pacific Ocean, with Taiwan to the north, and East Malaysia and Indonesia to the south.

ENVIRONMENT

The Philippines lie in an area of great tectonic instability – the "ring of fire" that surrounds the Pacific Ocean – and within the path of violent tropical storms.

The land

The archipelago, which extends 1,770 km (1,100 mi) north to south, is roughly triangular, and bounded by the South China, Sulu and Celebes Seas. The Philippine Trench, 10,500 m (34,500 ft) deep, runs along the eastern coastline. The islands are generally mountainous, have narrow coastal plains and some are heavily populated. Just 11 islands constitute 94 percent of the total land area.

Luzon in the north is the largest island, much of it mountainous and rugged. The Zambales Mountains on the west coast partly enclose a broad central plain – the country's only extensive lowland – running from the Lingayen Gulf in the north to Manila Bay, where the capital, Manila, is located. The long peninsula of southeastern Luzon has a landscape of scattered volcanoes.

Between Luzon and the second-largest island, Mindanao in the southeast, is a scattered range of islands including those of the Visayas group, such as Samar, Leyte, Cebu, Negros, Panay, Romblon and Mindoro. A chain of small volcanic islands, the Sulu Archipelago, extends southwest from Mindanao. North of Sabah (northern Borneo) is the long thin island ridge of Palawan.

Earthquakes are common, and there are some 50 volcanoes – at least 11 of them active – scattered across the Philippines. They include Mount Apo on Mindanao, a massive triple-peaked active volcano, and the previously dormant Mount Pinatubo, in the Zambales Mountains of Luzon, which in 1991 erupted violently, causing widespread havoc.

Climate

Like much of Southeast Asia, the Philippines are subject to seasonal monsoon winds blowing from the southwest between May and October, and from the northeast between November and February. On the western side the rainy season

Mount Mayon, overlooking paddy fields in southern Luzon (the largest of the Philippine islands) presents a quiet but simmering threat. Many areas face constant danger from active volcanoes, but ash from the eruptions makes soil fertile for growing crops.

lasts from May to November; the period December through February is dry and cool, and March and April both remain dry, but with rising temperatures and increasing humidity. The eastern side has no appreciable dry season, and receives the heaviest total rainfall.

Temperatures do not vary greatly from north to south, but they are affected by altitude; the high ground is always cooler, and also generally wetter. Tropical typhoon storms, normally occurring between June and December, are often severe and accompanied by flooding. There may be 25 or more in a single year, but they are rare on Mindanao.

on the island of Borneo) in the 15th century. It took strong hold on the islands of Palawan and Mindanao, but before it could take root in the northern islands, the first Europeans made contact. In 1521 the seafarer Ferdinand Magellan (1486–1521) visited the archipelago, where he claimed the country for Spain. In 1565 the first permanent Spanish settlement was established on the central island of Cebu, and the capital, Manila, was founded six years later on Luzon. The Spanish also named the islands after their king, Philip II (1527–98). As Spanish rule became more firmly rooted, the majority of Filipinos were converted to Roman Catholicism.

In the 1830s Manila was opened to foreign trade, ending centuries of Spanish monopoly. Demand for coffee, sugar and hemp encouraged the growth of new estates, many of which were run by Chinese-Filipino *mestizos*. By the 1880s the seeds of nationalism were being sown, and in 1896 there was an abortive armed revolt against Spanish rule. During the Spanish-American War of 1898 the Americans encouraged the drive toward independence. But with the Spanish defeat, the islands were ceded to the United States for $20 million. After resisting for six years, the Filipinos were forced to accept United States' rule in 1905.

NATIONAL DATA – PHILIPPINES				
Land area 300,000 sq km (115,800 sq mi)				
Climate		**Temperatures**		**Annual**
	Altitude m (ft)	January °C (°F)	July °C (°F)	precipitation mm (in)
Manila	15 (49)	25 (77)	28 (82)	1,719 (70.5)
Major physical features largest island: Luzon 104,684 sq km (40,419 sq mi); highest point: Mount Apo (Mindanao) 2,954 m (9,692 ft)				
Population (2000 est.) 81,159,644				
Form of government multiparty republic with two legislative houses				
Armed forces army 20,000; navy 23,000; air force 16,500				
Largest cities Manila (capital – 10,032,900); Davao (837,500); Cebu (733,000); Bacolod (434,900)				
Official languages Pilipino, English				
Ethnic composition Talalog 29.7%; Cebuano 24.2%; Ilocano 10.3%; Hiligayon Ilongo 9.2%; Bicol 5.6%; Samar-Leyte 4.0%; others 17.0%				
Religious affiliations Roman Catholic 84.1%; Philippine Independent Church 6.2%; Muslim 4.3%; Protestant 3.9%; others 1.5%				
Currency 1 Philippine peso (P) = 100 centavos				
Gross domestic product (1999) US $282 billion				
Gross domestic product per capita (1999) US $3,600				
Life expectancy at birth male 63.8 yr; female 69.5 yr				
Major resources nickel, copper, gold, silver, tin, zinc, lead, timber, rice, tobacco, fruit, sugar, coconuts, copra, fisheries				

Plants and animals

Forests range from tropical rainforest near the coasts to subtropical evergreens on the slopes, and pinewoods around the peaks of northern Luzon. Many areas have been cleared, leaving long, coarse grassland, but most upland regions have retained a dense covering of trees. The forests include valuable hardwoods and are home to some 800 kinds of orchids.

The islands are rich in wildlife, and isolation has encouraged the evolution of many animals that are unique to the area. These include several species of bat, the rare Philippine eagle (which attacks monkeys) and the tarsier, a primitive primate with very large eyes. Palawan has several bird species that are found nowhere else, while Mindoro is the exclusive home of a small water buffalo called the tamarau.

SOCIETY

The religion and culture of the Philippines reflect centuries of Spanish rule, whereas the system of government owes much to the subsequent administration of the United States' government.

History

The islands were first settled by waves of Malay-related peoples about 3000 BC. These early Filipinos provided themselves with food by hunting, fishing and slash-and-burn cultivation. The islanders lived in extended family groups called *barangays*, each led by a chief.

Between the 8th and 10th centuries the islands were trading with Chinese, Japanese and Malay merchants. However, the first major foreign influence was the arrival of Islam from Brunei (a sultanate

Filipinos took an increasingly active role in government, but progress toward full independence was slow. In 1935, an interim government was established but this was interrupted by the Japanese invasion in 1941. The United States recaptured the islands in October 1944 and on 4 July 1946, the Republic of the Philippines was finally declared. However, the United States obtained a long lease on several army, navy and air bases.

In 1969 Ferdinand Edralin Marcos (1917–89) became the first president since independence to be elected to a second term of office. However, the election of the so-called Constitutional Convention in the next year was unpopular and students took to the streets in protest. Martial law was declared in 1972.

The state of emergency officially ended in 1981, but Marcos retained enormous personal power. The assassination of the opposition leader, Benigno Simeon Aquino (1932–83), brought matters to a head. In the 1986 election Marcos was opposed by Benigno Aquino's widow, Corazon Aquino (b. 1933). Marcos was declared the winner, but public outrage at manifest electoral fraud developed into a popular revolution, which toppled him from power. He and his wife Imelda fled the country.

On assuming the presidency, Corazon Aquino faced a parlous economic situation, widespread poverty and threats from communist and Muslim insurgents. Her government drafted a new constitution, similar to that of 1935, which was ratified by referendum in 1987. Fidel Ramos succeeded to the presidency in 1992. In 1996 a peace agreement ended 25 years of civil unrest by Muslim insurgents. Joseph Estrada was elected president in 1998 but was toppled in a "people's revolution" in 2001 following a corruption scandal. Vice-president Gloria Arroyo took over the presidency.

Government

The 1987 constitution provides for a two-chamber parliament: the Congress of the Philippines. The 250 members of the lower house are mostly elected every three years from local districts. The 24 senators are elected on a national basis, and may hold office for, at most, two six-year terms. The head of state is the president, who is elected for a single six-year term and is responsible for appointing the cabinet, though these appointments are also subject to parliamentary approval. There is a large degree of autonomy in local administration

People

Few of the descendants of the first inhabitants – the Negritos – are left. Most of today's Filipinos are of Mongoloid origin whose ancestors came from Taiwan and the surrounding region. Over the centuries, however, there has been intermarriage with Chinese immigrants and with Spanish and American colonists.

Seventy or more languages are spoken in the Philippines. The Tagalog group of dialects has the majority of indigenous speakers. However, the national

An Igorot woman from the Cordillera Mountains of Luzon enjoying a smoke. The Igorot meaning "mountaineers" – have largely kept their traditional ways of life and belief in spirits. Most cultivate rice on mountain terraces or in gardens in the rain forests.

to exports and to the Filipino diet. The output of timber, however, has declined with reduced forest cover. Replanting has not kept pace with illegal felling and slash-and-burn cultivation.

Industry

The country is well endowed with mineral resources, especially nickel and copper; gold is also found in significant quantities. Nickel, copper, tin, zinc and lead are processed domestically in smelting and refining works. Recent irrigation projects have helped increase the output of hydroelectricity, while new geothermal plants and local oil have reduced the need for imported fuel.

Manufacturing industry is still at a relatively early stage of development. Many factories established by foreign companies use local labor to finish goods manufactured abroad. The chief local manufactures include textiles, electronics, clothing, chemicals and machinery. Natural disasters and political instability has hindered the development of tourism.

Transportation and communications

Only the islands of Luzon, Panay and Negros have railroads, but good road networks exist in all of the heavily populated areas. Manila, with a population of 10 million, is the main port, followed by Cebu city; each has an international airport nearby. All the main islands are linked to Manila by domestic airlines and shipping lines.

The Philippines' lively free press has enjoyed something of a renaissance since the overthrow of the Marcos regime, with newspapers published in English, Pilipino and main regional dialects. Local radio and television companies belong to a single national association, but are not subject to government control.

Welfare and education

Healthcare is centered on Manila; elsewhere treatment is often hard to obtain. Malnutrition remains a problem, especially in outlying areas, and there is a serious shortage of housing and proper sanitation around Manila. Many squatters were rehoused in model communities under the Marcos regime, but earthquakes, volcanic eruptions and floods have since aggravated the problem. Primary education is free and compulsory, and secondary schooling is also free, with a majority of children attending. There are about 50 state-run universities, and a few private institutions offering higher education.

"Jeepneys" (*left*), garishly decorated trucks serving as minibuses, are the main form of transport on the crowded streets of the capital, Manila. They were converted for public use from old United States' army jeeps by Filipinos after World War II. In recent decades they have become a characteristic sight in Manila.

Fragile, iridescent shells (*above*) are offered for sale to passing tourists. The Philippines is a major producer of shells, exporting mother-of-pearl (for buttons) to China and Hong Kong, and tortoiseshells to Singapore. Filipinos also cultivate pearls in the far south.

language, Pilipino, which is based on the Manila form of Tagalog, is fast gaining ground as both the first and second spoken language. English is also widely spoken, and is taught in schools.

The vast majority of Filipinos are Catholic, including the Aglipayans, members of the Philippine Independent Church that does not recognize the Pope as its head. There is a vigorous Muslim community in the south, and evangelical Protestants have a growing following.

ECONOMY

Development in farming and industry have both been encouraged by government investment and tax concessions.

However, industrial output has tended to benefit foreign investors more than the local economy, and prices for exports such as sugar and copper are vulnerable in a changing world market.

Agriculture and fisheries

The country is still predominantly agricultural, with a large rural labor force. The mountain slopes are terraced to grow rice. In recent decades rice production has become much more efficient because of improved irrigation and management techniques, and there is sometimes a surplus for export. However, the introduction of new strains has made it necessary to import expensive chemicals and fertilizers. Other major crops include tobacco and tropical fruits, such as pineapples; sugar, coconuts and copra are significant export crops.

Fishing contributes very significantly

REGIONAL PROFILES

Southeast Asia

Terraced paddyfields, Luzon, the Philippines

PHYSICAL GEOGRAPHY

The peninsula and islands of Southeast Asia extend over 6,000 km (3,700 mi) between the eastern end of the Himalayas and the continent of Australia to the south. They include over 20,000 tropical islands – the greatest archipelago on Earth. The loops and curves of the mountainous island arcs are bounded by the Java trench of the Indian Ocean and the Philippine trench of the Pacific. Here two great areas of the planet's crust – the Indo–Australian plate and the landmass of Asia – are in slow collision. Mantled by the dry teak forests of Myanmar, the luxuriant green rainforests of Indonesia and the eucalyptus and gum trees of Timor lie some of the world's fastest changing landscapes, in a region that is frequently subject to many of the Earth's more violent hazards – typhoons, tropical rains, earthquakes and volcanoes.

COUNTRIES IN THE REGION

Brunei, Cambodia, Indonesia, Laos, Malaysia, Myanmar, Philippines, Singapore, Thailand, Vietnam

LAND

Area 4,495,392 sq km (1,735,221 sq mi)
Highest point Hkakabo Razi, 5,881 m (19,296 ft)
Lowest point sea level
Major features mountain chains and flood plains, deltas of great rivers in north of region, mountainous and volcanic islands of Malaysia, Indonesia, Philippines, world's largest archipelago

WATER

Longest river Mekong, 4,180 km (2,600 mi)
Largest basin Mekong, 811,000 sq km (313,000 sq mi)
Highest average flow Irrawaddy, 12,660 cu m/sec (447,000 cu ft/sec)
Largest lake Tonle Sap, 10,000 sq km (3,860 sq mi)

CLIMATE

| | Temperature °C (°F) | | Altitude |
	January	July	m (ft)
Rangoon	25 (77)	27 (81)	23 (75)
Ho Chi Minh City	26 (79)	27 (81)	10 (33)
Manila	25 (77)	28 (82)	15 (49)
Cameron Highlands	18 (64)	18 (64)	1,449 (4,753)
Singapore	26 (79)	27 (81)	10 (33)
Jakarta	26 (79)	27 (81)	8 (26)

| | Precipitation mm (in) | | |
	January	July	Year
Rangoon	3 (0.1)	580 (22.8)	2,618 (103.1)
Ho Chi Minh City	6 (0.2)	242 (9.5)	1,808 (71.2)
Manila	18 (0.7)	253 (10.0)	1,791 (70.5)
Cameron Highlands	168 (6.6)	122 (4.8)	2,640 (104.0)
Singapore	285 (11.2)	163 (6.4)	2,282 (89.8)
Jakarta	335 (13.2)	61 (2.4)	1,755 (69.1)

Rainfall of 1,170 mm (46in) in 24 hours has been recorded at Baguio in Luzon, Philippines

NATURAL HAZARDS

Typhoons and floods, earthquakes and volcanic eruptions, landslides and mudslides

CLIMATE AND THE LAND

Southeast Asia is a tropical region. The islands straddle the Equator, but the Philippines and the continental peninsula extend farther north, so the region's climates are far from uniform. The areas nearest the Equator have a climate that is hot, wet and humid all year round. They include Sumatra, the Malay Peninsula, Borneo, Sulawesi, Halmahera and Mindanao. The annual rainfall averages over 2,000 mm (80 in), with at least 100 mm (4 in) every month, up to half of which comes in short, heavy downpours. During the day the temperature in the shade is 25–30°C (77–86°F), but just before dawn it falls to about 16–18°C (61–64°F) – hence the saying "in the tropics, winter comes every night".

Away from the Equator climates show the influence of the seasonal changes in winds (monsoons) and their accompanying summer rains. Both mainland Southeast Asia and the northern islands of the Philippines experience their wettest months from June through August. In the northern Philippines and in Vietnam, Laos and Cambodia rainfall patterns are strongly influenced by typhoons. Java and other islands to the south of the Equator have their heaviest rainfall from December through February.

Rainstorms and erosion

Typhoons are tropical storms, known elsewhere as hurricanes or cyclones. They travel from the western Pacific on erratic westerly courses toward the Asian mainland. The ferocious storms bring extreme rainfalls. Areas near the coast feel the effects most strongly. On Luzon, the main island of the Philippines, a fall of as much as 1,170 mm (46 in) in one day has been recorded. Even in the typhoon-free equatorial areas rain can be very heavy, with falls of 200 mm (8 in) in one day recorded in the Malay Peninsula.

The seasonal variation of rainfall causes the great rivers of mainland Southeast Asia, the Irrawaddy, Salween, Chao Phraya and Mekong, to have their peak flow in summer. They spill over their banks in the lowland and delta courses and inundate the ricefields.

The sudden heavy downpours can cause severe erosion on the ground. However, it is the same abundance of water, coupled with the continuously high temperatures, that encourages prolific growth of vegetation, which helps to retain the soil. Wherever rocks are weak, the streams and rivers erode them. The collapse of river banks, often triggered by fallen trees, and sand and silt churned up from the river bed are the main causes of the muddiness in the great rivers of this part of the world. This mud builds up the deltas and extends the great coastal mangrove swamps farther out to sea on many Southeast Asian coasts.

The patterns of climate help determine the types of vegetation. In the equatorial areas high humidity all year encourages the growth of the world's richest rain-forest. A monthly rainfall of 100 mm (4 in) or more is usually enough in the tropics to keep plants growing all year round, allow water to reach rivers and wash out chemicals from the soil. In the monsoon areas to the north and south, where there is a sequence of dry months with under 60 mm (2 in) of rain, there are deciduous woodlands, including teak, and some savanna grassland vegetation.

Phra Nang, a limestone island off the southwest coast of Thailand. Southern Thailand is part of the Malay Peninsula. The peninsula is fringed with thousands of tiny islands. Phra Nang was shaped by the chemical weathering of its limestone rock. The limestone is dissolved by rainwater that has become slightly acid by absorbing carbon dioxide from the atmosphere or from the soil. The water attacks the rock through the joints and bedding planes, producing distinctive "karst" landforms. In humid climates, such as that of the tropical Malay Peninsula, the rate of weathering is increased.

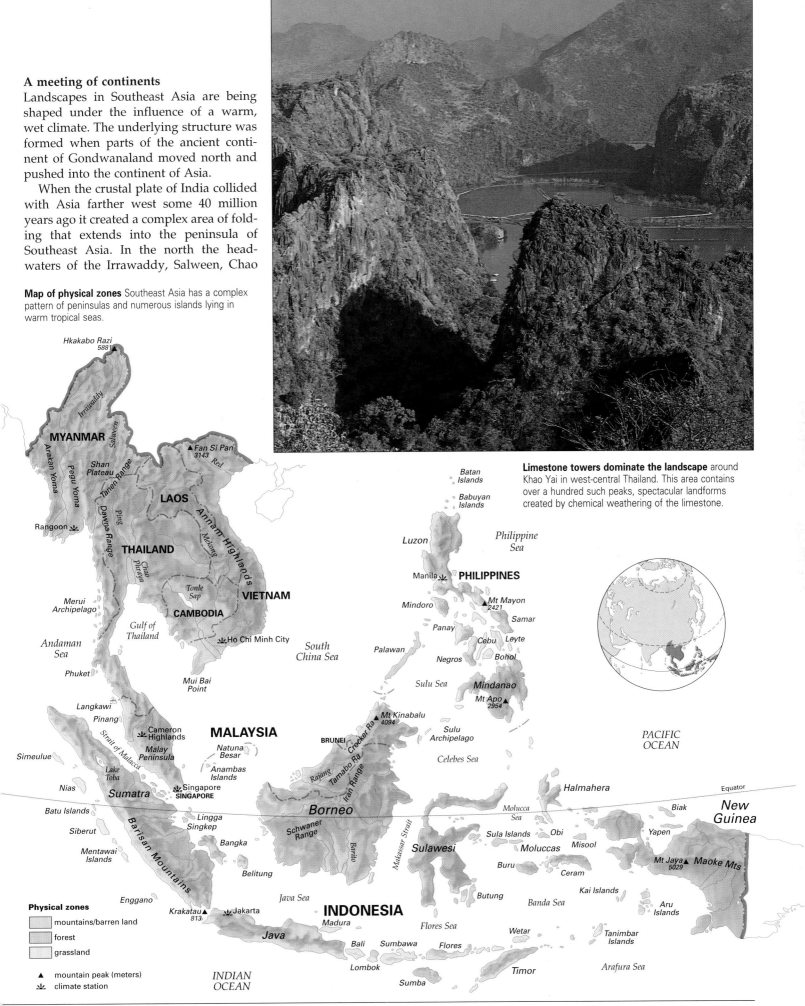

A meeting of continents

Landscapes in Southeast Asia are being shaped under the influence of a warm, wet climate. The underlying structure was formed when parts of the ancient continent of Gondwanaland moved north and pushed into the continent of Asia.

When the crustal plate of India collided with Asia farther west some 40 million years ago it created a complex area of folding that extends into the peninsula of Southeast Asia. In the north the headwaters of the Irrawaddy, Salween, Chao

Map of physical zones Southeast Asia has a complex pattern of peninsulas and numerous islands lying in warm tropical seas.

Limestone towers dominate the landscape around Khao Yai in west-central Thailand. This area contains over a hundred such peaks, spectacular landforms created by chemical weathering of the limestone.

Hkakabo Razi
5881▲

MYANMAR

Irrawaddy

Arakan Yoma

Pegu Yoma

Salween

▲ Fan Si Pan
3143

Red

Shan
Plateau

Tanen Range

LAOS

Annam Highlands

Rangoon

Dawna Range

Ping

THAILAND

Chao
Phraya

Mekong

Tonle
Sap

VIETNAM

CAMBODIA

Merui
Archipelago

Gulf of
Thailand

Andaman
Sea

Ho Chi Minh City

Phuket

Mui Bai
Point

South
China Sea

Langkawi

Pinang

Cameron
Highlands

MALAYSIA

Malay
Peninsula

Natuna
Besar

Simeulue

Strait of Malacca

Lake
Toba

Anambas
Islands

Nias

Sumatra

Singapore
SINGAPORE

Lingga
Singkep

Batu Islands

Barisan Mountains

Siberut

Bangka

Mentawai
Islands

Belitung

Enggano

Krakatau▲
813

Jakarta

Java Sea

Madura

Java

Bali

Lombok

Sumbawa

Sumba

INDIAN
OCEAN

Batan
Islands

Babuyan
Islands

Luzon

Philippine
Sea

Manila

PHILIPPINES

Mindoro

▲ Mt Mayon
2421

Samar

Panay

Cebu

Leyte

Palawan

Negros

Bohol

Sulu Sea

Mindanao

Mt Apo▲
2954

▲ Mt Kinabalu
4094

BRUNEI

Crocker Ra

Sulu
Archipelago

Celebes Sea

Tamabo Ra

Iran Range

Rajang

Borneo

Schwaner
Range

Barito

Makassar Strait

Sulawesi

Celebes Sea

Molucca
Sea

Sula Islands

Obi

Moluccas

Misool

Buru

Ceram

Butung

Banda Sea

Kai Islands

Flores Sea

Wetar

Flores

Tanimbar
Islands

INDONESIA

Timor

Arafura Sea

Halmahera

Equator

Biak

New
Guinea

Yapen

Mt Jaya▲
5029

Maoke Mts

Aru
Islands

PACIFIC
OCEAN

Physical zones

- mountains/barren land
- forest
- grassland

▲ mountain peak (meters)
☀ climate station

Phraya and Mekong rivers run south close together and parallel. So too do the upper courses of the Brahmaputra and Chang of India and China respectively. Mountain chains run between the rivers rather like the fingers of a hand. They extend east into China and southeast to form the Annam Highlands of Vietnam. To the south, the mountains and plateau of east Myanmar continue into the Malay Peninsula. To the southwest the Arakan Yoma extends down the western side of Myanmar. On the border with China lies Hkakabo Razi, at 5,881 m (19,298 ft) the region's highest peak. Away from the extreme north, only the summits of the Arakan Yoma exceed 3,000 m (10,000 ft).

Along the lower parts of the valleys are the great plains where most of the people of Southeast Asia live. The plains of the lower Red river and of the Mekong, the Chao Phraya central depression in Thailand and the Irrawaddy basin of Myanmar mostly consist of fertile river muds and sands that have been deposited in the last 2 million years.

THE ISLAND CHAIN

On the islands of Southeast Asia mountain slopes rise steeply from the sea. Parallel deep-sea troughs separate neighboring islands to north and south. The trench parallel to the coast of Java drops to 7,455 m (24,460 ft) below sea level, the deepest abyss of the Indian Ocean. This marks where the edge of the Indo-Australian plate of the Earth's crust is sliding under the Eurasian plate. On the eastern edge of the archipelago the Philippine trench of the Pacific Ocean is even deeper, plunging to as much as 10,497 m (34,444 ft).

Building the landscape

The islands of Java, Sumatra, Bali and Lombok and most of Borneo are peaks on an undersea extension of the Eurasian plate known as the Sunda shelf. Dry land once joined them and the continental peninsula of Southeast Asia when sea levels were lower during the last great ice age, 35,000 to 10,000 years ago, and a glacier topped Kinabalu, Borneo's highest peak at 4,094 m (13,432 ft).

In the south and east the pattern of smaller islands is much more complex. The long peninsulas of Sulawesi are different fragments of the Earth's crust that slid against one another, were twisted around and then became attached as a result of various plate movements. Mindanao, which is made of three such fragments, was also formed in this way.

Island Southeast Asia is a young landscape, much of which is still being created and built up by tectonic and volcanic activity, such as the great eruption that destroyed the island volcano of Krakatau between Sumatra and Java in 1883. Indonesia is the most active volcanic region in the world, and Java alone has over 50 active volcanoes out of the country's total of 150. Earthquake activity is also unmatched, most quakes taking place along the outer edges of the island arcs, for example along the Mentawai Islands on the southwestern flank of Sumatra.

The steaming volcano of Mount Bromo rises above the clouds in eastern Java. Mount Bromo is famous for its frequent activity, but it is only one of many mountain volcanoes in the region. Java alone has some 50 volcanoes. The slopes are frequently covered with tropical forest vegetation, and the lava and ash produce fertile soils that attract agricultural development despite the instability of the land.

Earthquake and volcanic zones
When earthquake epicenters and volcanoes are plotted on a map they show the major zones of tectonic activity and earth movement. These correspond to the boundaries of the Earth's plates. Southeast Asia lies where the Indo-Australian and Pacific/Philippine plates meet the extension of the Eurasian plate known as the Sunda shelf. Earthquake epicenters take place near the crust surface in ocean trenches, and at greater depths both under the island arcs and toward the mainland.

PACIFIC OCEAN

South China Sea

Luzon

Mindanao

Borneo

Sumatra

Sulawesi

INDIAN OCEAN

Java

Timor

Tectonic activity
▲ volcano
○ earthquake epicenter

THE WORLD'S LARGEST ISLANDS

The Malay Archipelago comprises the islands of Southeast Asia and is the largest island group in the world. It includes three of the world's 10 biggest islands. Including Greenland, the North American Arctic Contains four of them. Antarctica and Australia are regarded as continents, and are therefore excluded from the list.

	Area	
	sq km	sq mi
Greenland, Denmark	2,175,000	839,780
Irian Jaya (West Papua), Indonesia/Papua New Guinea	808,510	312,085
Borneo, Indonesia/ Malaysia	757,050	292,220
Madagascar	587,041	226,658
Baffin Island, Canada	476,070	183,760
Sumatra, Indonesia	473,700	182,900
Honshu, Japan	230,455	88,955
Great Britain, United Kingdom	229,870	88,730
Ellesmere Island, Canada	212,690	82,100
Victoria Island, Canada	212,147	81,910

Volcanic activity is now concentrated along the inner edge of the Asian plate: in central north Sumatra, the western mountains of central and southern Sumatra, and from west to east across Java into Bali, Lombok, Sumbawa, Flores and smaller islands. An arc of small volcanic islands stretches from Timor northeast to Ceram. There are parallel volcanic chains on the west coast of Halmahera and from the northern tip of Sulawesi to Mindanao. In west-central Mindanao there is a broad belt of volcanoes, while in the south of the island the peak of the Mount Apo volcano at 2,954 m (9,690 ft) forms the highest point of the Philippines.

Farther north, Canlaon in northern Negros is now the only active volcano in the Negros-Parnay-Samar-Leyte group of islands. Luzon has several active volcanic areas; in the south the present crater of Taal forms a small island in the center of the lake that shares its name. The lake occupies a vast caldera, produced by an explosive eruption in prehistoric times that blew the top off the volcano. Eruptions killed 1,200 people in 1911 and 2,000 in 1965. In 1991, nearby Mount Pinatubo erupted in what was the world's largest eruption for 50 years. The eruption coincided with a typhoon and caused 300 deaths and massive damage and disruption. In the far southeast of Luzon, Mount Mayon has a beautiful cone 2,421 m (7,943 ft) high, renowned as one of the most perfectly symmetrical volcanoes in the world.

THE RISE AND FALL OF CORAL REEFS

Sections of ancient coral now exposed many tens of meters above sea level have helped geologists to reconstruct the history of earth movements in Southeast Asia. The reefs are remnants of the old shorelines, providing traces of the system of coral reefs that developed in the past around many of the tropical islands of Indonesia strung out to the east of Java and Bali.

The great, relatively recent movements of the Earth's crust have had a dramatic effect on the land surface in some parts of these islands in Southeast Asia. In the center of the island of Timor, for example, reefs formed less than a million years ago have been lifted by as much as 1,300 m (4,260 ft) at a rate of 13 cm (5 in) per hundred years. To both the west and the east the rate of uplift lessens; at Tanimbar Island, more than 400 km (250 mi) to the east, there are no traces of the reefs being raised.

A great barrier reef on the edge of the stable Sunda shelf provides further evidence of old shorelines. Most of the shelf is now submerged, but when sea levels were lower 30,000 years ago it was exposed. The reef runs for more than 500 km (310 mi) off the southeast coast of Borneo. It is believed to have grown from a fringing reef that developed along the exposed eastern edge of the shelf. It did not grow fast enough to keep pace with the rising sea level, so it is now much farther offshore and most of it is submerged.

LANDFORMS AND LANDSCAPES

The climate and the upheavals of the Earth's crust have created a patchwork of landscape types in Southeast Asia. It is a region with a variety of scenery, though similar landforms are found in widely separated parts of the region. For example, the spectacular limestone tower karst scenery of the Red river delta in northern Vietnam, northwest Malaysia and the adjacent Langkawi Islands can also be found in scattered parts of Borneo, in Cebu in the Philippines and among the Indonesian islands, especially Java.

The dominant influences in many areas are the frequent earthquakes and volcanic eruptions that happen along the arc from Myanmar through Indonesia to the Philippines. Individual volcanoes erupt, earth tremors trigger landslides, earthquakes cause seismic sea waves (tsunami) that can destroy beaches, and extremely heavy monsoon rains and typhoons cause disastrous flooding. Riverbeds are often strewn with boulders, and there are great banks of gravel and sand where they emerge from the mountains onto the edge of the coastal plains.

A region of rugged terrain

The volcanic areas have the most fertile soils of all Southeast Asia. In Java, Bali and much of the Philippines the lower slopes are intricately terraced for rice cultivation. Higher up the slopes, much of the original forest has been replaced with plantations. Elsewhere patches of forest remain, as on Sumatra and many of the smaller islands.

The sandstones and shales that were folded and tilted by the collision of the tectonic plates form another kind of rugged terrain, particularly extensive in Borneo. Typically a succession of deep river valleys is overlooked by precipitous slopes, sometimes separated from another set of hills and valleys by a gently undulating plateau or plain. The land is covered with tropical rainforest.

Older rocks form the backbone of the most stable highlands, such as those of the Malay Peninsula, whose succession of granite peaks continues through the islands of Singapore, Bangka and Belitung unto western Borneo. Except where used for farming, as in the cool, damp Cameron Highlands in the center of the southern part of the peninsula, the ranges are generally still forested. The summits, often shrouded in mist, rise to 2,000 m (6,500 ft) or more. From the steep-sided slopes boulders are released by the weathering of blocks of granite. These roll down and accumulate in the narrow river channels, where they are gradually broken down into sand. Where the rivers begin to enter the lowlands their channels widen, and they meander from side to side, creating a broad, flat-floored valley where rice may be cultivated.

Long-eroded landscapes

In stable areas the land surface has been worn down over long periods, and the uplands are low plateaus or gently undulating hills and valleys. Chemical weathering has penetrated deeply into the rocks, and some of the soils formed on them have a hard layer where iron has accumulated (laterite or ferricrete).

West of the mountains of Vietnam these uplands comprise sandstones, in places overlain by basalt forced between the rocks during mountain-building about 20 million years ago, when the South China Sea was opening up.

The major low tableland in continental Southeast Asia is the southern plateau of southern Thailand. It resembles a tilted saucer, with a low, mountainous rim that separates it from the rest of the peninsula to the south and west. The plateau is one of the drier areas of Southeast Asia, with

PLANTS AND THE LAND

Some habitats are so limiting that they can accommodate only a single plant species. In the lush unspoiled tropical rainforest that is the natural vegetation of Southeast Asia, however, there are over a hundred different plant species in a single hectare (2.5 acres). The diverse plant community supports a host of birds, animals, insects, fungi, bacteria and other microorganisms.

In northern Myanmar, Laos and Thailand the luxuriance of the subtropical and temperate vegetation is limited by cold at high altitudes and by drought in the dry season. These deciduous forests include teak, but in drier areas they may be replaced by scrub and bamboo.

At the opposite end of the region, in Timor, the length of the dry season and the island's closeness to the plant species of Australia result in a dry tropical flora of eucalyptus and gum trees. Nearby, in western Sumbawa, the dry lowlands up to 800 m (2,600 ft) were originally covered with deciduous forest. Above 800 m the higher rainfall supports evergreen rainforest. On the dry summits of the mountains at 1,500 m (4,900 ft) this becomes stunted montane forest. Here the effects of seasonal drought and altitude can result in contrasting vegetation on different sides of the same mountain.

Individual rock types have developed characteristic vegetation. A special heath forest (kerangas) grows on the sandy beach ridges of the eastern Malay Peninsula. Behind the ridges, river outlets may be blocked and create waterlogged areas that are occupied by freshwater swamp forest. At the mouths of major rivers and along the coasts of eastern Sumatra and southern Borneo there are great mangrove swamps, the tropical equivalent of the salt marshes of temperate zones. Eventually a mangrove swamp may become dry and high enough to develop into coastal swamp forest.

---

less than 1,000 mm (25 in) of rain each year. Its sandy soils are thin and poor. Deciduous forests were once widespread, but with the help of irrigation rice is now cultivated. The plateau of southern Vietnam also has poor soils. The tablelands of Java are often limestone areas with dry surfaces, but there are water supplies below ground. The largest cave in the world, the Sarawak Chamber, is in a limestone area in northwest Borneo. It is 700 m (2,300 ft) long and an average 300 m (980 ft) wide and 70 m (230 ft) high.

Valleys, plains and deltas
In the upper reaches of the Irrawaddy, Chao Phraya and Mekong rivers, and on the eastern margin of the mountains of

The Irrawaddy floodplain The Irrawaddy flows south through central Myanmar and enters the sea through numerous river mouths. The waters are swollen both by mountain snowmelt and by the monsoons. The huge delta has been built up with river silts, producing fertile soil in which rice is widely grown.

Sumatra, there are old flood plains and river terraces well above the level of modern river channels. Their soils are easily irrigated by diverting tributary streams. The dry plain of the Irrawaddy in Myanmar lies in a rain shadow, cut off by mountains from the southwest monsoon; the upper Chao Phraya plain of Thailand is much less dry.

There are two major types of landscape in the geologically more recent flood plains. On the deltas of the Irrawaddy,

Chao Phraya, Mekong and Red rivers the land is intensively managed for rice cultivation. Along the coasts of eastern Sumatra, the Malay Peninsula and Borneo there are forests and mangrove swamps. The great deltas are built up of river silt that is often rich in nutrients, so the soil is very fertile. In the coastal swamps, on the other hand, decaying vegetation builds up peat deposits that even when drained are acidic and unsuitable for many crops without further treatment.

Southeast Asia's sliding slopes

Landslides play an important part in shaping the landscapes of Southeast Asia. Landslides are triggered wherever there is enough energy to set loose material moving down steep slopes. Such energy is abundant in Southeast Asia in the form of earthquakes and prolonged torrential rain, and is often found in combination with steep mountain terrain.

Much of Southeast Asia lies in a zone where different plates of the Earth's crust have collided in geologically recent times and continue to do so, raising the land and creating steep slopes. Deep chemical weathering under the hot and wet conditions has provided a mantle of rotted rock several meters deep. Torrential rainfall is common both in the equatorial belt and in areas subject to typhoons, such as the Philippines. The slopes are already unstable, and once the soil and rotted rock have become saturated with water there may be so much pressure caused by the water in the tiny spaces between individual rock particles that they start to slide over each other. When this happens, part or all of the hillside begins to move downslope as a landslide

Causes and effects

A landslide can be set in motion and accelerated by vibration of the ground, as occurs in an earthquake. In Indonesia, especially around the large islands of Sumatra and Java, relatively few earthquakes happen on land compared with the frequent quakes that originate in the ocean trench offshore to the southwest. Nevertheless, most of the economic damage and social disruption on land is caused by earthquakes. One earthquake in 1962, in the steep-sided mountains near the city of Padang in central west Sumatra, caused numerous landslides and much damage to buildings and other structures. It also lowered the floor of a lake so places that were previously above the shoreline became submerged beneath 10 m (33 ft) of water.

Most large Indonesian cities have been built on relatively stable ground away from the main earthquake zone. Batavia, on the site of Jakarta in northwest Java, was devastated in 1699 by an earthquake that caused landslides in the catchment area of the Liwung river; great masses of mud and uprooted trees hurtled down into the river, causing widespread flooding and silting up of channels downstream in the city.

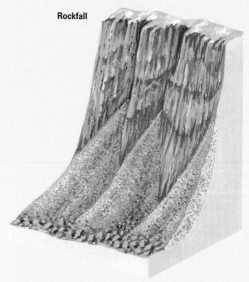
Rockfall

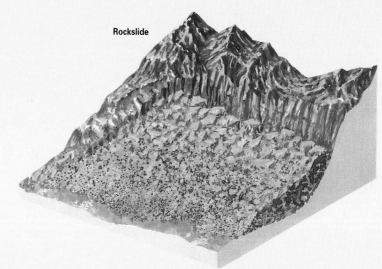
Rockslide

Forested slopes in mountainous Sabah, northeast Borneo. Where vegetation cover is removed by logging or during road or building construction, the soil is exposed to erosion and the risk of landslides. On the steep slopes of Southeast Asia torrential rain results in many landslides. Volcanic eruptions and earthquakes also trigger landslides.

Rockfalls and rockslides are the fastest types of mass movement – the downslope shiftings of weathered material. A rockfall (*left*) is a free fall of fragments on a mountainside or other precipitous slope. In high mountains, fragments accumulate as scree at the foot of slopes. In a rockslide (*below*), masses of rock slip down a slope. The term avalanche is used to cover both types of mass movement. Slides cause more damage to people than rock falls do because they take place on lower slopes, which are closer to human settlements.

From the offshore islands and oceanic Java trench southwest of Sumatra and Java, the active zone of earthquakes passes through Flores in an arc east through Sulawesi to the Philippines. Earthquakes that trigger landslides are particularly strong close to the Philippine trench of the Pacific and in eastern Luzon. Weaker earthquakes occur in western Mindanao and southwestern Luzon.

Many landslides are also triggered by volcanic eruptions. Mount Mayon on Luzon is one of the most active volcanoes of Southeast Asia, with a peak period of major eruptions between 1814 and 1928. Some of the landslides that develop form mud-and-lava mixtures (lahars) and pour into rivers, fill the channels and cause widespread flooding. The 1963 eruption of Goenoeng Agoeng, the sacred mountain of northeast Bali, started flows of mud, stones and boulders that buried the houses of a nearby village in up to 3 m (10 ft) of debris.

In the Philippines the effects of earthquakes and volcanic eruptions are often aggravated by heavy rain. Other landslides are associated simply with heavy rain on unstable slopes. Major typhoons, such as those that struck central Vietnam in 1953 and Manila in 1999, cause extensive landslides, as do heavy rains in equatorial areas, especially where hill slopes have been modified by cuttings for roads or excavation for building construction. One or two major storms may cause so many landslides and such high river flows that more eroded rock material is carried away by them than by all the rest of the rains during the year.

MAJOR LANDSLIDE DISASTERS

Torrential rainfall often triggers landslides, in Southeast Asia as elsewhere, but many are triggered by events some distance away. In 1920 earthquakes started the catastrophic landslides in the loess region of northern China that cost some 200,000 lives. Volcanic eruptions caused the landslides and mudflows of 1970 and 1985 in the Andes mountains of South America.

Year	Location	Deaths
1963	Italy	2,500
1966–67	Brazil	2,700
1970	Peru	21,000
1971	Peru	600
1972	Hong Kong	300
1972	United States	400
1981	Indonesia	500
1983	China	277
1985	Colombia	26,000
1985	Philippines	300
2000	Sumatra	100

Mudflow

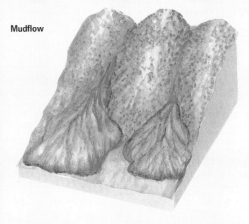

Soil creep

Slump

Earthflow

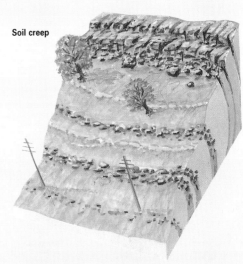

Sliding rocks slump (*left*) when they tip backward (rotate) as they move downslope, often where clay or shale underlies more solid rocks.

An earthflow (*above*) can be triggered by heavy rain. The slipping rocks can break into steps, and at the foot of the slope a "toe" forms.

In a mudflow (*top*) the saturated earth flows down even a gentle slope. The consequences can be catastrophic. Soil creep (*below*) is much slower; imperceptible to the eye, it is revealed by displaced rock layers, trees, soil and walls.

HABITATS AND THEIR CONSERVATION

A SPECTACULAR WILDERNESS · STRATEGIES FOR CONSERVATION · VANISHING HABITATS

Southeast Asia extends from the Tropic of Cancer to south of the Equator, and from the Himalayan foothills of Myanmar to the tropical islands of the Philippines and Indonesia, a distance of more than 6,000 km (3,730 mi) west to east. It encompasses a wide variety of habitats, and is the meeting place for species from two continents. Myanmar, Thailand, Indochina and most of Malaysia mark the southernmost limit for Asian species, and the islands of eastern Indonesia, including Irian Jaya (now West Papua), lying on the Australian continental shelf, contain many Oceanian species. This warm, fertile region contains some of the wildest places still remaining in the world, both on land and in the seas, though they are increasingly threatened by the pressures of ever-increasing numbers of local inhabitants and tourists.

COUNTRIES IN THE REGION

Brunei, Cambodia, Indonesia, Laos, Malaysia, Myanmar, Philippines, Singapore, Thailand, Vietnam

Major protected area	Hectares
Alaungdaw Kathapa NP	160,667
Cibodas NP BR	15,000
Cuc Phuong NP	25,000
Dumoga-Bone NR	300,000
Gunung Leuser NP BR	792,675
Gunung Lorentz NP	2,505,000
Gunung Mulu NP	52,865
Gunung Niut NR	110,000
Huai Kha Khaeng WS WH	622,200
Khao Yai NP	216,863
Komodo NP BR WH	75,000
Lore Lindu NP BR	231,000
Mae Sa-Kog Ma R BR	14,200
Mount Apo NP	72,814
Mount Kinabalu NP	75,370
Palawan BR	1,150,800
Red River Estuary RS	12,000
Siberut NP BR	56,500
Taman Negara NP	434,351
Tanjung Puting NP BR	355,000
Teluk Laut Cendrawasih NP	1,453,500
Ujung Kulon NP WH	78,619
Ulu Temburong NP	48,859

BR = Biosphere Reserve; NP = National Park; NR = Nature Reserve; R = Reserve; RS = Ramsar site; WH = World Heritage site; WS = Wildlife Sanctuary

A SPECTACULAR WILDERNESS

Southeast Asia was created between 15 and 3 million years ago when outlying fragments of ancient drifting supercontinents collided in the vicinity of the island of Sulawesi. Molded by its geological past, at a crossroads for animal and plant migrations, the region has some of the most spectacular and diverse tropical habitats in the world. These range from muddy coastal mangroves and peat swamp forests to moss-draped cloud forests and shrubby alpine plant communities; from tall, lowland dipterocarp (two-winged fruited) forests to the palm-thick jungles of the eastern islands; from tidal wetlands to the multicolored crater lakes of still-active volcanoes; from craggy limestone hills with spearlike pinnacles and vast underground cave systems to harsh, nutrient-poor heathlands.

The region has had a long history of human settlement, and people have left their mark on the landscape. The open rolling grasslands of Thailand, east Java and the Lesser Sunda Islands, which extend from Bali to Timor, are great swathes of once forested land that was cleared for agriculture a long time ago and subsequently abandoned.

A species-rich ecosystem Tropical rainforest covers much of the region. It supports many rare and unusual plants and animals, which are specially adapted to living in a particular layer of the tree canopy, in the understorey or on the forest floor.

Mist clings to a forested mountainside Highland cloud forests contain fewer species than lowland rainforest. Their inaccessibility means that they are less vulnerable to human disturbance and encroachment.

Biomes

- tropical humid forest
- tropical dry forest
- mountain and highland system
- island system
- lake system

- ◆ major protected area
- ○ Biosphere Reserve
- × World Heritage site

Map of biomes Two continents – Asia and Australia – meet in Southeast Asia, and it is a mixing ground for plants and animals from both of them. The large number of islands increases the diversity of species.

The variety of terrestrial habitats is matched offshore by a marine world of superb diversity. Meadows of sea grass make lush feeding grounds for sea cows (dugongs) and turtles, while vast numbers of colorful fish and other sea creatures live and breed in the complex world of the coral reefs that fringe the islands, among the richest ecosystems on Earth. The southern seas are rich grounds for marine mammals: schools of sperm whales and dolphins, following their traditional migration routes into the Indian Ocean, sport in the straits between the Lesser Sunda Islands.

The luxuriant forests

With an equable climate, year-round sunshine and regular rainfall, Southeast Asia has ideal growing conditions for plant life. Temperate oak, teak and conifer forests in Myanmar give way farther south to dry deciduous forests and then to a broad band of tropical rainforest.

Seasonal monsoon rains mean that these rainforests are among the most luxuriant and species-rich habitats on Earth. Giant trees stretch upward, sometimes 60 m (200 ft) or more, and each hectare (2.5 acres) of forest may contain 100 different species of trees. Clinging to the taller trees, other plants strain to reach the life-giving light: orchids and bird's-nest ferns festoon the highest boughs; spiny rattans (climbing palms) thrust their tendrils upward; and gnarled vines and berry-laden climbers wind round the trunks. Strangling figs, which begin life high in the canopy, develop arched roots that eventually strangle the unfortunate host tree.

Distinct communities of plants and animals occupy layers of the tropical forest between the ground and the topmost tree canopy. The whole habitat is thus so complex that as yet little is understood of its

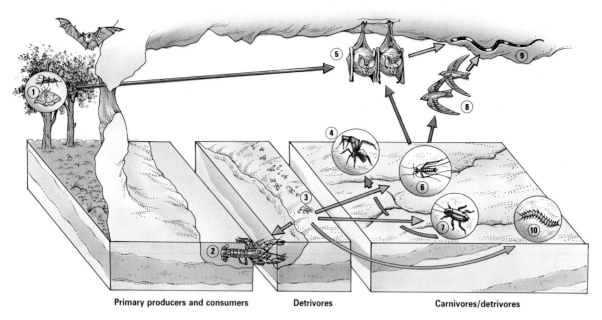
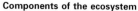

Components of the ecosystem
1 Forest insects
2 Cave crayfish
3 Bat guano
4 Cave spider
5 Roosting bats
6 Cave cricket
7 Cave beetle
8 Cave swiftlets
9 Cave snake
10 Cave millipede

Energy flow
→ primary/secondary consumer
→ secondary/tertiary consumer
→ dead material/consumer

A cave ecosystem is based on nutrients brought into the cave by bats, birds and underground streams.

Primary producers and consumers   Detrivores   Carnivores/detrivores

tangled interrelationships or even of all the species it contains. There are many strange and unique plants and animals: the giant parasitic rafflesia, the world's largest flower, the delicate maiden's-veil fungus, and the insect-eating pitcher plants and ant plants that flourish on the nutrient-poor soils of Borneo. The forest is the home of the solitary orangutan, territorial gibbons, big-eyed tarsiers, flying lemurs and a host of other "flying" mammals, lizards and frogs that have adopted ways of gliding through the trees. Indonesia alone boasts more than 400 mammal species, including such rarities as Sumatran and Javan rhinos, tree kangaroos, babirusa hogs and pot-bellied proboscis monkeys, as well as a wealth of colorful birds, ranging from tiny iridescent sunbirds to birds of paradise, helmeted cassowaries and the magnificent hornbills that are so important in Bornean culture and folklore.

STRATEGIES FOR CONSERVATION

The idea of conservation is not new to Southeast Asia. The first nature reserve in the Indonesian archipelago was established in southern Sumatra as early as the 7th century by decree of one of the first kings of Srivijaya; it reflected the early Hindus' appreciation of all animal life. Traditionally, communities harvested natural resources wisely and sustainably. Today, however, much greater demands are being made on wilderness areas, and conservation has consequently become a matter for governments rather than individual villages.

During the period of European colonization a network of game and forest reserves was established throughout Southeast Asia. These set out to prevent overexploitation of certain species rather than give total protection. This tradition of conservation contin-

ued after independence, and emphasis has been given to improving the protected area systems of the region, and expanding them to cover the whole range of natural habitats, from coral reefs to rainforests.

Indonesia has recognized the importance of its biodiversity to the world; it has 47 ecosystem types and approximately 17 percent of the total number of species in the world including about 11 percent of the world flowering plant species, 12 percent of mammals, 15 percent of amphibians and reptiles, 17 percent of birds and over 37 percent of the world's fish. The government has a national biodiversity strategy and action plan and there are over 350 protected areas covering 10 percent of the land area. Thailand also has some well-run reserves and a network of national parks and wildlife sanctuaries covering nearly 14 percent of its land. Vietnam created its first national park, Cuc Phuong, in 1962 and now has 54 protected areas. Cambodia, where the area around Tonle Sap was damaged by warring factions in the country's civil war, has recently developed a network of 23 protected areas including 7 national parks. One of the poorest nations in the world, Laos, also created 17 National Biodiversity Conservation Areas throughout the 1990s.

Governments have come to appreciate the need to preserve natural habitats. Many parks and reserves protect important watersheds that control the flow of water to the surrounding country. The Dumoga-Bone National Park in Sulawesi was established to protect the watershed around a large irrigation scheme. To establish the

Lowland swamps in Irian Jaya (West Papua). These unspoilt wetlands are inhabited by many species of animals, and preservation of the habitat is essential to safeguard their diversity. But the surrounding land is being encroached on by coconut plantations.

THE SUMMIT OF BORNEO

Towering dramatically above the coastal plains of northern Borneo, Kinabalu at 4,094 m (13,432 ft) is the island's highest peak. Kinabalu National Park was established in 1964, and is one of the best-managed parks in the region. The mountain has one of the richest communities of plants in the world, with representatives from more than half the families of flowering plants. There are a thousand or more species of orchids, 24 species of rhododendrons, 5 of them unique to Kinabalu, and 10 species of insect-eating pitcher plants.

As the land rises, lowland rainforest gives way to montane chestnut and oak forest, succeeded by cloud forest and rhododendron thickets. On the windswept pavement of the granite summit a few hardy alpines struggle to survive. Tens of millions of years ago the spine of Borneo was much higher than it is today, and supported a rich variety of alpine plants; Kinabalu is a refuge for these plants of cooler climes. The mountain plants include many living fossils, such as the celery-top pine and the tree oak, the missing link between the oaks and the beeches. At higher altitudes there are several plants more typical of temperate latitudes, isolated here when the climate warmed at the end of the most recent ice age some 10,000 years ago.

The animals of the park are as varied as the plants, though less conspicuous. More than 100 species of mammals and over 250 bird species have been recorded, including the orangutan, gibbon, mouse deer, clouded leopard and ferret badger. Even the elusive Sumatran rhino is rumored to have been sighted.

Sheltered crevices on the bare summit of Mount Kinabalu provide a refuge for alpine plants isolated since the last ice age some 10,000 years ago. The harsh climate allowed them to survive here.

reserve cost only a fraction of the World Bank loan that subsidized the development, yet the reserve protects the forest and extends the life of the irrigation canals, so that both the people of the island and Sulawesi's unique wildlife enjoy the benefits of the scheme.

The long-term security and survival of protected areas in densely populated Southeast Asia depends upon the support of local communities. Increasingly, conservation programs will need to establish buffer zones outside the most strictly protected areas to provide sources of income, firewood and forest products for the local people. In the protected areas at Khao Yai in Thailand and Gunung Mulu in Sarawak there has been a determined effort to employ local guides and guards, so that the growing ecotourism industry is able to benefit both local communities and the national economy.

Reserves under pressure
Even officially protected areas are not yet secure. Forest clearance and hunting continues unchecked in many parts of the region. Reserves are threatened by all kinds of development, from landfilling of estuaries to resettlement schemes or even the creation of prestigious golf courses. Protected areas also face such pressures as low local community participation, poor management and inadequate staffing as well as lack of funding. Mount Apo park in the Philippines, the last stronghold of the monkey-eating eagle and other rare wildlife, has been partly reduced in status in order to provide agricultural land for settlers. Gunung Niut in Borneo is threatened by logging and by goldmining; both industries would upset the park's ecosystem.

Many of these protected areas are of global as well as national significance, and the world community is responding to the challenge. For many years international organizations such as the World Wide Fund for Nature (WWF) and the World Conservation Union (IUCN) have helped to identify conservation needs and improve management in reserves in Southeast Asia. There is an encouraging trend as financial institutions such as the World Bank and – through their aid agencies – Western governments take on a more active role in sponsoring conservation activities; in this way they often protect their investments. The beneficiaries will be the forests and their wildlife, and the local and worldwide human communities.

VANISHING HABITATS

The demands of agriculture place tremendous pressures on wilderness areas in the region. Forests are being felled by farmers who cultivate the land and then move on, for plantations, and to satisfy the world's seemingly insatiable appetite for hardwoods. Tropical rainforests are disappearing at an alarming rate. In Malaysia, where an average of 37 million cubic meters of roundwood are cut each year, is facing a loss of about 2.5 percent of its natural forest annually. It has been estimated that nearly half of its frontier forest and 737 tree species are threatened.

Forests have also been lost as a consequence of war, as in Vietnam where 2 million ha (5 million acres) of forest and mangroves were sprayed with herbicides such as Agent Orange during the conflict with the United States between 1964 and 1975. Large areas of the region, particularly in Indonesia, have been lost to fires. In 1997, forest fires burned continuously for several months destroying about 1 million ha (2.4 million acres) of forest in Kalimantan and Sumatra and creating a smoke haze that spread over Southeast Asia affecting some 70 million people. The fires were started by farmers clearing forested land for agriculture. Indonesia is now taking steps to conserve parts of its forest and has also initiated a forest fire prevention program.

Most countries in Southeast Asia have already lost at least half their forest cover. In densely crowded Java only 9 percent of the island remains forested. Even on Borneo, renowned for its vast tracts of tall dipterocarp and swamp forests, the forest boundaries are being pushed back farther and farther inland and every major river is congested with floating logs. Until people throughout the world become aware of the threat and there is a dramatic reduction in the use of tropical hardwoods, the destructive deforestation of Southeast Asia will continue.

Where the loggers go the farmers follow. Traditional peoples living at low densities were once able to practice shifting cultivation in ecological balance with their environment. The Land Dayaks of Borneo, the Muong people of Laos and the hill tribes of Myanmar all cleared land, grew their crops and then let the land lie fallow for several years before returning to cultivate it again. As human populations have grown and remote areas have been opened up for new settlers, more forest areas have been cleared, often on vulnerable lands with nutrient-poor soils. These fields may provide crops for a year or two, but with regular burning they cannot return to secondary forest.

Eventually these abandoned fields become a sea of alang-alang (cogon) grasslands. These are becoming increasingly common throughout tropical Asia. The tough, tall grass is difficult to supplant, has little value except for new grazing and thrives on burning. Fires sweep through the grasslands, destroying adjacent planta-

Cloudy moss forest at 3,500 m (10,500 ft). Northern Borneo is one of the wettest places on Earth, and in the highlands it is also very cold. The trees are stunted, being no more than 10 to 15 m (30 to 45 ft) high; as there is only a single canopy layer enough light penetrates to promote the growth of hanging lichens, mosses and other epiphytes, as well as ground plants.

Life from the ashes As lava and ash on a volcanic peak weather to a fertile soil, the radiating ridges and channels formed in the lava flows are colonized by wind-blown seeds, and vegetation begins to cover the mountainside.

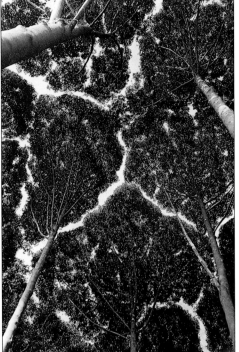

Looking up through the canopy The tops of these giant dipterocarp trees do not overlap. One explanation for this "crown shyness" is that it inhibits the spread of leaf-eating caterpillars. It also allows light to penetrate through the trees, and has led to the evolution of jumping and gliding mammals and reptiles.

tions of newly planted trees and eating into the natural forest.

Sometimes the need for conservation is understood only too well by the local people but ignored by governments and business interests, more concerned with short-term profit than the long-term cost of environmental folly. The Penan of Sarawak, hunter-gatherers who harvest wild meat and a few minor forest products for their own use, have blockaded roads to halt the timber trucks of the companies that are destroying their traditional lands. Local people, struggling for a livelihood from shifting cultivation, are often blamed for starting the fires that lead to forest losses, but the areas that burn most intensely are those that have already been logged.

Paying the price of "progress"

Many countries in the region are suffering the environmental consequences that follow the loss of natural landscapes – droughts where there was once rain, floods sweeping down deforested valleys, and erosion of coasts and hillsides. Lowland habitats, particularly on the fertile alluvial lands along river valleys, are the first to disappear. Swamps, mangroves and wetlands are drained for development

WALLACE'S LINE

During the last ice age the countries of mainland tropical Asia and the Greater Sunda Islands – Sumatra, Borneo and Java – were connected by dry land; they were separated as melting ice caused sea levels to rise again. Before this wildlife was able to move along the land bridge, and the islands still have plant and animal species in common with those of the mainland, characterized by tall dipterocarp trees and by monkeys, native deer and hornbills. These habitats, together with their plants and animals, fall within the Indomalayan biogeographical region.

By contrast the islands of eastern Indonesia – Irian Jaya (western New Guinea), Kai and Aru – lie on the Australian continental shelf and belong within the Oceanian biogeographical region. Here there are mound-building birds, bowerbirds, parrots and birds of paradise, while wallabies take over the ecological niche of deer.

On the edges of these two biogeographical regions the islands of Sulawesi, the Philippines, the Moluccas and the Lesser Sundas form a mixing ground for plant and animals from both east and west. They include many species that are found only here.

It was the renowned 19th-century British naturalist, Alfred Russel Wallace (1823–1913), co-publisher with Charles Darwin (1809–82) of the theory of natural selection, who first recognized the pattern of species distribution in the area. Wallace's line runs through the islands between Bali and Lombok, Borneo and Sulawesi, and Palawan and the rest of the Philippines. It is still recognized as the biogeographical boundary for many families of plants, and of birds, mammals, insects and other animals, and is a reminder of Southeast Asia's turbulent geological past.

and agriculture, forests are cleared, limestone hills are quarried for cement, coral reefs are mined for lime and damaged by blasting to kill the fish.

As these habitats are lost, so too are the benefits they provide: natural products, fish nurseries, coastline and watershed protection. Their value is often appreciated only after they are gone. Very few wildlands, apart from inaccessible mountain areas, will remain inviolate outside protected areas. The 21st century will be a time for decision, a last chance to save many natural areas which once destroyed will be lost forever.

Ujung Kulon National Park

Situated on Java's westernmost point, the Ujung Kulon National Park is Indonesia's premier reserve and one of the few remaining wilderness areas on this densely populated island. The park includes the Ujung Kulon peninsula, connected by a narrow isthmus to the Gunung Honje massif, and the offshore islands of Panaitan and Peucang, with their spectacular coral reefs. Its boundaries extend seaward to embrace the island remnants of the famous volcano Krakatau in the Sunda Strait between Java and Sumatra. Protected on three sides by the sea and to the east by Gunung Honje, Ujung Kulon provides a last refuge for some of the unique wildlife on an island where 100 million land-hungry people have cleared most of the original vegetation.

The reserve was created to protect one of the last surviving populations of one of the world's rarest animals, the one-horned Javan rhinoceros, which is found in the lowlying swamps of Ujung Kulon. Other rare animals living in the park include the leopard, native Javan gibbon and troops of leaf monkeys (surili). The Javan tiger, which survived in the reserve until recently, is now extinct.

The landscape was shaped by the eruption of 1883, when the island of Krakatau was rent by a massive explosion. After the explosion came devastating sea waves, which destroyed the coastal forests of Ujung Kulon. Today these forests are characterized by dense thickets of rattan and salak palms, gingers and bamboos, so tangled that only the thick-skinned rhinos can pass with ease.

Several open grazing grounds are maintained within the park and here the Javan wild cattle (banteng) come to graze in the early morning and late afternoon. Here, too, sambar deer come to feed, as well as peacocks and the green junglefowl that are found only on Java. On the golden beaches on the south coast of the park green turtles nest, though even in this sanctuary their eggs are not secure from natural predators such as pigs and monitor lizards.

Ujung Kulon is a paradise for birds, from the forest-ranging hornbills to tiny sunbirds and the waterbirds and storks that enjoy the wetlands of the Nyiur swamps. The park's marine and river life includes the archerfish, which fells insects by shooting jets of water at them, and the beautiful and colorful animals of the coral reefs. Scenically the park is outstanding, with white coral beaches, lofty rainforest, strangling figs with cathedral-like roots and the rich plant life of the forest floor – exotic fungi, intricate palm fronds and twisting lianas that wind their way up to the canopy.

Ujung Kulon's most dramatic spectacle is the crater of Anak Krakatau (child of Krakatau). The smoking cone bears witness to the fact that the volcano is only sleeping; during its restless phases the sea and night sky are lit dramatically by showers of sparks from its glowing core.

People have probably lived on Ujung Kulon since early times. At the time of the 1883 eruption there were several coastal settlements practicing shifting cultivation

A forest stream carries away the excess water deposited by the area's heavy rainfall. By acting as a sponge, the forests form a natural reservoir, regulating the supply of water to the surrounding country. Without the forest, water flow becomes erratic.

A last refuge for wildlife Ujung Kulon's forests shelter some of Java's most endangered animal species, including the one-horned Javan rhinoceros. The park is a reminder of how the densely populated island must have been before the original vegetation was cleared.

A mangrove swamp in Ujung Kulon. These salt-tolerant trees form a very rich ecosystem in many estuaries and coastal waters of the tropics. Their leaves and twigs fall into the water and decompose to make the first link in the food chain.

and growing rice. These were swept away by the tsunami that followed the eruption. The ash from the volcano smothered the peninsula and its vegetation, making the land much less productive, so the human population of Ujung Kulon declined. The region's wildlife benefited further when the area was evacuated by government decree because of the danger from disease and from man-eating tigers.

Protection of Ujung Kulon began in 1921; it was granted national park status in 1980. The WWF has had an important role in conservation since 1965, working closely with the Indonesian Conservation Department to improve the protection and management of the reserve. Today it is probably one of the better protected Indonesian reserves, though its eastern borders have been encroached on by village farmers. Vigilance is needed against poachers (the rhino is particularly vulnerable) and collectors of turtle eggs; local fishermen not only overfish the reef areas but can cause serious damage from untended campfires.

Living in the dark

In parts of Southeast Asia huge cave systems have been formed by underground streams, which have eroded the limestone rocks. The most famous are the Niah Caves of Borneo and the Batu Caves of Malaysia.

These caves form islands that contrast with the sea of forest around them. They are an ecosystem with special characteristics, the main feature of which is the complete absence of light.

Away from the entrance no green plants can survive, so the animal community within the cave needs another source of energy and nutrients. These are provided by bats and swiftlets, which feed outside the caves and return to breed and roost. They form the basis of a food chain, being preyed on by snakes, lizards, rats and civets, while their corpses and droppings fall to the cave floor and are scavenged by a variety of animals. Cockroaches, springtails, flies and beetles swarm over the cave floor in vast numbers and are eaten by spiders, scorpions, whip-scorpions and centipedes. Many of these invertebrates are colorless and blind, color and sight being of little use in the dark. Touch and smell are the secret to successful predation and scavenging.

The vast entrance to a cave in Mulu National Park, Sarawak, Malaysia provides the link between the outside world and the specialized ecosystem within.

ANIMAL LIFE

UNIQUE ANIMAL LIFE · ANCIENT FOREST LIFE · NATURE IN RETREAT

Southeast Asia is home to an extremely diverse collection of animals and an enormous variety of habitats; there are some 150,000 species in the region. The animal life forms part of the Oriental realm, a zoogeographic region which comprises most of Asia. Consequently many of the region's animals also occur in adjacent parts of the Indian subcontinent and southwestern China. New species have evolved on a number of the islands: for example, the Proboscis monkey and the Flying frog of Borneo. On the easternmost islands Asian mainland animals, such as forest pigs and civets, mingle with animals of Australasian origin, such as the marsupial tree kangaroo. The rich Indo-Pacific coral reefs and warm seas support a wealth of marine life, including sea turtles and schools of Sperm whales.

COUNTRIES IN THE REGION

Brunei, Cambodia, Indonesia, Laos, Malaysia, Myanmar, Philippines, Singapore, Thailand, Vietnam

ENDEMISM AND DIVERSITY

Diversity Very high (second only to South America)
Endemism High to very high

SPECIES

	Total	Threatened	†Extinct
Mammals	650	75	2
Birds	*2,000	200	3
Others	unknown	141	0

† species extinct since 1600 – including Panay giant fruit bat (Acerodonlucifer), Schomburgk's deer (Cervus schomburgki), Japanese wattled lapwing (Vanellus macropterus), Caerulean paradise-flycatcher (Eutrichomyias rowleyi), Four-colored flowerpecker (Dicaeum quadricolor)
* breeding and regular non-breeding species

NOTABLE THREATENED ENDEMIC SPECIES

Mammals Pileated gibbon (Hylobates pileatus), orangutan (Pongo pygmaeus), Flat-headed cat (Felis planiceps), Malayan tapir (Tapirus indicus), Javan rhinoceros (Rhinoceros sondaicus), Kouprey (Bos sauveli), Tamaraw (Bubalus mindorensis)
Birds Philippine eagle (Pithecophaga jefferyi), Giant ibis (Pseudibis gigantea), Gumey's pitta (Pitta gurneyi), Salmon-crested cockatoo (Cacatua moluccensis)
Others River terrapin (Batagur baska), False gharial (Tomistoma schlegelii), Komodo dragon (Varanus komodoensis)

NOTABLE THREATENED NON-ENDEMIC SPECIES

Mammals Asian elephant (Elephas maximus), Gaur (Bos gaurus)
Birds Lesser adjutant (Leptoptilos javanicus), Green peafowl (Pavo muticus), Asian dowitcher (Limnodromus semipalmatus)
Others Estuarine crocodile (Crocodylus porosus)

DOMESTICATED ANIMALS (originating in region)

Bali cattle (Bos javanicus), Water buffalo (Bubalus 'bubalis'), Asian elephant (Elephas maximus), duck (Anas platyrhynchos), chicken (Gallus gallus)

UNIQUE ANIMAL LIFE

The rainforests, mangrove swamps and myriad islands of Southeast Asia support a very high number of endemic species. Many of these animals evolved in the tropical rainforests that cover most of the region. Some of the oldest forests in the world are found here, and have provided a stable habitat long enough for new species to evolve. There are in fact whole families and orders of animals that occur nowhere else. These include the tarsiers, tree shrews, flying lemurs, leaf monkeys and gibbons, and the leaf birds. Other birds, such as hornbills and pheasants, are especially characteristic of Southeast Asia. The forests also provide a refuge where many rare large mammals maintain a precarious foothold: tigers, the Indian elephant, rhinoceroses, tapirs, bears, numerous monkeys and the large distinctive orangutan.

Centers of evolution

Southeast Asia's great diversity of animals is attributable in part to the presence of thousands of islands, some of them very large. The western islands of Sumatra, Java and Borneo were once connected to the Asian mainland during past periods of glaciation. Under these conditions land bridges were formed, enabling mammals and birds gradually to colonize the area before the islands had formed. The islands between the Asian mainland and Australia have experienced animal immigration from both east and west. For example, there are marsupials (pouched mammals) in West Papua (formerly Irian Jaya), rhinoceroses in Sumatra and Java; orangutans in Sumatra and Borneo and tapirs in southern Sumatra. After the land bridges were submerged and the islands became isolated, some animals continued to colonize by island hopping.

In Indonesia and on the surrounding islands, remote fragments of tropical forests have served as miniature centers of evolution, and are home to many endemic species. These animals have diversified in many cases into individual island species or races that are specially adapted to the local conditions. Wild cattle are good

Gentle giant The orangutan is superbly adapted for life in the trees, with long arms, hooked hands and handlike feet for gripping. Already decimated by collection for zoos, the orangutan population is now threatened by destruction of its rainforest habitat.

The Rhinoceros hornbill feeds mainly on fruit, which it picks up with the tips of its large mandibles. The large, horny growth above the bill may help the bird to recognize sex, age and species; in the larger species it may also be used when fighting.

examples of different species having adapted to particular environments: the large gaur lives in upland forests, the wild Water buffaloes in swampy areas, the banteng only in Java and the small anoa in the hills of Sulawesi.

Another species that has diversified is the Sulawesi macaque – related to the Pig-tailed and Crab-eating macaques of nearby Borneo: over time it has evolved not only into a new species but also into several distinct races in different parts of the island.

In 1858 the naturalist Alfred Wallace (1823–1913) proposed a boundary to mark the easternmost extent of the Oriental zoogeographic region. The Wallace line has been recently modified, and now runs along the edge of the Sunda continental shelf, just east of Java, Borneo and the Philippines. A later line was proposed in 1902 by the Dutch zoologist Max Weber to mark the westernmost extent of Australasian wildlife. The recently amended Weber's line runs just west of Australia and New Guinea, following the edge of the Australian continental shelf. In between these two lines lie Sulawesi, the Lesser Sunda Islands and many other islands in which both Australasian and Oriental animals are mixed.

ANCIENT FOREST LIFE

Tropical Asia's ancient forests have been the focus of evolution of several groups of animals that are highly adapted to life in the treetops. These include the tree shrews and the tarsiers, both of which are found only in Southeast Asia.

Tree shrews are small, squirrel-like mammals. The ground-dwelling species are larger, with short tails, long snouts and well-developed claws that they use to dig for insects. Tree-dwellers tend to be smaller, with eyes more forward-directed for judging distance, and long tails for balancing. They are thought to resemble closely the early ancestors of the simians (monkeys and apes) and are therefore placed in the prosimian ("forerunners of the simians") animal suborder.

Tarsiers are small, nocturnal mammals confined to Sumatra, Borneo, Sulawesi and a number of small islands in the Philippines. They have huge eyes for night vision which – as in owls – take up so much room in their sockets that they cannot move much; the animal compensates by turning its head through a wide angle. The eyes are directed forward to give good stereoscopic vision, useful to the animal when catching prey with its long, slender fingers, which act like a cage to ensnare swift-moving insects. Tarsiers also use their large, sensitive ears to locate prey. They can easily jump up to 2 m (6.5 ft), landing feet first on neighboring trees, using their enlarged adhesive finger pads for better grip.

The tarsiers' carnivorous diet has led to controversy over their taxonomic position – or classification – in the animal world. Current opinion regards them as intermediate between the prosimians (the suborder that also includes lorises, lemurs and bushbabies) and the primates.

Another prosimian, the Slow loris, is found from Vietnam to Borneo. Like the tarsiers it is nocturnal, and does not compete with other primates. Its fingers are shorter, and it creeps up on its unwary prey, rather like a chameleon. The Slow loris has a remarkable ability to eat prey that other animals find repulsive.

Movement through the canopy
Various primates employ different ways of moving among the trees. Orangutans move slowly, walking along the branches, but will use their heavy weight to bend

Stump-tailed macaque
Macaca arctoides

Pig-tailed macaque
Macaca nemestrina

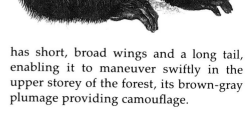

Moor macaque
Macaca maura

trees until the gap between one tree and the next has narrowed sufficiently for them to traverse it. The gibbons swing from branch to branch using their long arms and hooked hands alternately, but they walk upright on two feet on broad branches and on the ground.

Animals from many other groups have evolved the habit of gliding from tree to tree. The Gliding gecko has broad flaps of skin along both sides of its abdomen, webbed limbs and toes and a flattened tail that is used as a rudder while gliding. The Flying dragon, another lizard, has broad, often brilliantly colored, winglike membranes. They serve two purposes: gliding, and attraction of the female during courtship. When the lizard alights on a tree trunk, the thin membrane presses close to the bark, concealing the animal's shadow. Flying squirrels also use membranes between their limbs for gliding; this not only helps them to travel easily through the canopy, but also provides a useful means of escape from predators.

Perhaps the most remarkable gliding mammals are the flying lemurs or colugos, which belong to an order of mammals with no known relatives. Their gliding membranes extend from the tips of their fingers and toes to the tip of their long tails, forming an impressive parachute. Other perhaps unexpected gliders are the Flying frog and the Gliding snake. The frog uses widely spread webs between its toes to glide through the air, spreading its limbs and toes wide to present as large a surface area as possible to the air. The Gliding snake controls its fall by curving its undersurface into a concave shape.

Birds also need certain adaptations for flying among trees. The Philippine eagle, the main predator of the Philippines jungle, is capable of attacking monkeys, taking them by surprise from branches. It

has short, broad wings and a long tail, enabling it to maneuver swiftly in the upper storey of the forest, its brown-gray plumage providing camouflage.

Pastures of the sea
The shallow lagoons that lie behind many coral reefs in this region support extensive meadows of sea grass, a favorite food of sea turtles and the unusual mammal, the Sea cow or dugong. Sea cows and their relatives, the manatees, are the only vegetarian marine mammals. The Sea cow has a fat, streamlined body with plenty of blubber to keep it warm and aid buoyancy, along with paddlelike forelimbs and a flattened tail resembling a dolphin's. Its short snout ends in a fleshy horseshoe-shaped disk armed with stiff bristles around a slitlike mouth. The sea cow has few teeth; it chews using the rough horny pads on its upper and lower palates. It feeds at night, raking up food from the seabed with its muscular disk – earning it the popular name of Sea pig. Its slow movement and relative inactivity enable it to survive on a diet low in nutrients.

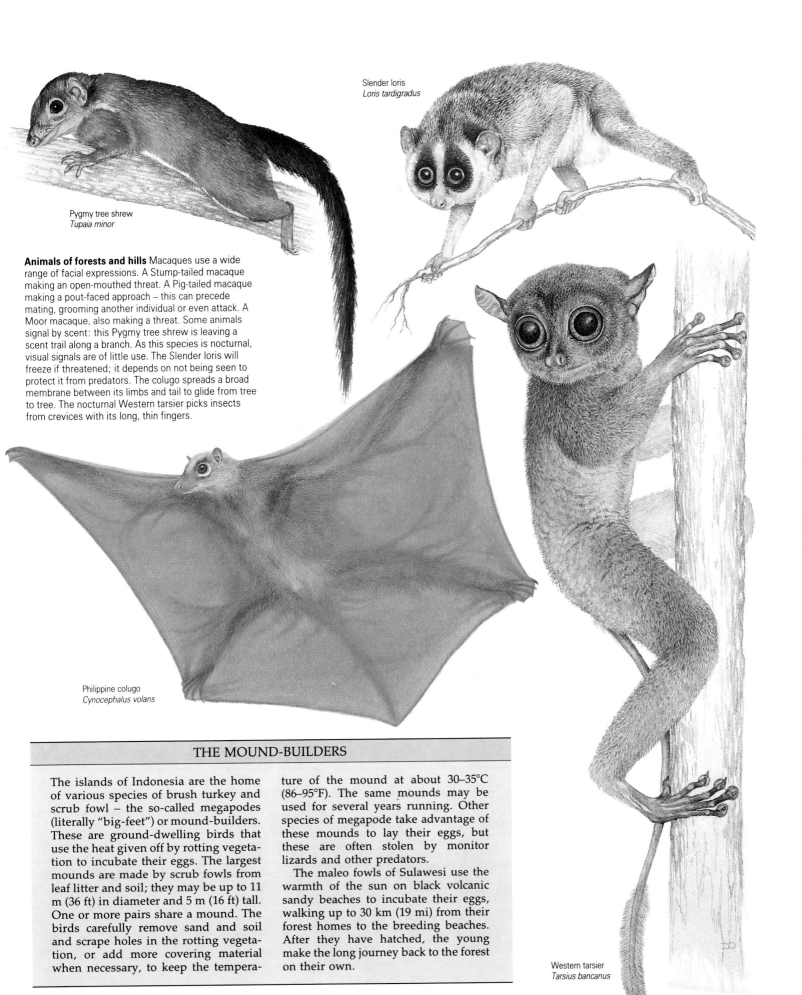

Slender loris
Loris tardigradus

Pygmy tree shrew
Tupaia minor

Animals of forests and hills Macaques use a wide range of facial expressions. A Stump-tailed macaque making an open-mouthed threat. A Pig-tailed macaque making a pout-faced approach – this can precede mating, grooming another individual or even attack. A Moor macaque, also making a threat. Some animals signal by scent: this Pygmy tree shrew is leaving a scent trail along a branch. As this species is nocturnal, visual signals are of little use. The Slender loris will freeze if threatened; it depends on not being seen to protect it from predators. The colugo spreads a broad membrane between its limbs and tail to glide from tree to tree. The nocturnal Western tarsier picks insects from crevices with its long, thin fingers.

Philippine colugo
Cynocephalus volans

THE MOUND-BUILDERS

The islands of Indonesia are the home of various species of brush turkey and scrub fowl – the so-called megapodes (literally "big-feet") or mound-builders. These are ground-dwelling birds that use the heat given off by rotting vegetation to incubate their eggs. The largest mounds are made by scrub fowls from leaf litter and soil; they may be up to 11 m (36 ft) in diameter and 5 m (16 ft) tall. One or more pairs share a mound. The birds carefully remove sand and soil and scrape holes in the rotting vegetation, or add more covering material when necessary, to keep the tempera-

ture of the mound at about 30–35°C (86–95°F). The same mounds may be used for several years running. Other species of megapode take advantage of these mounds to lay their eggs, but these are often stolen by monitor lizards and other predators.

The maleo fowls of Sulawesi use the warmth of the sun on black volcanic sandy beaches to incubate their eggs, walking up to 30 km (19 mi) from their forest homes to the breeding beaches. After they have hatched, the young make the long journey back to the forest on their own.

Western tarsier
Tarsius bancanus

NATURE IN RETREAT

It is estimated that since 1850 some 25 percent of the region's forests have been removed, more than 225 million ha (555 million acres), with a deforestation rate of 1.3 percent lost each year. The deforestation rate of Indonesia alone is about 1 percent a year and Indonesia has also lost about 1 million ha (2.4 million acres) from continuously burning forest fires since 1997. In the Philippines, forest cover is down to under 3 percent of its original extent and the forests are now not able to support the population leading to domestic wood shortages.

Such largescale habitat destruction inevitably has an enormous impact on the region's biodiversity. The fruit-bearing trees are a haven for fruit-eating birds such as the spectacular hornbills, as well as squirrels and monkeys. Flowers attract nectarsipping butterflies and tiny, iridescent sunbirds, and the leaves are food for a great many herbi-

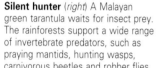

Silent hunter (*right*) A Malayan green tarantula waits for insect prey. The rainforests support a wide range of invertebrate predators, such as praying mantids, hunting wasps, carnivorous beetles and robber flies.

vores such as monkeys and small insects. The abundant insect life is in turn preyed on by birds such as flycatchers, babblers and leaf birds.

Coastal reclamation schemes have now cleared more than 1 million ha (2.5 million acres) of primary swamp forest. Up to 600,000 people have been resettled in the environmentally sensitive wetlands of Sumatra, Borneo and Irian Jaya (West Papua). Present economic policies favor short-term resource exploitation and under-value long-term benefits of conservation.

With the continuing loss of natural habitats, biological diversity is being swiftly reduced. Large mammals such as tigers and rhinoceroses need sizable areas in order to sustain viable populations. Despite full legal protection, the Bali tiger became extinct in the 1960s, and the Javan tiger disappeared in the early 1980s. The future of the Sumatran tiger and the Sumatran rhinoceros looks extremely bleak. They are now both categorized as "critically endan-

gered" with wild populations of under 400–500 and 250–400 respectively.

Large mammals that exhibit traditional migratory patterns, such as elephants, are the most likely to be affected by habitat fragmentation. It will be impossible to protect the entire range of a population or Sumatran elephants, which could be as large as 1 million ha (2.5 million acres).

Attempts have been made to increase the orangutan population, now classed as "vulnerable", by reintroducing to the wild individuals that have been rescued as orphans or captured for the pet trade. Such programs prove very difficult, as the animals have to be taught how to feed and survive in the wild.

Of the 1,000 or so globally threatened species of bird, more than 200 occur in Southeast Asia. The Gurney's pitta may have under 25 breeding pairs left, at Khao Phra Bang Khran in Thailand. Indonesia harbors more endangered bird species than any other country in the world: a total of 128, of which 91 are endemic. Some species are already in peril. The Bali starling, although numerous in zoos, numbers 30–35 in the wild.

The threat of overexploitation
Overhunting is another problem that particularly affects the larger mammals. The Indian cheetah is already extinct, and the tigers and rhinoceroses have been greatly reduced in numbers as a result of overhunting; added to this they have suffered from loss of habitat in more recent decades. Another modern trend has been the largescale trapping of monkeys for medical research. The magnificent Philippine eagle has been brought to the brink of extinction by trophy-hunters; there are estimated to be less than 500 individuals left. It seems likely that this majestic bird will be finally exterminated by the loss of its remaining fragments of forest habitat.

Crocodiles have been hunted for their skins and eggs and are now scarce in much of their former range. The taking of shells and eggs threatens several species of sea turtle. Collecting has also reduced numbers of the giant Robber crab or Coconut crab, possibly the largest terrestrial arthropod in the world, measuring 1 m (3 ft) across its legs.

Malayan tapir
Tapirus indicus

Lone wanderer (*left*) A Malayan tapir browses in the forest. It uses its muscular prehensile lips to twist and tear off leaves and twigs. Tapirs are skilled swimmers, and often browse on water plants, or submerge themselves in the water to cool off or to rid themselves of parasites.

THE KOMODO DRAGON

The tiny Indonesian islands of Komodo, Rinca, and Flores, the larger neighboring island, are the home of the world's largest lizard, the Komodo dragon, known locally as the Ora. This enormous monitor lizard can reach up to 3 m (10 ft) long and can weigh as much as 150 kg (330 lb). It is related to the carnivorous dinosaurs: fossils strikingly similar to the Komodo dragon have been unearthed in Australia from chalk deposits dating back 130 million years.

The lizard has no predators on these islands. With its huge powerful body, jaws that can be disarticulated like those of snakes, and sawedged teeth, the lizard preys on deer and Wild boar. Its powerful jaws can also excavate the egg mounds of megapode birds, and it will scavenge carrion. Its stomach juices are so strong that the lizard digests almost every part of its prey, including bones, hair and hooves. It will even devour its own offspring – young Komodo dragons spend most of their first two years hiding in trees, out of sight of the adults.

The world population of Komodo dragons is thought to be some 5,700. The species is under threat from the loss of its prey to human hunters, and the loss of its natural habitat to urbanization and agriculture. However, the area has become a National Park and World Heritage Site providing the Komodo dragons a measure of protection. They have also become a lucrative ecotourism attraction.

The world's largest lizard The powerful Komodo dragon is a formidable predator, its only enemy being humans.

Overexploitation is nowhere more prevalent than in the seas of Southeast Asia and the Pacific. When coral reefs are mined for building material and lime, the resulting clouding of the water kills the remaining living corals and with them the rich life of the reef. Reefs are frequently plundered so that resorts can be built for the tourists whose very aim is to see the unspoilt beauty of underwater life.

Commercial fishing is wreaking havoc in the Indo-Pacific. Invisible rot-proof gill nets of up to 40 km (25 mi) long drift through the ocean, often abandoned. Every year in the north Pacific alone they kill hundreds of thousands of seabirds, seals, turtles, porpoises and dolphins.

The future outlook

Environmental awareness among the governments of Asian countries is growing. Over the last 25 years Indonesia has set aside 20 million ha (50 million acres) as conservation areas, and aims to protect 20 percent of its land. In 1988 Thailand banned logging in an attempt to halt forest degradation. However, conservation must be linked to economic development among the poor of the region if a real solution to habitat destruction and species loss is to be found.

Dolphins

Dolphins are really small whales. They have elongated jaws forming the so-called beak and a high, rounded forehead, which is called the melon. Their jaws are lined with conical pointed teeth that are often curved for a better grip on their slippery prey. Most dolphins feed on fish, but a few species feed on squid or crustaceans; these species tend to have more rounded foreheads, blunter beaks and, in some cases, fewer teeth.

Marine specialists

Dolphins have managed to exploit virtually all types of marine, estuarine and riverine habitats except for the deepest parts of the ocean. They are found in the open ocean, along muddy shores and in clear rivers. Unlike most mammals, they are well adapted to a marine existence. Their bodies are streamlined, and well endowed with fat for insulation against the coldness of the water. Their forelimbs have been modified to form paddles, and they have a horizontal finlike tail for propulsion. Some species are able to dive to depths of 300 m (1,000 ft), remaining submerged for eight minutes or more. During these prolonged dives, the heart rate and peripheral blood flow are considerably reduced. In dolphins it has been estimated that 80 to 90 percent of the air in the lungs is replaced during each inhalation – a far more efficient process than human breathing. Unlike seals, dolphins give birth in the water. The calves, which are born tail first, are generally large in relation to the size of the mother – this increased surface area to volume ratio minimizes heat loss to the water.

Dolphins have either reduced or absent taste and smell organs, which are of little use in water, but they have very acute hearing, and some species use highly sensitive echolocation to find their prey. The various river dolphins rely on this method to guide them to their prey in the murky water; indeed, the Indus and Ganges dolphins have no eye lenses at all. Species that hunt in clear waters, however, probably rely on vision.

In Southeast Asia only four species live in estuaries and rivers, but no fewer than 21 species of oceanic dolphin migrate through the offshore waters of the tropical Pacific and Indian Oceans. Dolphin migration is usually a response to seasonal changes in water temperature, caused by the monsoons, which also affect the availability of food.

Purse-net danger

In some dolphin species individuals are solitary, while in others they are highly gregarious. The Spotted dolphin and other ocean dolphins may make up enormous groups of 1,000 to 2,000 individuals. They cooperate to concentrate a shoal of fish, and this has proved their undoing when hunting tuna. Every year tens of thousands of dolphins drown in the purse-seine nets of tuna fishermen, particularly from the South Korean and Japanese industrial fleets. Research has revealed that at least one dolphin dies – mostly Spotted and Long-snouted spinner dolphins – for every nine tuna caught. In the eastern Pacific fishermen use the dolphins to lead them to the tuna.

An international campaign to highlight the threat to dolphins began in the 1980s with consumers, particularly in the US, boycotting tuna. US legislation in 1990 provided for a "dolphin-safe" label on cans of tuna and canneries stopped using fish caught by encircling hunting dolphins. Fishermen then changed their practice to encircling schools of tuna but this had disastrous effects as huge numbers of other species were killed including shark and endangered sea turtles. A further bill, signed in 1997, called for dolphins caught in encircling purse-seine nets to be freed. However, these measures will not do anything to save the tens of thousands of dolphins and porpoises that are drowned each year by becoming entangled in fishermen's vast drifting gill nets that are suspended vertically in the water.

Bottle-nosed dolphin
Tursiops truncatus

Rough-toothed dolphin
Steno bredanensis

Risso's dolphin
Grampus griseus

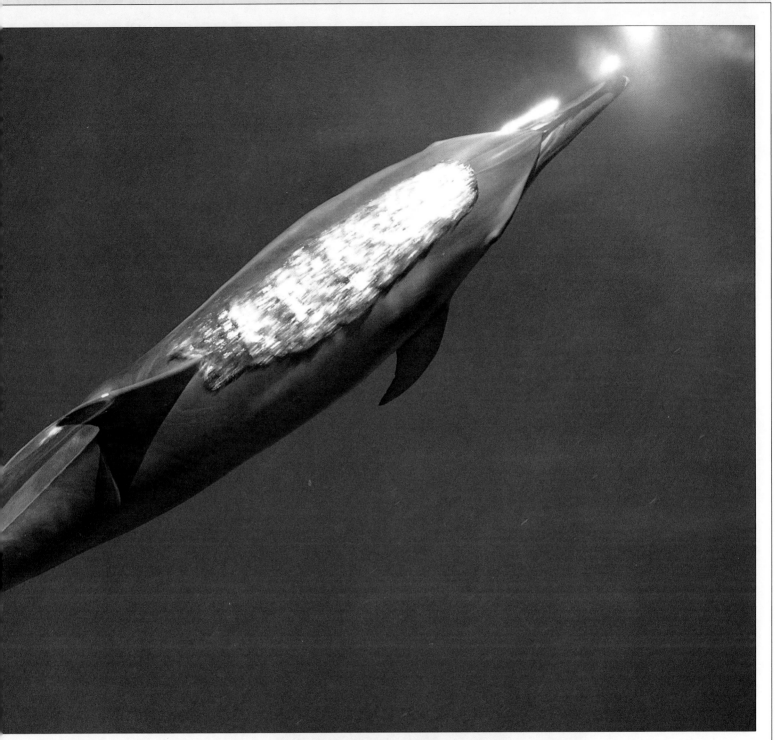

Common dolphin
Delphinus delphis

Dolphins of Southeast Asia (*left*) A Bottle-nosed dolphin scanning the world above the water. This is the species most commonly seen in dolphinaria. A coastal species, it likes to ride the bow waves of boats. The Rough-toothed dolphin is named for the wrinkled enamel on its teeth. Risso's dolphin, or grampus, lives in herds with stable group relationships, and is found in the open ocean throughout the world. The skin of males becomes very scarred with age, due to fights with other males. The Common dolphin often forms herds of several hundred individuals. They give a spectacular display when swimming close to the surface, sometimes leaping clear of the water.

Spinner dolphin (*above*) Bubbles streaming from its blowhole, a dolphin rises to the surface. Spinners are named for their acrobatic displays, usually performed in the evening, when they leap out of the water and spin round before dropping back. Many thousands are killed every year by tuna fishermen.

An engaging smile (*left*) The smile of the Bottle-nosed dolphin is a feature of its anatomy rather than of its temperament, but it makes this the most popular of dolphins. Lone individuals sometimes befriend swimmers and sailors, playing games with them and allowing themselves to be stroked. The Bottle-nosed dolphin is large; its only natural predators are Killer whales and sharks.

Conservation or collection?

As the human population has increased, the threat to wildlife from collectors, who take specimens either for pets, ornaments or trade, has grown dramatically. The region as a whole is notorious for its lack of controls over trade in wild species and has a reputation as a center of illegal trade and smuggling.

Trade in birds for the pet trade and collectors' market, both domestic and international, has drastically reduced local populations of certain bird species, particularly cockatoos and parrots.

In the Philippines hundreds of coral reef fish are caught for the aquarium trade. They are doped with cyanide, which damages their livers, so they die within six months of capture, creating further demand for replacements. Stress and disease in the overcrowded conditions of storage and transportation result in a high mortality rate among the fish. Rare corals and mollusk shells are also great collectors' items, and are taken by the thousand as tourist souvenirs.

Tropical butterflies, particularly the birdwing butterflies, are highly prized collectors' items. The Queen Alexandra's birdwing of the forests of New Guinea has been protected since 1966 from unauthorized collecting. Butterfly farms in the region are increasing in number. However, in many places habitat loss is now undoing this valuable conservation work.

The Great mormon butterfly, common throughout Southeast Asia, is remarkable for the great variety of form and color of the females; these mimic several other species of swallowtail butterflies.

PLANT LIFE

LUXURIANT FORESTS · ADAPTATION IN THE FOREST · SPICES, EBONY AND ORCHIDS

Southeast Asia is particularly rich in plant species, with a total of about 20,000 flowering plants. Almost all the region was once covered by dense forest, but logging for valuable timber trees has substantially reduced their extent. In both the north and the south there is a moderately dry season for part of each year, and plant growth depends on the heavy monsoon rains. Here semi-deciduous, seasonal tropical forests grow. Nearer the Equator the climate remains hot and wet all year round, and tropical rainforests flourish. The highest rainforests in the world are on the Malay Peninsula, Sumatra and Borneo. The conditions are perfect for luxuriant plant growth. There is also great variety – more than 2,000 species of orchid grow on Borneo alone. Many important food plants also originated in this region.

Widespread palms Members of the palm family can be found in many parts of Southeast Asia. Most produce a huge inflorescence below the crown of leaves; this sealing-wax palm (*Cyrtostachys renda*), a palm of peaty soil, is no exception.

COUNTRIES IN THE REGION

Brunei, Cambodia, Indonesia, Laos, Malaysia, Myanmar, Philippines, Singapore, Thailand, Vietnam

DIVERSITY

	Number of species	Endemism
Brunei	6,000	high
Indonesia	29,375	high
Malaysia	15,500	high
Singapore	2,168	high
Vietnam	10,500	20%

PLANTS IN DANGER

	Threatened	Endangered	Extinct
Little information; many species threatened or lost because of extensive deforestation			
Brunei	25	—	—
Indonesia	264	24	1
Malaysia	490	84	3
Singapore	29	4	1
Vietnam	341	6	—

Examples *Allobunkillia* species; *Amorphopallus titanum* (titan arum); *Johannesteijsmannia lanceolata* (umbrella leaf palm) *Maingaya* species; *Maxburretia rupicola*; *Nepenthes* – Mount Kinabulu species (pitcher plant); *Paphiopedilum rothschildianum* (Rothschild's slipper orchid); *Phyllagathis magnifica*; *Rafflesia* species; *Strongylodon macrobotrys* (jade vine)

USEFUL AND DANGEROUS NATIVE PLANTS

Crop plants *Artocarpus altilis* (breadfruit); *Camellia sinensis* (tea); *Citrus limon* (lemon); *Cucumis sativa* (cucumber); *Durio zibethinus* (durian); *Eugenia caryophyllus* (cloves); *Mangifera indica* (mango); *Musa* species (banana); *Myristica fragans* (nutmeg)
Garden plants *Cyrtostachys renda* (sealing wax palm); *Ficus benjaminia* (weeping fig); *Pandanus sanderi*; *Paphiopedilum barbatum*
Poisonous plants *Antiaris toxicaria*; *Croton tiglium*; *Gloriosa superba* (glory lily); *Strychnos nux-vomica*

MAJOR BOTANIC GARDENS

Bogor, Manila (10,000 taxa); Penang (1,000 taxa); Rangoon; Singapore (3,000 taxa); Rimba Ilmu University, Kuala Lumpur; Hanoi Botanic Garden

---

LUXURIANT FORESTS

The type of forest found in Southeast Asia is not only determined by the climate; soil also influences the distribution and growth of plants. In areas with a strongly seasonal climate, such as central Myanmar and the Indochina peninsula, scrubby savanna forests or thorn forests grow. On the flat coastal plains there are extensive swamplands dominated by mangroves. Mangroves also grow in the brackish tidal swamps along the muddy coasts, supported by sturdy prop roots that rise up out of the murky water. Inland, where the soil is fertile, many of the former freshwater swamps have been converted into rice paddies, producing the most important staple food crop of Southeast Asia. A distinctive kind of swamp is also found over areas of acidic inland peat, which is extensive in Sumatra, the Malay Peninsula and Borneo.

In the high mountain ranges throughout Southeast Asia the climate is cooler than on the lowland plains, as it is in mountainous zones throughout the world; plant growth here may be more limited. Close to the Equator, however, the climate even of mountain altitudes tends to remain fairly

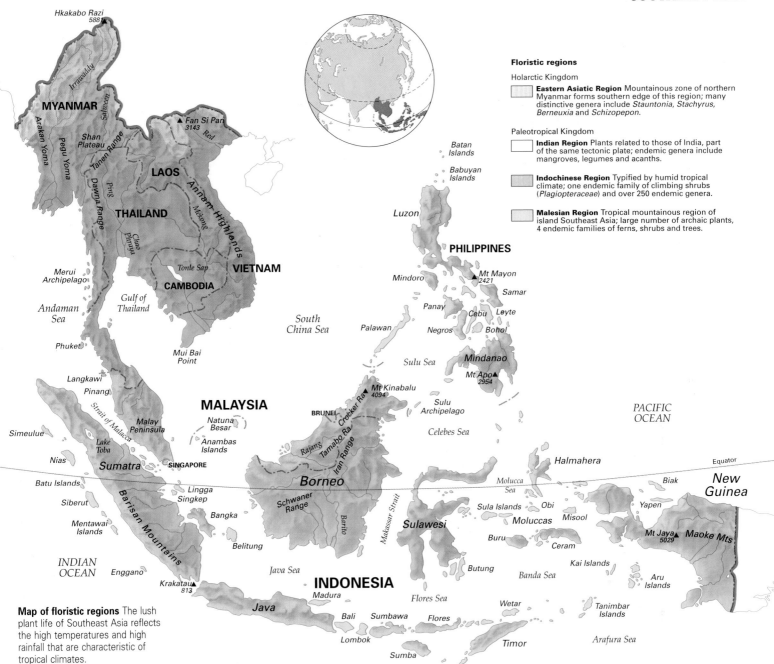

Floristic regions

Holarctic Kingdom

Eastern Asiatic Region Mountainous zone of northern Myanmar forms southern edge of this region; many distinctive genera include *Stauntonia*, *Stachyrus*, *Berneuxia* and *Schizopepon*.

Paleotropical Kingdom

Indian Region Plants related to those of India, part of the same tectonic plate; endemic genera include mangroves, legumes and acanths.

Indochinese Region Typified by humid tropical climate; one endemic family of climbing shrubs (*Plagiopteraceae*) and over 250 endemic genera.

Malesian Region Tropical mountainous region of island Southeast Asia; large number of archaic plants, 4 endemic families of ferns, shrubs and trees.

Map of floristic regions The lush plant life of Southeast Asia reflects the high temperatures and high rainfall that are characteristic of tropical climates.

A glorious lily *Gloriosa superba* is a climbing lily, seeking support from trees to which it clings by its tendril-like leaftips. This region has a profusion of flowering herbs, brilliant in color and often remarkable in appearance.

constant and relatively humid, conditions that support the growth of rainforest.

An abundance of species

The lowland Malaysian rainforests, which are warm and humid for most of the year, support a vast number of species. The most distinctive family is the Dipterocarpaceae. These are largely lofty, timber-producing giants that are the dominant trees in most kinds of lowland forest. The seasonal tropical (monsoon) forests to the north and south support fewer species. The most famous timber tree here is teak (*Tectona grandis*). Bamboo also grows abundantly, and particularly in areas where tree felling or land disturbance has allowed these highly opportunistic plants to invade, colonizing any open spaces.

To the north of the region, where the climate is less humid, temperate genera become increasingly common, such as ash (*Fraxinus*) and elm (*Ulmus*). Some of the more temperate genera, such as *Rhododendron* and *Vaccinium*, extend toward the Equator in the cooler, more mountainous rainforests. Above the treeline alpine plants such as gentians (*Gentiana*), primroses (*Primula*) and buttercups (*Ranunculus*) grow. On the high Himalayan ranges temperate plants are widespread. Among the trees are included fir (*Abies*), spruce (*Picea*) and pine (*Pinus*).

In Malaysia a few Australian families are found, such as she-oaks (Casuarinaceae) and Australian heaths (Epacridaceae). These are especially abundant in the heath forests that grow – most extensively on Borneo – on silica-rich sands in which the topsoil has been leached of minerals such as iron. Some temperate Australasian plants also grow among the high mountain herbs, such as the mat-forming species of *Gunnera* and *Nertera*, for example.

ADAPTATION IN THE FOREST

The Dipterocarpaceae are a family of trees strongly centered in Southeast Asia. They are most numerous in the lowland rainforest, where they are the dominant family of large trees. The trees are unique in several respects. In an area of a few square kilometers up to five or six genera, comprising 30 or 40 different species, can be found growing together; the genera *Dipterocarpus*, *Hopea* and *Shorea* have particularly large numbers of species. They are the commonest large canopy-top trees of the rainforest, growing in dense stands and developing straight, unbranched trunks that frequently reach 40 m (130 ft), and occasionally 50 or even 60 m (165 or 200 ft), in height, with a diameter of up to 1.5 m (5 ft), as they compete for light. When a giant grows successfully and emerges through the canopy, it produces a huge spreading crown in the bright sunlight.

Trees of the Dipterocarpaceae flower at about the same time over large areas. When this happens, once or twice a decade, the whole of the upper canopy bursts spectacularly into white, pink or red blossoms. Different species flower in sequence over a period of several weeks; the air becomes fragrant with their scent and is later filled with falling petals. The fruits of the various species mature at slightly different rates, so they all ripen simultaneously and fall to the ground together to provide a feast for the forest animals. Not all the harvest is eaten, however; the fruits that escape germinate immediately, rapidly forming crowded carpets of several million seedlings per hectare. Almost all these will die over the next few years; only when a tree falls, leaving a sunlit gap, can a young sapling grow to form a replacement canopy.

This mass production of seedlings can be exploited, because large numbers of the young plants can easily be persuaded to grow up to form a new forest if care is taken not to damage them while logging, and provided that the gaps in the overhead canopy are not allowed to become too large, which would destroy the warm, moist atmosphere they require for growth.

Prickly palms

Throughout the region, and especially in the lowland rainforests of Malaysia and

Slipper orchid (*above*) *Paphiopedilum sukhakulii* is a ground dweller, endemic to northeastern Thailand. Behind the central column, above the pouched lip, are concealed two pollinia (pollen balls). These stick on pollinating insects as they investigate the flower, attracted by its lurid markings.

Mangrove swamps (*below*) Mangroves fringe many low muddy coastlines in Southeast Asia. To overcome the problem of living in waterlogged soil all mangroves possess specialized roots. These develop kneelike growths (pneumatophores) capable of absorbing air when they are exposed at low tide.

Borneo, climbing prickly palms called rattans are abundant. These palms belong to the subfamily Calamoideae, all of which bear scaly fruit. The rattan stem varies from pencil-thin to the thickness of a human arm. It is covered in very sharp, spiny leaf sheaths. These palms scramble through the forest canopy in their search for light, hanging on by means of long grappling hooks that are either modified flowering parts or the prolonged tips of their feather-shaped leaves.

Sun-loving pioneers

Macaranga is a huge genus of small to medium-sized trees. The genus comprises 280 species, with a range that extends from Africa to the Pacific, and is strongly concentrated in Southeast Asia: Borneo has 44 species and New Guinea 73, though between them the two islands

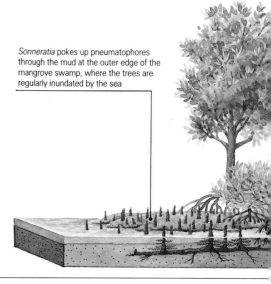

Sonneratia pokes up pneumatophores through the mud at the outer edge of the mangrove swamp, where the trees are regularly inundated by the sea

have only a handful of species in common. *Macaranga* are gap-opportunists – sun-loving trees that grow to form closely packed stands in large forest clearings or where other plants have been swept away by landslides, and along river banks. They bear all the hallmarks of pioneer trees – rapid growth, pale, low-density timber and the production, for most of the year, of copious small seeds. These are dispersed by birds, which are further attracted by the fleshy extra seed covering of some species.

Ants and scale insects inhabit the hollows within the twig stems of some *Macaranga* species. The trees produce starch grains that provide the ants with food, while the scale insects feed on the trees' sap. In the same way that herders guard a herd of goats, the ants keep the scale insects inside the twig hollows, protecting them against predators and periodically "milking" them to collect the sweet secretions they produce.

This relationship benefits the trees as well as the ants. A *Macaranga* that is free of ants will have its leaves damaged by herbivorous insects; ants have been seen removing would-be leaf eaters and insect eggs, and also the tips and tendrils of climbers that might otherwise eventually smother the tree.

Ants scurry busily around the protective hollows on the twigs of *Macaranga*. These trees are not alone in forming close associations with animals. In tropical zones competition between plants is fierce, and an animal partner can help in the fight for survival.

TORRENT-LOVING PLANTS

Throughout the tropics the swiftly flowing rocky streams are liable to flood when they are swollen by sudden heavy rain. Their banks are often fringed by wiry-stemmed shrubs and small trees, such as the evergreen *Garcinia cataractalis*, herbs and even ferns like *Dipteris lobbiana* of Borneo. These plants are known as rheophytes. They have narrow, willow-like leaves and form a very distinctive community in places where swift, powerful currents of water would damage broader, less tough leaves. Botanists have not yet established why rheophytes are far more abundant in some parts of the world than in others; they are extremely common in Southeast Asia, and especially in Borneo.

Rheophytic species are found within many different families of plants. Their narrow, leathery leaves are often so similar, even in plants that are totally unrelated, that the species can only be positively identified by studying their flowers or fruits.

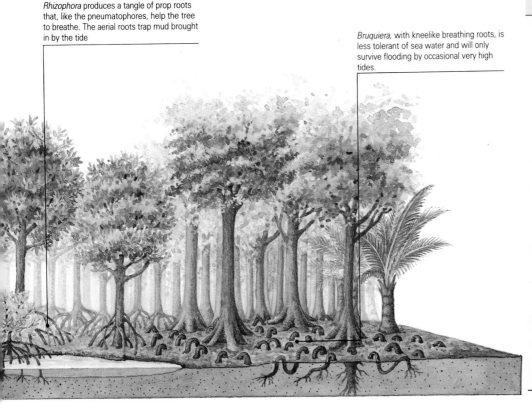

Rhizophora produces a tangle of prop roots that, like the pneumatophores, help the tree to breathe. The aerial roots trap mud brought in by the tide

Bruguiera, with kneelike breathing roots, is less tolerant of sea water and will only survive flooding by occasional very high tides.

SPICES, EBONY AND ORCHIDS

Some of the most important food plants have come from Southeast Asia. Archeological findings have suggested that agriculture, based on a type of rice (a grass called *Oryza sativa*), may have developed here earlier than anywhere else in the world. Citrus fruits such as oranges and lemons all originated in this region. Other export crops from the rainforest include bananas (*Musa*), of which many species grow wild in wet open places, and mangoes (*Mangifera*), which grow on medium-sized forest trees. Numerous other fruits are widely grown, such as the delicately flavored mangosteen (*Garginia mangostana*) and the rambutan (*Nephelium lappaceum*). Most famous of all, perhaps, is the durian (*Durio zibethinus*), notorious for its dreadful smell and delicious taste.

In the past several European powers laid claim to territories in the archipelago, drawn by the riches of the spice trade, principally nutmeg (*Myristica fragrans*) and cloves (*Syzygium aromaticum*) from the Moluccas in eastern Indonesia (often known as the Spice Islands). Cardamom (*Elettaria cardamomum*), cinnamon (*Cinnamomum rerum*) and ginger (*Zingiber officinalis*) were also highly prized.

Resin and timber

Resins taken from the giant coniferous kauri tree (*Agathis*) and from Dipterocarpaceae and Burseraceae species were once widely used in the manufacture of paints and varnishes. Together with a yellow gum known as gambodge, obtained from various *Garcinia* species, and named after Cambodia, which is its principal source, these resins have been important items of trade for some 2,000 years.

An extraordinary flowerhead The banana is a huge herb with a stem made up of the bases of the enormous leaves. The fruit develops in large bunches called hands; after fruiting the plant dies, to be replaced by suckers arising from its base.

In the 19th century a major market developed for the solidified latex guttapercha (*Palaquium*), which was once used to insulate underwater cables and for making golf balls, and is still used today to make adhesives. In the 1920s an international trade developed in jelutong (*Dyera costulata*), a tasteless latex that formed the basic ingredient of chewing gum. The market for chewing gum in the United States increased greatly during this period as a result of the prohibition of alcoholic drink.

Fine timbers exported from the region include teak, especially from Myanmar and formerly from Java and Thailand, where the forests have been so heavily depleted that logging activities were suspended at the end of 1988. Ironwood grows in Sumatra and Borneo. This heavy, durable timber was traditionally used to make houseposts; it can also easily be split into the shingles that are still widely used as a roofing material.

The rainforests support numerous species of *Diospyros*. Most are small trees of the gloomy undergrowth, but a few reach medium size and develop the black heartwood known as ebony, of which Sulawesi is a major exporter. Despite the large number of species that grow in this region (155 in Malaysia; 267 in Borneo), the timber they produce is so similar that it can be grouped for sale into only a handful of categories.

Dipterocarp trees that produce heavy, dark, durable timber have long been valued, especially the chengal (*Neobalano capus*) of the Malay Peninsula. Recently dipterocarp species that produce softer, paler, non-durable timbers have become more important. These include light red meranti, which comes from certain species of *Shorea*, keruing (*Dipterocarpus*) and kapur (*Dryobalanops*). Most of these woods are of low and medium density, excellent for plywood or furniture.

Other important timber species are pines (*Pinus kesiya* and *P. merkusii*), which also give resin for turpentine production. Yemane, a relative of teak, grows wild in slightly seasonal forests and is one of the few species that has proved successful when grown on timber plantations.

Two sizable trees that are common throughout the region and are now well-known houseplants everywhere are the banyan or weeping fig (*Ficus benjamina*) and the rubber tree (*Ficus elastica*).

Orchids and palms

The most important Southeast Asian plants in horticulture are the orchids and the palms. With the Singapore Botanic Garden as an important innovator, a major industry has developed, based on cultivating native orchids and their hybrids and exporting cut flowers by air to many parts of the world.

In contrast, only a few of the wide range of native palms have been cultivated; many have great potential, such as the sealing-wax palm (*Cyrtostachys renda*) of peatswamp forests, which develops slow-growing clumps and has attractive red leaf sheaths. The fishtail palms, such as *Caryota mitis*, are sometimes seen in the

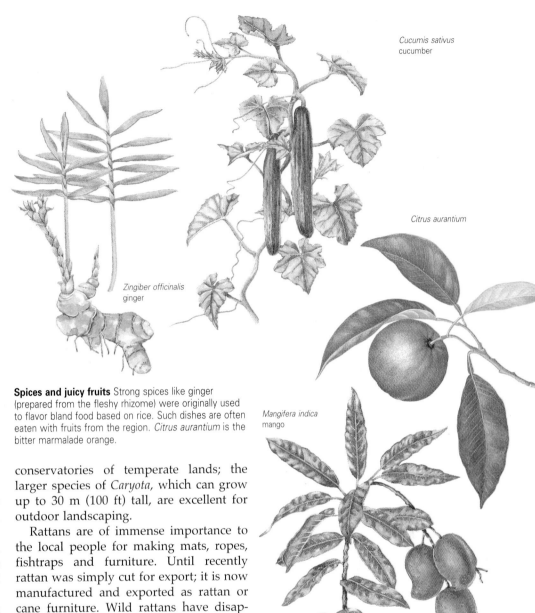

Cucumis sativus
cucumber

Citrus aurantium

Mangifera indica
mango

Zingiber officinalis
ginger

Spices and juicy fruits Strong spices like ginger (prepared from the fleshy rhizome) were originally used to flavor bland food based on rice. Such dishes are often eaten with fruits from the region. *Citrus aurantium* is the bitter marmalade orange.

conservatories of temperate lands; the larger species of *Caryota*, which can grow up to 30 m (100 ft) tall, are excellent for outdoor landscaping.

Rattans are of immense importance to the local people for making mats, ropes, fishtraps and furniture. Until recently rattan was simply cut for export; it is now manufactured and exported as rattan or cane furniture. Wild rattans have disappeared with the clearance of the lowland rainforests in the last fifty years, but attempts to cultivate them have recently been successful.

THREATS TO THE FOREST

Many countries in Southeast Asia have high levels of land degradation caused by deforestation. The rapid rise in population in the region has placed enormous pressure on the forests but it is debatable whether this has been the main cause of deforestation. Commercial timber felling, based for a long time on the high value of hardwoods such as teak, has been responsible for the clearance of millions of hectares of tropical rainforest. Roads constructed for the logging industry have also opened up the forest for conversion to farmland, rubber and oil palm plantations, resettlement or industrial development. In Indonesia, the World Bank has estimated annual sources of deforestation as smallholder conversion 500,000 ha (1.2 million acres); development projects 250,000 ha (617,750 acres); logging 80,000 ha (197,680 acres); and fire loss 70,000 ha (172,970 acres).

As the forests diminish, the region's biodiversity is threatened. The full extent of species and habitat loss cannot be quantified because of lack of up-to-date information – few countries have adequate listings of species. However, estimates suggest that about two-thirds of the major vegetation types have been lost which include forests and wetlands.

Parasites and carnivores

Rafflesias, the most distinctive of parasites, obtain nutrition entirely from the living host. The genus contains about 14 species. The largest of these, *Rafflesia arnoldii*, has the biggest flower in the world: it can measure up to 80 cm (32 in) across and weigh as much as 7 kg (15 lb). The tiny seed germinates on *Tetrastigma*, a stout liana that is a member of the vine family. Inside its host the *Rafflesia* develops fungal-like threads, but grows neither a stem nor leaves; instead it produces only a huge flower, with blotched red and white petals, that forms on the stem of the vine. The blossoms smell of rotting meat, attracting flies that act as pollinators by carrying pollen from male to female flowers. Local people have long believed that the flower has special medicinal properties, and this has contributed to its rarity in the wild.

Saprophytes

Another group of plants that are dependent on a host for their nutrition are saprophytes, which take sustenance from the rotting plant material on which they live. They do not themselves cause this material to decompose, but live in close association with the fungi that do. Most saprophytes are small and inconspicuous, growing among the dark forest undergrowth. Like other parasites, they lack the green pigment chlorophyll that is used by most plants to make their food by the process known as photosynthesis.

The tropical forests of Southeast Asia also harbor partial or hemiparasites, including plants of the family Viscaceae and a related family, the Santalaceae. Many members of these families grow as epiphytic shrubs, tapping their host tree for water and mineral nutrients; however, they do possess chlorophyll and are able to manufacture their own food. The Santalaceae contain ground-growing bush

The biggest flower in the world (*right*) The center of the evil-smelling *Rafflesia arnoldii* flower contains a spiky disk, which conceals the stamens in the male flowers and the ovary in the female flowers. Large, squashy fruits contain the tiny seeds.

Pitcher plant (*below*) Once an insect has crawled over the slippery overhanging lip of *Nepenthes macfarlanei*, just one of the many striking species of pitcher plant, there is no escape. The lid prevents rain from diluting the digestive fluid at the base.

and tree hemiparasites that take moisture and nutrients from the roots of other tree species. This group includes sandalwood (*Santalum album*), much prized for its perfumed wood.

Carnivorous pitcher plants

In Southeast Asia the most spectacular carnivorous plants are the Old World

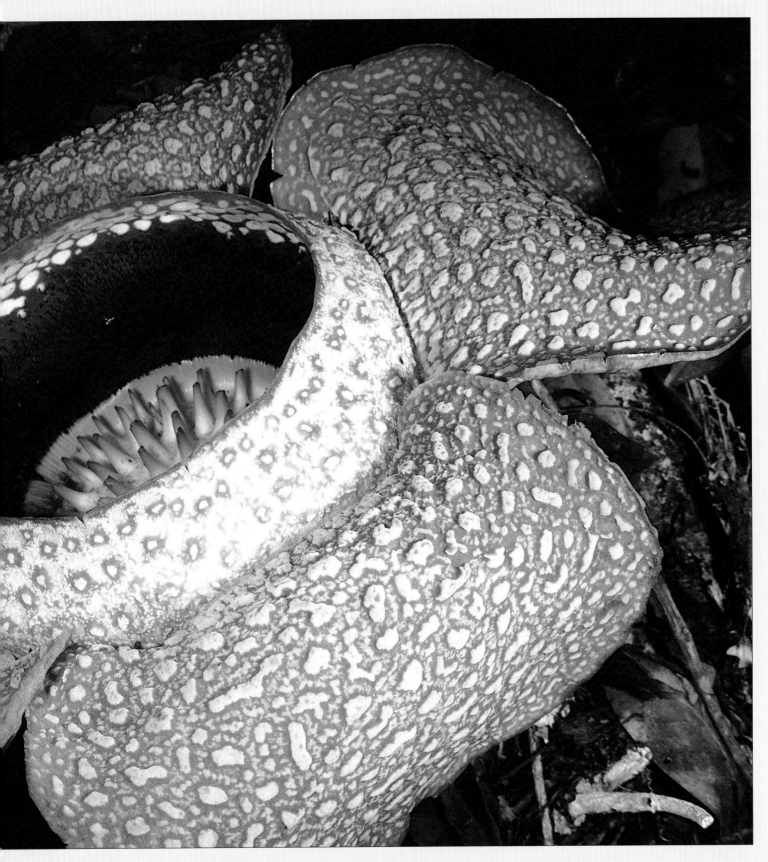

pitcher plants, *Nepenthes*, a genus of 70 species. The stems and leaves of *Nepenthes* bear nectaries, and the leaves also produce terminal tendrils that aid the plant in climbing. Behind these tendrils most leaves develop a pitcher-shaped pouch with an overhanging lid. These pitchers are often bright red, green, yellow or brown; digestive fluids collect in the base of each one. Unsuspecting insects are attracted by the nectaries and the brightly colored pitchers; they walk down on to the slippery pitcher walls and fall to the base, where they are eventually dissolved in the juices.

Nepenthes species are especially common on poor rocky or sandy soils, and it is thought that the insects they devour help to supply them with essential nutrients that they are unable to find in the soil. *Nepenthes rajah* has the largest pitchers, 30 cm (12 in) long, which hold up to 2 liters (3.5 pints) of liquid. The stems of the scrambling and climbing species provide tough cords that are traditionally used in Borneo for binding longhouse floors and to make matting.

The sacred lotus

The sacred lotus (*Nelumbo nucifera*) is an ancient plant. Fossil evidence of it growing 160 million years ago shows that is has changed little over eons of time. Yet, like the waterlily to which it is related, its blossoms are sophisticated for a plant that evolved so long ago.

It lives in still water. Some of the circular leaves float on the water, but as the plant matures the leaves become more like an inverted cone and are held above the surface. When young, these are rolled tightly to emerge between the floating leaves. In the center of each exquisite flower is a strange receptacle whose circular holes are the stigmas.

In the east almost all parts of the sacred lotus are eaten, and this may have a bearing on its religious significance. The leaf stalks provide a salad, the rootstock is roasted and the pearlike seeds taste of almonds.

It is a sacred plant in many lands – from Egypt to Japan, where it is planted for devotional purposes. In India it is Padma, symbol of the Ganges; from there it traveled eastward with the spread of Buddhism, across southern Asia to China, where it was depicted as the seat of the Buddha and became a symbol of feminine beauty.

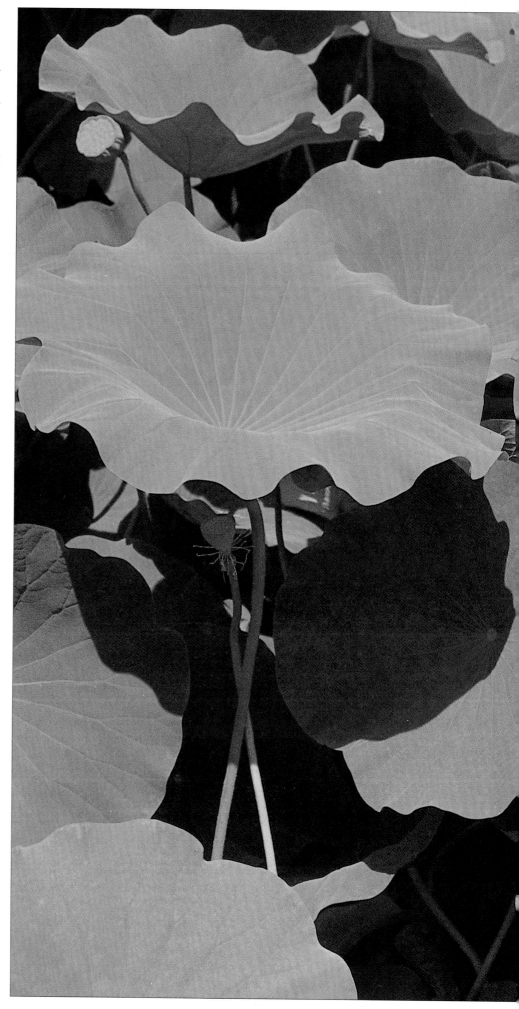

The sacred lotus, a plant of great beauty revered for many hundreds of years.

AGRICULTURE

FROM EARLY BEGINNINGS · SMALLHOLDINGS, PLANTATIONS AND SWIDDENS · PRESSURE FOR CHANGE

The complex interaction of environment, economics, politics and society gives Southeast Asia its variety of agricultural systems. These range from the capital-intensive estates of the Malay Peninsula, where plantation crops such as rubber – introduced from South America by British colonists – and palm oil are grown for export, to the socialist agriculture of Vietnam, where the state maintains a firm hold on production and marketing, and on all other aspects of rural life. Extensive upland areas and unproductive forest soils mean that much of the region is unfavorable for farming. The mountains of Borneo, for example, remain largely forested; farmers are shifting cultivators, maintaining a traditional farming system in which they clear a forest plot and grow crops for a few years before abandoning it.

COUNTRIES IN THE REGION

Brunei (B), Cambodia (C), Indonesia (I), Laos (L), Malaysia (Ma), Myanmar (My), Philippines (P), Singapore (S), Thailand (T), Vietnam (V)

LAND: Total area 4,495,392 sq km (1,735,221 sq mi)

% cropland	% pasture	% forest/woodland
20 % (883,340 sq km)	4% (193,787 sq km)	53% (2,371,439 sq km)

FARMERS	Highest	Middle	Lowest
Agriculture as % of GDP	59% (My)	26% (V)	0% (S)
% of workforce	80% (C, L)	45% (I)	<10% (S)

MAJOR CROPS: Agricultural products fruit: bananas, mangoes, coconuts; pineapple; rice, cassava, corn; soybeans; palm oil; sugarcane; rubber; coffee, cocoa, tea; copra; pepper; pou.try, pork, water buffalo meat; fish; timber

Total cropland (000 ha)	30,987 (I)	10,151 (My)	1 (S)
Cropland (ha) per 1000 people	363 (C)	231 (My)	< 1 (S)
Irrigated land as % of cropland	25% (T)	16% (I,P)	0% (S)
Number of tractors	149,500 (T)	43,300 (Ma)	65 (S)
Average cereal crop yields (kg/ha)	3,915 (I)	2,947 (My)	1,785 (C)
Cereal production (000 tonnes)	59,029 (I)	17,938 (My)	1,670 (L)
Change since 1986/88	27%	26%	32%

LIVESTOCK & FISHERIES

Meat production (000 tonnes)	1,848 (P)	989 (Ma)	71 (L)
Change since 1986–88	182%	160%	103%
Marine fish catch (000 tonnes)	2,864.9 (I)	1,503 (P)	7.9 (S)
Change since 1986/88	72%	20%	–51%

FOOD SECURITY

Food aid as % of total imports	47% (My)	11% (My)	0% (I, Ma, S)
Daily kcal/person	2,977 (Ma)	2,484 (V)	2,048 (C)

FROM EARLY BEGINNINGS

Some of the world's earliest agriculture appears to have developed in Southeast Asia. Evidence found at two important archaeological sites, at Baan Chiang in northeast Thailand and around the Red river in northern Vietnam, suggests that the change from hunting and gathering to agriculture on the mainland took place between 5500 BC and 3500 BC. The practice and technology of farming appeared later on the islands, probably having spread from the mainland; there are signs of food production in Sulawesi dating back to 2500 BC.

Rice, the key to life in most areas of modern Southeast Asia, was probably not domesticated until 3000–2000 BC. Since then its cultivation has spread throughout the region, and it has become the dominant agricultural crop. It is only in the more arid locations such as the Indonesian island of Timor that the inhabitants rely on other crops like cassava to meet their needs. These alternative staples are regarded locally as "poor man's food".

Examples of all three stages through which farming has developed – hunting and gathering, shifting cultivation and set-tled agriculture – are still to be found in the region. No type is more advanced than another; they are merely geared to the diverse environments and to different levels of population pressure. The commercialization of farming dominates much of the region's agriculture (though less so in socialist countries in mainland Southeast Asia); it is a recent development in most areas. Until shortly after World War II subsistence was the keynote of agriculture. Farmers used traditional technology, family labor and locally procured seeds and manures. Subsistence farming has now almost entirely disappeared. Farmers grow crops for the market: they buy and use chemicals, hire labor, use machinery, and plant newly developed, high-yielding crop varieties.

Some forms of agriculture have become industrialized following this commercialization. The forests of the region are extensively logged, and crops such as sugar cane, rubber, oil palm and pineapples are grown under industrial conditions on large estates that are often owned by

Irrigated rice terraces in Bali, Indonesia reflect the evening light. These fertile volcanic lowlands are among the most intensely cultivated in the world, often bearing three crops of rice a year. Rice remains the staple crop throughout the region, as it has been for thousands of years.

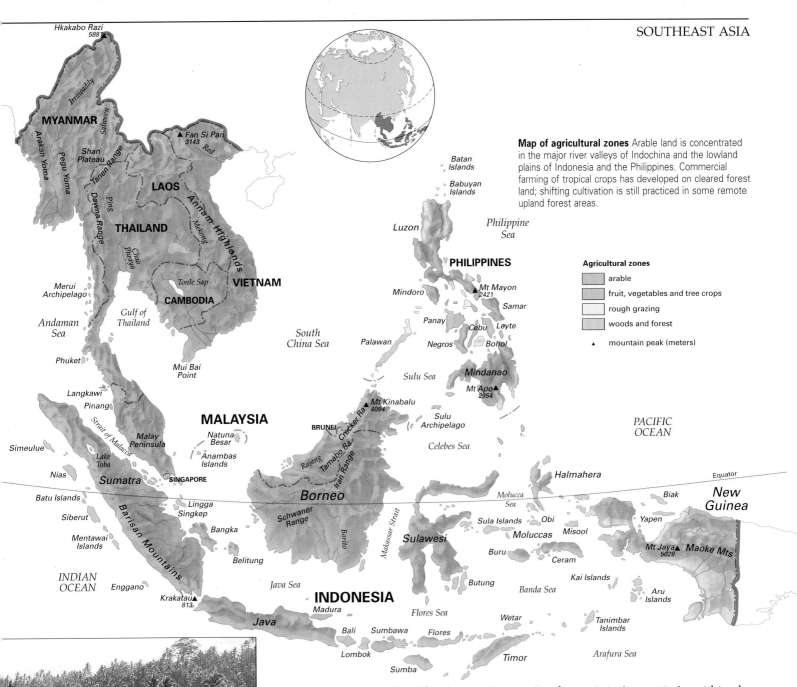

Map of agricultural zones Arable land is concentrated in the major river valleys of Indochina and the lowland plains of Indonesia and the Philippines. Commercial farming of tropical crops has developed on cleared forest land; shifting cultivation is still practiced in some remote upland forest areas.

Agricultural zones

- arable
- fruit, vegetables and tree crops
- rough grazing
- woods and forest
- ▲ mountain peak (meters)

multinational companies. The destruction of Southeast Asia's forests is now viewed internationally as an environmental disaster. The tropical forest soils are shallow; once the vegetation cover is removed nutrients are leached downward through the soil, which is then easily eroded by the wind and rain.

Rivers and rains

Southeast Asia has few favorable niches for agriculture – often a result of too much or too little water. Even on the limited lowlands farming is plagued by swampy conditions. However, suitable places do exist, particularly along the valleys of major rivers such as the Chao Phraya in Thailand and the Red in North Vietnam. The volcanic soils of Luzon in the Philippines and central Java in Indonesia are also fertile; here farmers grow up to three crops of rice a year, and agricultural population densities often exceed 1,000 people per sq km (0.39 sq mi).

Southeast Asia lies entirely within the humid tropics. Close to the Equator rain falls evenly throughout the year, and in some places exceeds 4,500 mm (177 in). However, traveling north and south from the Equator, it decreases in amount and becomes increasingly seasonal. Over much of the mainland between 80 and 98 percent of the year's rain falls within the seven months from April to October – the period of the southwest monsoon. It is this seasonality of rainfall, rather than the total quantity, which presents farmers with their greatest problems. In northern Thailand various systems of irrigation have been developed over many hundreds of years to overcome the vagaries of the rainfall. In other places farmers have developed sophisticated strategies of rain-fed cultivation. They carefully select and grow local varieties that are resistant to floods or drought, matching the plants to the conditions of the microenvironment in which they will be cultivated.

SMALLHOLDINGS, PLANTATIONS AND SWIDDENS

Farming in Southeast Asia is predominantly based on wet rice production, and is carried out by family farmers on small areas of land. The world average cropland per capita is 0.24 ha (0.6 acres) but Southeast Asia's average is well below this at 0.09 ha (0.2 acres). However, farmers still often manage to produce enough for all their subsistence needs. The way in which farmers have continually managed to squeeze that little bit extra out of their land is called "agricultural involution".

Where the environment allows, they not only keep a diverse and well-stocked home garden and raise livestock, but also cultivate cash crops such as maize, cotton and cassava. Children help to herd buffaloes and cattle, and both husband and wife are involved in the day-to-day running of the enterprise. Land tends to be owner-occupied, though tenancy and landlessness are both on the increase throughout the region. Although agriculture is becoming increasingly commercial, farmers nevertheless still largely operate a strategy that will minimize risk, rather than maximize profit. Their one essential guiding principle is that a certain critical level of production must be maintained from year to year, through conditions of flood and drought. Such farmers have sometimes been criticized for falling behind technologically, but this is unfair – they are conservative in their outlook. To experiment with new methods and techniques may not only be risky, but could also make all the difference between survival and starvation.

Farming for profit

Plantation systems differ radically from smallholdings. They are large, nontraditional, highly commercialized and geared to export. They also use new scientific techniques, employ large numbers of wage laborers and are organized and run as commercial enterprises, not as family concerns. What determines decision making is the profit margin – and because the crops are sold all around the world, profit is related to prices in the fluctuating international economy.

Plantation agriculture accounts for over two-thirds of all cultivated land in Malaysia with the world's most important rubber growing area producing one-fifth

of the world total. However, the men and women who work on these largescale plantations do not own the land. To counteract the social and political disadvantages arising from this, governments have been promoting smallholder production of the traditional plantation crops. In Malaysia, over 80 percent of land planted to rubber is now operated by smallholders (about 2 ha/6 acre plots). They often do not have the capital to invest in modern cultivation techniques and processing facilities, but building central processing plants has married the social and political advantages of smallholder production with the agricultural and economic advantages of estate management. Unfortunately, smallholder production is of very variable quality, which makes processing considerably more complex.

At the other end of the political spectrum is the state-controlled agriculture of Vietnam. In the early years of the communist regime, huge state-owned communes were set up, each supporting some 5,500 farming families. These stifled incentive: available figures suggest that commune members produce over 50 percent less than private farmers on the same amount of land. In 1988 a disastrous rice harvest threatened the northern provinces with famine, and the government was forced to reform the system, allowing families tenures of 15 years or more on the land they farmed. Family-owned farms now pay tax based on the fertility of the land, decide what to grow, and sell their surpluses on the free market.

Productive in its own way

Shifting cultivation is another common farming system in Southeast Asia. Land is partially cleared through burning, and crops such as hill rice are grown in the fertile ash. After the temporary plot (a swidden) has become exhausted it is abandoned for between 15 and 30 years before being cultivated once again. Some shifting cultivators live in settled communities. They practice an extensive form of rotation in which the fields shift but the settlement does not. Other groups are migratory, shifting fields and settlement.

Clearing land and then moving on may seem to be primitive and environmentally ruthless, but it has proved sustainable for thousands of years and can be carried out on steep slopes. Shallow cultivation, partial clearance, multiple cropping and the small size of the plots all help to reduce

Traditional agriculture (*above*) Shifting cultivation is still practiced by people in upland areas. Pigs and poultry are often raised by these subsistence farmers, and a wide range of crops are grown, typically including rice, maize and manioc or yam.

Fish ponds in Vietnam (*right*) Fish plays an important part in local diets, and the region provides a wide range of habitats for marine and freshwater fish. Inland fish breeding in specially adapted ponds and lakes can provide a profitable alternative to farming.

erosion because they imitate the natural forest ecosystem. The Kantu people of Kalimantan in Indonesia plant an average of 17 different rice varieties and over 20 crops on their small cleared plots each year. They know the land intimately, and what it can support.

Although shifting cultivation is an extensive system of farming, the yields are low. It has therefore been characterized by some as inefficient; however, land was not formerly a scarce resource in the upland forested areas of Southeast Asia. It was,

MALAYSIA'S RUBBER CROP

Rubber is among Malaysia's most important exports – it produces about 20 percent of the world total. In 1999 Malaysia's crop was 984 million tonnes worth nearly US $603 million. The rubber tree *Hevea brasiliensis*, from which most commercial rubber is obtained, was introduced into colonial Malaya from Brazil in the late 19th century, and rapidly spread as international demand for the commodity grew. Initially it was grown on estates that were under European control, but Chinese and Malay smallholders quickly appreciated its profit-making capabilities, and also began to plant the crop. Today, about 1.7 million ha (4.2 million acres) are planted to rubber of which less than 20 percent is grown on large estates. The rest is cultivated by smallholders.

The new, quick-maturing and high-yielding rubber trees take some five years to come into production, and last about 25 years before yields begin to decline. The latex, the milky-white fluid from which the rubber is processed, is drawn from the tree through cuts made in the bark, and collected in bowls strapped to the trunk. After collection the rubber is processed into sheets or blocks and sold.

Over half the workers on rubber estates are Indians, the descendants of indentured laborers brought in to meet a shortage of workers at the beginning of the 20th century. Wages are low, conditions poor, and the rubber estates remain sinks of poverty in a fast-developing country. Fluctuations in the international price of rubber and competition from synthetic materials, as well as the high costs of modernization and replanting, are responsible for the fall in estate rubber since the 1940s.

rather, people who were in short supply. Now the pressures of population growth, commercialization and deforestation are radically changing the way that upland areas are being used. Shifting cultivators have been forced to move to marginal land, or to settle and to intensify production; fallow periods are being reduced as land becomes ever more scarce. Traditionally the land was communally owned through customary law or *adat*, but now individual landownership is spreading. The whole system of shifting cultivation is being radically reworked and, in some cases, destroyed.

PRESSURES FOR CHANGE

Farming is still an important sector in Southeast Asia's economy, despite rapid urban and industrial growth; in Cambodia, Myanmar, Indonesia, Philippines, Thailand and Vietnam it involves over 40 percent of the population. At a superficial glance it may appear to cling to its traditional roots and follow the age-old rhythms and patterns, but beneath the surface the changes have been dramatic. Population growth has put pressure on farmers to raise yields. At the same time, technological advances have provided farmers with new crops and methods. Increasingly, land and labor are owned, operated, hired and paid for in new ways and the aspirations of farmers have changed dramatically.

Meeting new needs

In 1800 Southeast Asia's population was 32 million. By 2000 it had risen to well over 500 million. In addition to this rapid population growth, farmers are now demanding far more goods and services if they are to live, by their own standards, a creditable existence. These twin pressures have altered the very nature of farming, while urban growth means that there is less land available for farming.

Farmers have responded to the pressing need to raise yields by planting new crops and using increasing amounts of agricultural chemicals such as fertilizers and pesticides. Between 1988 and 1998, cereal yields in many countries in the region increased substantially; by 10 percent in Indonesia, 24 percent in Cambodia, 26 percent in Laos and 38 percent in Vietnam. Correspondingly, fertilizer use also increased, for example, from 73 kg per ha to 92 kg per ha in Indonesia and from 76 kg per ha to 206 kg per ha in Vietnam. As a result countries such as Indonesia and the Philippines have been able to reduce their dependency on imported cereals, and also to export large

Sun dried cassava in Java (*above*) Cassava, a traditional subsistence crop in many tropical regions, is now also grown as a cash crop. It is favored because it is very easy to grow, and gives high yields. The root is soaked in water, then dried in the sun to leave the white starch, which has many commercial uses.

Destruction of the forests (*left*) These dipterocarp trees in Sabah, Malaysia are being stripped of their bark. Forests are being felled more quickly than they can grow, with serious environmental consequences.

quantities of high value crops such as cocoa, coffee, fruit, spices and tea.

While technical advances have helped to offset the decline in available land, the fragmentation of farms, as plots are subdivided between family members, and the rising number of tenancies, are creating serious problems. Inequalities have widened, and some farms have become so small that subsistence needs can no longer be met. Farmers either sink into poverty, or search for alternative employment outside agriculture. The pressure to increase yields sometimes leads to a decline in fertility as more is taken from the soil than is put into it. The levels of mechanization have increased sharply. The number of tractors, between 1987 and 1997, increased by nearly 300 percent in Indonesia and Thailand and by 412 percent in Vietnam. This has deprived farm workers of their livelihoods, forcing many to migrate to the rapidly expanding urban areas in search of work. The population of Bangkok city, for example, rose from 1 million in the early 1950s, to over 6 million by 2001. Rural decline is a source of concern to all the region's policymakers.

Farming as big business

The move toward more commercialized farming means that more and more nontraditional crops are being grown for cash. Rubber, oil palm, jute, coffee and tobacco are all widely cultivated. The ratio between the area planted to food and to nonfood crops is 70 to 30, and even tradi-

tional subsistence crops such as rice are now partially grown for sale.

Farming, then, is making the transition from being a way of life to becoming a business. Money is borrowed (in some cases at rates of interest of 100 percent a year), profit margins have to be carefully calculated and the relative prices of different crops assessed as part of the decision-making process. Farmers can now earn incomes to buy consumer goods and to pay for services. One effect is that they have been drawn more tightly into the international cash economy, making them more vulnerable to fluctuations in the international market place.

Within this context of change, government policies provide a framework through which the transition process can be helped or hindered. For example, government agricultural research stations and extension programs have aided the promotion and diffusion of new technologies and techniques. In Malaysia a government-funded smallholders' association has been instrumental in modernizing and revitalizing smallholdings by providing advice, technology and interestfree loans. Nearly all smallholdings that grow rubber have been replanted with new high-yielding varieties.

Throughout Southeast Asia governments have supported prices and helped to establish cooperatives and marketing agencies for both crops and livestock. However, some government actions have not always been to the benefit of farmers. The taxes on certain crops, such as the rice premium that has operated in Thailand for many years, for example, significantly lowered farmers' returns.

Maintaining the pace

The pace of change is not slackening. New technologies and crops will be still more widely adopted: they include new chemical pesticides and herbicides; the adoption of genetically engineered crop varieties, and improved labor-saving machinery. Commercialization is likely to proceed in tandem. These changes will bring about fresh problems, two of which stand out: the need to raise yields and absorb a surplus rural population as land becomes an increasingly scarce resource; and the need to promote sustainable agricultural growth so that production can continue to rise at a rate relative to population growth and so ensure that there will be enough food for future generations.

NEW LAND FOR FARMING

Indonesia is the world's fourth most populated country. Over 50 percent of its 224 million inhabitants live on the island of Java, only 7 percent of the country's land area. Elsewhere, in Irian Jaya (West Papua) and Borneo, huge areas of land are forested and seemingly underpopulated and underutilized. Since 1950 the Indonesian government has tried to redress this population imbalance by promoting settlement on the "outer islands".

This exceptionally large transmigration scheme has resettled over 5 million people. Huge areas of forest have been cleared to accommodate and feed them – but there are problems. The shallow, heavily leached, infertile forest soils deteriorate under cultivation, so yields quickly decline. The wet rice system that dominates the scene is thought by some experts to be environmentally inappro-

priate: soils are more suited to upland crops and shifting cultivation, while irrigation facilities are either nonexistent or perform poorly. Settlers find it hard to market their produce or buy agricultural inputs in these remote areas. To add to the difficulties many of the areas, far from being unpopulated, are inhabited by shifting cultivators.

Inevitably there has been a certain amount of conflict between the old and new inhabitants, and some settlers have returned to Java. However, the Indonesian government has recently made much greater efforts to adapt its schemes so that they do not encroach on the traditional way of life of the indigenous inhabitants. It is also considering ways of basing the agriculture of these new areas on more suitable tree crops, such as rubber or coconuts.

The "rice bowl" of Asia

Thailand is a kingdom of rice farmers. Nearly two-thirds of crop land – some 1.2 million ha (3 million acres) – is planted to rice. It is both the staple crop of the country and the most important cash crop. Thailand is the largest rice exporter in the world; it exports about 6 million tonnes a year. Its annual harvest is around 20 million tonnes and most of this is produced on small, family-owned farms: over half the average holding of 4.5 ha (11 acres) will usually be given to rice.

The cultivation of rice by the wet or paddy system begins between May and July during the southwest monsoon. The land is carefully leveled, producing small plots where water collects. Farmers first broadcast pregerminated rice seed into a meticulously prepared nursery bed. The main field is plowed and puddled using either buffaloes or, increasingly, handheld rotavators. After about a month the seedlings are transplanted. The harvest of the main rice crop takes place from November through January. Once the rice has been stored safely in the rice barns the farmers turn out their livestock to graze the stubble. They then begin to prepare for the work and festivals of the dry season. "Having rice in the barn," say the villagers, "is like having money in the bank."

Treasures of the paddyfield

Although rice production is at the core of the system, the paddyfield is also used to raise fish; the frogs and crabs that live in the bunded fields provide the people with an important source of animal protein as

Preparing the rice fields The rice cycle begins as soon as enough rain has fallen to soften the soil. The banks (bunds) are repaired, and the weeds removed and left to rot. When the fields are covered with water plowing begins, ready for transplantation of the seedlings from the nursery bed.

well. At the end of the rice season the farmer sometimes uses the field to grow a second crop such as beans or sesame, taking advantage of the moisture that has been retained in the soil.

More than any other staple crop, wet rice is heavily dependent on an ample and stable supply of water. In the central plains and the north of Thailand, where irrigation helps to control the water, double-cropping is sometimes possible. In comparison to systems in Java and the Philippines, however, irrigation methods are crude. There is only limited control over water supplies, and deep inundation remains a problem in the wet season, while insufficient water handicaps farmers in the dry season. Consequently, yields in the central plains are lower.

In most areas, though, farmers still grow rice in rainfed conditions where water availability is less certain. This means that yields tend to be both lower and more variable. Nevertheless, using sophisticated cultivation methods, and one of the thousands of traditional varieties of rice, some of which can grow in several meters of water, farmers can usually grow enough to meet their own needs and to contribute to Thailand's substantial rice exports. In the delta areas of the central plains a system particularly characteristic of Thailand has evolved – deepwater

Transplanting seedlings (*above*) The young rice plants are carefully pulled up and bundled to be taken for replanting in the prepared rice field.

Threshing with water buffalo (*right*) Trampling by people or animals is the usual way of separating the grain. This method retains the protein- and vitamin-rich part of the seed (endosperm).

rice cultivation. Seed is broadcast directly onto the dry field; it grows in dry conditions until the rains arrive in earnest perhaps 50 days after germination. Then the plants must compete with the rising water, which can eventually exceed 1 m (3 ft) in depth. Yields are low, perhaps only 1.5 tonnes per hectare (3.7 tonnes per acre), and the system is being replaced in many areas by transplanted rice as water control improves.

Like all farming in Southeast Asia, wet rice cultivation has undergone many drastic changes. Production is becoming increasingly mechanized, the new high-yielding varieties are being more widely planted, and farmers may use large quantities of chemicals.

Rice plant

Panicle, or head,
of ripe grain

The rice plant Rice is one of the world's most important food crops. It grows best in shallow water; the hollow stem allows oxygen to reach the roots submerged in the flooded soil. The plants grow to a height of 80–180 cm (31–70 in), and have several stems, each one bearing a head (panicle) of rice kernels. The grains mature 110 to 180 days after planting. Rice is a good source of carbohydrate, though it is slightly lower in protein than other cereals.

These modern techniques are not without their problems. Social inequalities have widened as some households within a village have benefited at the expense of others, causing friction between neighbors. At the same time, some scientists now believe that farmers are courting ecological disaster by planting the same varieties of rice over large areas, instead of rotating a large number of varieties as traditional farmers did. It has been estimated that over 1,500 rice varieties have been lost in the region since 1975. Genetic variability is reduced, the chance of catastrophic pest attack increased, and the land becomes prone to deterioration as excessive demands are placed upon it. Yet modern techniques and irrigation have raised yields in environmentally favored areas by up to 6 tonnes per hectare (2.5 tonnes per acre), four to five times higher than in the less advantaged provinces. Whatever methods are used, rice remains a central part of the traditional way of life in most of rural Southeast Asia.

INDUSTRY

SUPPLYING THE WORLD WITH TIN · ADDING VALUE TO RESOURCES · VERSATILITY AND AMBITION

Southeast Asia has been a rich source of precious metals, minerals and gemstones for hundreds of years. The region is famous for its jade (mostly from Myanmar) and for its hardwood, made into intricately carved furniture and boxes. More recently Southeast Asia has become a leading exporter of tin, particularly from Thailand, and has significant reserves of oil and natural gas. These resources help to fund new industrial growth. Since the 1960s, a young labor force has provided the impetus for expansion into high-technology electronics. However, progress has been affected by political events. Vietnam, Laos, Cambodia and Myanmar have been isolated from their neighbors, and internal wars during the past 50 years have forced a decline in their traditional mining and manufacturing, preventing new opportunities to diversify.

COUNTRIES IN THE REGION

Brunei, Cambodia, Indonesia, Laos, Malaysia, Myanmar, Philippines, Singapore, Thailand, Vietnam

INDUSTRIAL OUTPUT 1997 (US $ billion)

Thailand	61
Singapore	34
Philippines	26
Malaysia	47
Indonesia	92

INDUSTRIAL WORKERS (% of total labor force)

	Mining	Manufacturing	Construction
Singapore (1996)	—	406,300 (23.2%)	115,000 (6.6%)
Thailand (1995)	64,000 (0.2%)	4,839,500 (15.4%)	2,649,100 (8.5%)
Indonesia (1995)	64,332 (0.8%)	10,127,047 (12.7%)	3,768,080 (4.7%)

MAJOR PRODUCTS (INDONESIA)

Energy and minerals	Output change 1970	Output change 1995
Coal (mill tonnes)	0.1	42
Natural gas (thou terajoules)	46	2,508
Oil (crude, mill tonnes)	43	77
Tin (thou tonnes)	5.2	44
Nickel ore (thou tonnes)	18	87
Cement (thou tonnes)	515	23,316
Gold (tonnes)	0	74
Silver (tonnes)	9	161

Manufactures		
Radio receivers (thou)	393	3,500
Televisions (thou)	5	1,000
Tyres (thou)	358	15,000
Coconuts (thou tonnes)	5,892	13,868
Palm oil (thou tonnes)	114	4,480
Coffee (thou tonnes)	186	485 (1998)

SUPPLYING THE WORLD WITH TIN

The countries that make up the region of Southeast Asia are richly endowed with metals and minerals, especially in the older mountain chain running south from the border between China and mainland Southeast Asia to the Indonesian islands around Bangka, north of Java. Rubies, sapphires, gold, silver, and other valuable resources have been mined extensively in past centuries, but as it enters a new industrial era the region has made its fortune extracting modern riches: for example, tin, oil and gas.

About 200 years ago Chinese settlers began to mine tin in parts of the peninsula. By the second half of the 19th century they had developed the richest tin fields in the world in the Kinta Valley in southeast Malaysia. Largescale European interest was not awakened until the early 20th century when dredgers – machines that suck metal from the mine floor – were imported to boost mining activities. Until World War II Malay was the dominant source of tin, but afterward there was rapid expansion in Indonesia and Thailand as world demand strengthened. Malaysia's output continues to fall gradually as the richest fields become depleted and only 25 percent of the mines operating in 1985 were still working in 1990. The expensive large dredgers of the 1960s and 1970s are less successful today and cheaper gravel pumps, which are more flexible in poor mining conditions, are being reintroduced.

In Indonesia, where tin resources are still relatively plentiful, 28 state-owned dredgers contribute to 60 percent of the country's tin production. Thailand is seeking to increase offshore output from extensive undeveloped tin deposits near Phuket, an island lying off the southwest coast of Thailand. Even so, production is dropping due to dwindling resources. In 1995 Indonesia, Malaysia and Thailand together accounted for 35–40 percent of

Tin bath (*below*) Plentiful in Malaysia, but scarce worldwide, tin is usually found mixed with mud in alluvial deposits in streams, rivers or oceans. Sucked up from the water bed, the tin is laundered – washed and separated – and the concentrate collected.

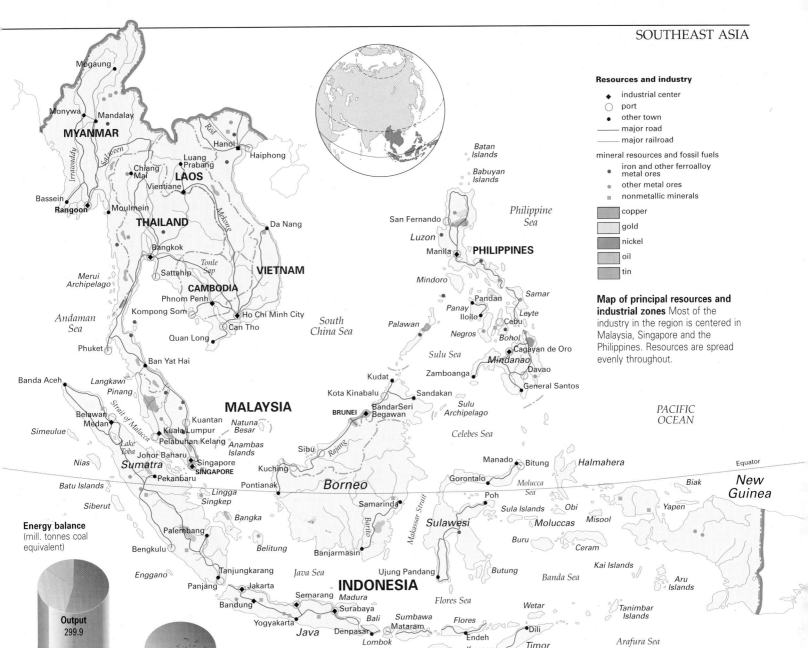

Resources and industry

- ◆ industrial center
- ○ port
- ● other town
- — major road
- — major railroad

mineral resources and fossil fuels
- ● iron and other ferroalloy metal ores
- ● other metal ores
- ■ nonmetallic minerals

- copper
- gold
- nickel
- oil
- tin

Map of principal resources and industrial zones Most of the industry in the region is centered in Malaysia, Singapore and the Philippines. Resources are spread evenly throughout.

Energy balance
(mill. tonnes coal equivalent)

Output 299.9
Exports 145.5
Consumption 131.8
Imports 27.2

Sources of energy output

- coal
- gas
- oil
- other

Energy production and consumption – Indonesia
(above) Not only is the region a net exporter of oil and natural gas, it also has the third largest oil refinery complex in the world. Coal is the only other major fuel. Indonesia is exploring nuclear power possibilities.

world output compared with over 60 percent in the 1960s, and the output of tin in Myanmar has also fallen.

The fossil fuel boom

During the second half of the 20th century, Brunei, Malaysia, Indonesia and Vietnam all became net energy exporters. However, exploitation of oil and natural gas in the region has barely kept pace with demand – between 1990 and 1997 regional oil demand grew by more than 6 million barrels per day driven by the economies of India, China, Japan and Indonesia. Extensive deposits, and a small variety of other minerals, are found in Myanmar, Malaysia, Borneo, Sumatra and Java. The giant oilfield at Seria in Brunei (north-eastern Borneo) has passed its peak of production but oil and gas revenues still contribute over 50 percent of Brunei's GDP and exploration for new fields continues, particularly offshore. Indonesia has become a major regional exporter of oil: in the late 1990s crude oil production was around 1.5 million barrels per day. At the end of the 1990s Malaysia experienced declining reserves due to a lack of significant new discoveries, nevertheless, total oil production increased steadily to an estimated 803,000 barrels per day in 1998. The majority of oil was exported to Japan, Thailand, South Korea and Singapore.

There are rich natural gas reserves in the region and these are being explored with the intention of reducing reliance on imported oil. Thailand is developing off-shore natural gas reserves which estimated to amount to 202 billion cu meters in 1997. Agreement was reached with Malaysia in 1998 to share equally offshore reserves in previously disputed territory and in 1997 a similar agreement was made between Thailand and Vietnam. The Philippines has recently discovered a large natural gas field off the island of Palawan.

Natural gas supplies about 60 percent of Indonesia's energy needs, most of which comes from the Arun field in northern Sumatra. The majority of the extracted gas is used in the domestic market. Malaysia had proven natural gas reserves of 81.7 trillion cubic feet in the late 1990s and production was rising to supply the main markets of Japan, South Korea and Taiwan. An important potential oilfield is beneath the waters of the Spratley Islands in the South China Sea. However, six surrounding nations, including China, claim the islands' development has been halted until territorial disputes are resolved.

ADDING VALUE TO RESOURCES

In the 1950s and early 1960s a number of countries in Southeast Asia built up manufacturing industries to exploit their natural resources. Their aim was to establish processing industries, particularly oil refining, metalworking, food packaging, textiles and electrical assembly to add value to local raw materials, and to reduce the region's reliance on imports.

Oil refining is by far the most significant processing industry in the region. Singapore, which was a British colonial trading center from the early 19th century until just after World War II, has transformed itself since independence into a leading processing center for oil, as well as rubber, tin and oil palm. The tiny island state is now the third most important center for oil refining in the world after Houston (Texas, the United States) and

Rotterdam (the Netherlands), and has developed rapidly since 1961. It has five major refining complexes with a total capacity of 43 million tonnes. Singapore can more than fulfill the needs of the region, and has enough capacity to export processed petroleum across the world. Recently the industry has become more sophisticated and also produces chemical byproducts, plastics and synthetic fibers.

Following Singapore's lead, other oil producers in the region are anxious to develop their own refining capacity to serve at least their domestic needs for fuel oil, gasoline and kerosene. Pertamina, the Indonesian state-owned company, has six refineries in Sumatra and one in Kalimantan with a similar capacity to Singapore. It is also developing liquid propane gas (LPG) plants with Japanese investment, particularly in Bontung and Bodak in eastern Kalimantan. Malaysia, with 10 million tonnes of oil-refining

capacity, has gone a step further by building an export-oriented refinery at Lutong in Sarawak to compete with Singapore. Continuing high demand for plastic, a byproduct of the refining process, attracts further investment in the industry from multinational giants including Kellog-Thyssen and Rheinstahl.

Stagnation caused by war
Many of the poorer countries in the region, including Laos and Cambodia, have very little largescale manufacturing industry, and war has prevented any effective development. Vietnam's industrial economy regressed in the second half of the 20th century as a result of the Vietnam war (1955–75). Some manufacturing industries, such as cement, paper, metals, glass, cotton textiles, food, drink and tobacco, had been developed in the north (mostly in Hanoi, Haiphong and Cholon) before hostilities commenced.

The written word (*above*) Southeast Asia, especially Singapore, has become a major center for printing and color reproduction. The combination of cheap labor, good transportation and vast improvements in printing technology has fueled this growth.

Economic driving forces (*left*) Although some United States' automobile manufacturers are well established in the region, the past two decades have seen a big increase in Japanese investment and development of joint venture and licensee automobile factories. Companies such as Toyota are able to take advantage of cheap labor and tax incentives.

There were also some specialized craft-based industries in the Tonkin delta, but more recently Vietnam has lacked sufficient funds to modernize them. After 1976, reconstruction efforts created a revival in the cement, steel and power-production industries.

Myanmar, too, has lagged in industrial development in the late 20th century. Its inward-looking military government has halted the potential growth of the tourist industry, which in turn stunted development of the country's traditional craft industries, particularly jewelry (made from local gemstones, gold and silver), woodcarving and textiles.

Fostering joint ventures
In the countries belonging to the Association of Southeast Asian Nations (ASEAN) prior to 1990 – Brunei, Indonesia, Malaysia, the Philippines, Singapore and Thailand – industries

processing the area's rich resources attracted international attention. A number of multinational companies have developed manufacturing bases in Singapore, because of the oil and rubber refining there. Similarly, the palm oil industry in the Philippines is bringing in considerable investment from foreign countries. A joint venture between Shell and Mitsubishi has invested US $1.3 billion in an olefin plant in Indonesia making textile fibers.

Japanese and American investment is very important in maintaining copper smelting in the Philippines and aluminum smelting in northern Sumatra using local hydroelectric power. However, it is less vital to the older tin-smelting industries in Pinang, Phuket and Pelim near Bangkok, where local Chinese capital is used. A new development has been the expansion of Krakatau Steel at Cilegon near Jakarta in Indonesia; it produces large quantities of steel products mainly for export north to Japan.

High-tech and electronics industries are also beginning to transform several manufacturing sectors across the region. Malaysia and Thailand have been most successful in this field to date, Malaysia in particular having developed a semiconductor and integrated circuit (IC) chip industry, exporting products all around the world. Manufacturing automobiles, trucks and motorcycles is also growing in importance, with help from abroad. Expansion in this area reflects increased domestic demand and international confidence in manufacturing in Southeast Asia.

MICROCHIP TECHNOLOGY FROM PINANG

The tiny Malaysian island of Pinang is known as the Silicon Island of the Pacific basin due to its rapid and successful development in the microelectronics industry. A cheap labor force and good communications with the mainland – the island has a port, an international airport and a road link – have made it an attractive prospect to multinational companies.

It has particular expertise in the production of semi-conductor devices (so-called because they are neither good conductors nor good insulators) used in electronic circuits as switches, amplifiers, light-detectors and for numerous other functions. They can be put into complex but easily manufactured microelectronic circuits and are the key elements for the majority of electronic systems from computers to communications equipment. Their versatility owes much to their compact size, reliable performance and low cost.

Originally Pinang imported most of the components, and was responsible for only the last two stages of chip making, the labor-intensive assembly and final testing and sorting. However, the island was able to attract investment to upgrade production, recruit skilled workers and go into silicon wafer processing. The multinational company, National Semiconductor, has a plant in Malaysia and is a world leader in the manufacture of semiconductors and silicon chip technology. The company is investing heavily in the communications and consumer electronics fields especially in the development of information appliances – electronic items that will access the Internet without a computer.

VERSATILITY AND AMBITION

Southeast Asia has a population of over 531 million people, the majority of whom are young. The potential workforce is therefore enormous, and this wealth of human resources has already begun to play an important part in the region's development. Levels of urbanization are still low – below 30 percent in Thailand, Vietnam, Cambodia and Myanmar – and a large proportion of the population works in agriculture and fishing (more than 45 percent in most countries). There are few very large industrial cities in the region given the overall size of the population. Bangkok and Jakarta, with agglomerations of more than eight million, stand out as being exceptionally large.

Recently, education has become more readily available to the younger generations and literacy has increased, except in Laos and the remoter islands of Indonesia. A young, educated workforce is essential to expansion in the emerging labor-intensive light industries such as garment manufacture and electronics, particularly as the region is becoming increasingly competitive with the West. Whereas Malaysia, Singapore and, to a lesser extent, Thailand have been relatively successful in meeting the more sophisticated aspirations of these educated workers, in Indonesia and the Philippines they have struggled to find jobs. This has led to an explosion of people going overseas to areas of shortage, most significantly to the Gulf areas in the Middle East, though this may change in time.

Filipinos are the most numerous migrant workers; because English is one of the country's two official languages, it makes it easy for them to travel to the United Kingdom, continental Europe, Australia, Hong Kong and the United States. With the development of inter-ASEAN economic zones such as the one based in Singapore, the region should be able to provide employment for most of its own workforce. Recently, Singapore has even begun to take in guest workers to cover its own shortages.

Shifting patterns of employment
As the region has developed modern manufacturing industries, a noticeable divide has grown up between a commercial, capitalized and technologically-oriented sector and one that is often family oriented and more traditional, using a low level of technology, and with informal labor and wage arrangements. Over time, the traditional sector has been drawn into providing products and services for the commercial sector, and the high-tech sector has come to specialize in labor-intensive products. Traditional wood-carving skills are used in the manufacture of furniture and plywood, for example, and long-standing expertise in paper and metal processing has been turned toward high-quality color reproduction and printing for Western and Japanese markets.

One consequence of this shift in emphasis is that the traditional resource-based

Following the pattern (*above*) The majority of industry in the region is in the middle ground between cottage and high-tech industries. Manufactured goods, usually clothes and household items, are either for domestic consumption or limited export.

Like father, like son (*below*) Very smallscale manufacturing, such as this explosives workshop in Indonesia, is being squeezed out of the region. Except in Thailand, Myanmar and Vietnam, family-owned workshops mainly produce trinkets for tourists.

industries are becoming less attractive areas for employment, and generally offer wages that support a much lower standard of living. The mining sector now accounts for a tiny proportion of the labor force in all countries where figures are available, except Brunei. Even the plantations (producing rubber, sugar and coconuts) that, historically, were very large employers, operate with many fewer people today. Throughout the 1980s and 1990s the workforce began to move away from subsistence farming and was increasingly absorbed into the manufacturing and service sectors.

Low levels of unionization
In spite of the spread of education among the growing young adult urban population, there has been little union activity in manufacturing centers. Demands for improved wage levels and conditions of work are usually the result of rising standards of living, though improvements have sometimes been introduced by paternalistic governments. There is often a powerful work ethic among the population, particularly driven by the motivation to acquire enough wealth to marry, buy homes or consumer goods, fund further education or set up small businesses. The lack of union activity is one of the features that attracts foreign companies seeking new locations for factories to satisfy their global markets. Most of the governments in the region actively encourage foreign investment and frown on trade unionism. In Myanmar, for example, trade unions are not permitted, although centrally controlled workers'

SINGAPORE – CROSSROADS OF THE EAST

A tiny island at the meeting points of the Indian and Pacific oceans, northern Asia and Australasia, Singapore is one of the world's most exotic commercial centers. Colonial traditions – including the widespread use of English as a first language – and a long history of trade have helped Singapore become a magnet for various multinational companies. Singapore's commercial significance is due largely to the free port status it had in colonial times. At its height in the mid 20th century, Singapore was the largest port in Asia and the fifth largest in the world. Although shipping is still a leading industry, it is no longer the most important.

The island is heavily and efficiently promoted as a tourist and conference destination. Tourists go there for the superb food, luxury hotels, and duty-free electrical and photographic equipment. They also use it as an attractive and convenient gateway to or from Australasia or the rest of Asia.

Alongside tourism, international business flourishes. Branches of multinational firms and a thriving workforce provide the capital and service industries to make Singapore a significant commercial center. The island has been particularly successful in establishing oil and petrochemical industries as well as electrical and electronics manufacture, industrial chemicals, printing and publishing. Metalworking, especially for ships and oil-rig repair, is a more recent spinoff from the old shipbreaking industries that were set up on the Jurong industrial estate in the 1970s.

Space is a recurring problem in such a heavily urbanized country and Singapore has joined forces with its neighbors, Jahore to the north and Riau islands to the south, in developing a growth triangle. In addition, the free trade economic zone on Batam Island, 12 miles away, has attracted industrial development by international giants including Philips, Sony and Toshiba.

The pulse of industry In Singapore most factories, such as this medical supplies company, are manufacturing outposts of multinational organizations, specializing in the production of high-tech electronic and miniaturized equipment.

councils and local conciliation committees mediate in labor disputes. Northern Vietnam has a similar government-controlled system to mediate in any labor disputes that may occur.

Among the foreign investors in many of these countries are the Chinese, who act as a local source of wealth to fund entrepreneurial ventures. This is important in countries such as Thailand and Indonesia that particularly favor joint industrial ventures. The few individuals who have become very wealthy in business have often expanded from a modest beginning, and such people act as a motivating example to others. The ultimate wish of most working Asians is to improve on their traditional low-waged employment status in order to own and run their own small business.

Carving up the forests

Timber is undoubtedly one of the most important exports of the region, especially to Japan where it is a mainstay of the construction industry. Hardwood from Southeast Asia is used to make wooden houses, or as shuttering in the manufacture of concrete slabs. The more valuable woods are exported in large quantities to Europe and Japan to be used as high-quality veneers or in cabinet making. Teak, prized for its visual appeal and durability, is frequently used for interior fittings in ships or luxury cars or for domestic utensils, particularly wooden bowls. Its exceptional resistance to acid makes it popular for laboratory benches and other fittings. At the other end of the spectrum, kempas and kapur are heavy-duty timbers used extensively in the construction of bridges, farm buildings, wharf decking, industrial flooring and in railroad sleepers.

Meeting insatiable demand

Southeast Asia was originally covered with extensive tropical rain forest, but exploitation of hardwood as an industrial resource has accelerated in recent years, causing extensive depletion. Much of the wood has been used to produce furniture, timber for the building trade, paneling, flooring, plywood, paper and other commercial products.

During the 1980s output of processed wood more than doubled in most of the region except Vietnam and the Philippines, and increased tenfold in Indonesia. The development of the printing industry in the region has meant that the consumption of pulp and paper is growing twice as fast in Asia as in Europe and North America, and the product is seriously underpriced in terms of the real costs of soil depletion, the drain on the water supply, atmospheric pollution and global warming. While the scale of forest depletion is not comparable to the much more extensive areas disappearing in South America, Southeast Asia is still selling a valuable resource for shortterm gains and longterm losses.

Demands for timber and for its byproducts, woodchip and paper goods, have encouraged tree-felling practices in the

Awaiting the chop (*above*) Log felling and the timber trade is an important part of the region's economy. Nearly half of the labor force in the area is involved in forestry or some aspect of wood processing. After petroleum and rubber, timber is Malaysia's biggest foreign export earner.

From tree to toothpick (*left*) There is little wastage in wood processing. The bark is used for compost and fuel, and the rounded outer portion is processed into chipboard. The inner sections of wood are cut into either planks of beam depending on the quality of the wood.

Heartwood, cut for lumber. The central core is made into thick planks or beams

Outer, round-sided slabs, chipped and used for chipboard

Carving a niche There is a long tradition of wood carving and furniture making in the region, but most of it is small scale. Attempts are being made to develop this industry to benefit both the timber trade and local skilled craftsmen.

region that prevent woodland from renewing itself. Thailand finally banned logging after discovering that forest cover in the country fell from 29 to 19 percent between 1985 and 1988. Furthermore, the high level of demand for this versatile resource has forced the lumber industry to expand into the neighboring countries. In consequence, there is a considerable amount of illegal cutting and smuggling from both Myanmar and Laos.

Less wood, more income

One possible way to slow down the rate of tree felling would be to generate a higher level of income from less of the raw product. In effect, this would mean adding value to the wood while it is still in the region, by processing it or using it in manufacturing industries and then exporting the finished goods. Manufacture of wooden furniture in the region remains small scale, but is an obvious candidate for expansion.

The traditional craft of decorative carving is currently only a very small part of the modern wood products industry since the vast majority of timber is exported in its raw state to be worked on by European and Japanese craftsmen. Manufacturers specializing in furniture are scattered in hundreds of small factories, often employing a large, skilled workforce but making slim profits. In terms of productivity these firms rank about 20th in the region compared with other ventures, though they have a much higher position in terms of numbers of employees.

At the beginning of the 1990s, the wood-processing industries making plywood, veneer sheets, sleepers, chipboard and fiberboard were still relatively small, but the emphasis for the future was on growth. A program to promote this sector has already had some success in Indonesia. Exports of raw timber have been banned, and as a result plywood has recently become one of the country's important nonoil exports. With average prices for logs and sawn timber staying at a standstill during the 1980s, it was doubly important for the industry to find other ways to expand and sustain themselves apart from increasing the volume and rate of cutting.

ECONOMY

PRIMARY CONCERNS · GROWTH FALTERS · LONGSTANDING POVERTY AND NEW WEALTH

Southeast Asia was recognized as a major subdivision of the world economy only after World War II, when the region gained independence from its former colonial masters. Since then, Southeast Asia has transformed itself from a supplier of raw materials into a thriving manufacturing region with booming export sales. Despite a background of political conflict, particularly in former Indo-China, cheap labor costs and a powerful work ethic have encouraged foreign investment, especially from Japan and the United States. The communist states of Vietnam, Laos and Cambodia remained cut off from the world economy until the late 1980s. The other countries have pursued diverse economic philosophies, ranging from Singapore's rigid system of economic control to Thailand's "freewheeling" capitalism.

PRIMARY CONCERNS

Southeast Asia occupies an important strategic position linking China and east Asia with India and the Middle East. From the 15th century, the region became a vital connection in the emerging world economy, initially as a supplier of high-value spice and transshipper of Chinese silk, drugs and porcelain. Later it became a supplier of bulk primary goods such as rice, tin and rubber and a large market for manufactured goods from the West.

During the 19th century virtually the whole region passed under direct Western rule. Only Thailand – much reduced in size – retained a measure of political independence. Broadly based patterns of trade and production gave way to the production of

a narrow range of primary products. After the signing of the Bowring Treaty (1855), Thailand also came under British economic control. The removal of tariff barriers opened the Thai economy to a flood of cheap British manufactured goods that pushed domestic manufacturing into rapid decline. Textile production was largely replaced by the export of raw cotton. Rice, which accounted for under 3 percent of exports in 1850, constituted 70 percent in 1890 and dominated production.

By the late 1930s the economies of Southeast Asia were geared toward primary production. Trade and investment were locked into the imperial trading systems of Britain, France, the Netherlands and the United States. However, in Southeast Asia, as elsewhere in the world, the colonial structures were beginning to

COUNTRIES IN THE REGION

Brunei, Cambodia, Indonesia, Laos, Malaysia, Myanmar, Philippines, Singapore, Thailand, Vietnam

ECONOMIC INDICATORS: 1995–97

	*HIE Singapore	*LMIE Thailand	*LIE Indonesia
GDP (US$ billions)	96.3	157.2	214.6
GNP per capita (US$)	29,000	6,590	3,450
Annual rate of growth of GDP, 1990–1997 (%)	8.5%	7.4%	7.5%
Manufacturing as % of GDP	24.3%	28.4%	25.6%
Central government spending as % of GDP	15.9%	15.8%	14.7%
Merchandise exports (US$ billions)	125.8	56.7	56.3
Merchandise imports (US$ billions)	124.6	55.1	46.2
% of GNP received as development aid	—	0.5%	0.5%
Total external debt as a % of GDP	—	62.6%	65.3%
Industrial production growth rate 1999	14%	12.6%	1.5%

WELFARE INDICATORS

Infant mortality rate (per 1,000 live births)			
1965	26	145	128
1995–2000	5	29	48
Population per physcian (1993–4)	709	4,416	7,028
Teacher–pupil ratio (primary school, 1995)	1 : 25.3	1 : 19.3	1 : 22.3

Note: The Gross Domestic Product (GDP) is the total value of all goods and services domestically produced. The Gross National Product (GNP) is the GDP plus net income from abroad.

* HIE (High Income Economy) – GNP per capita above $9,360 in 1997. LMIE (Lower Middle Income Economy) – GNP per capita between $761 and $3,030. LIE (Low Income Economy) – GNP per capita below $760.

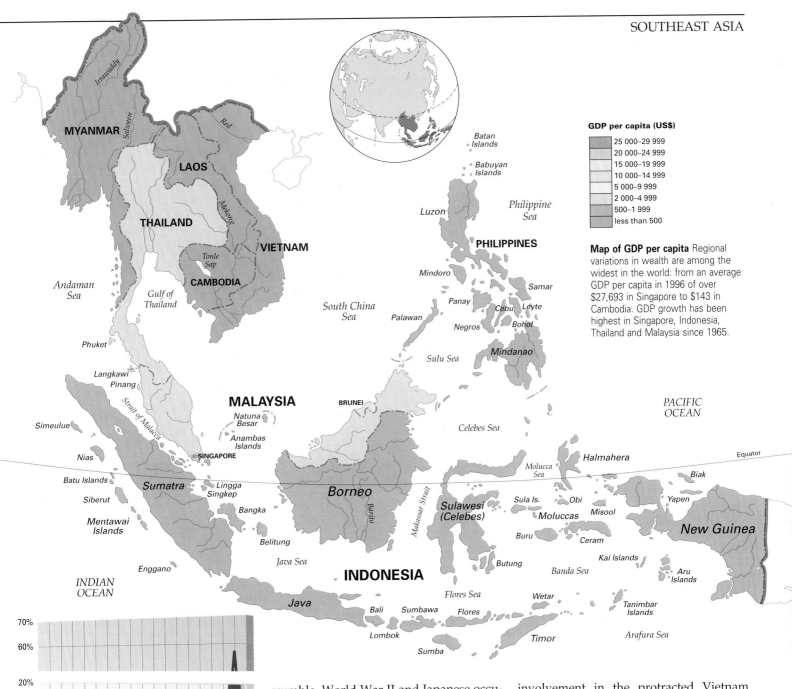

Map of GDP per capita Regional variations in wealth are among the widest in the world: from an average GDP per capita in 1996 of over $27,693 in Singapore to $143 in Cambodia. GDP growth has been highest in Singapore, Indonesia, Thailand and Malaysia since 1965.

GDP per capita (US$)

- 25 000–29 999
- 20 000–24 999
- 15 000–19 999
- 10 000–14 999
- 5 000–9 999
- 2 000–4 999
- 500–1 999
- less than 500

Profile of inflation (*above*) Indonesia's inflation soared to over 50 percent between 1997 and 1998, which was the time of the Asian financial market, and dramatically dropped to under 5 percent thereafter. Singapore achieved zero inflation during 1998–99, in part because of its social controls and tight monetary policies.

Sea of wealth (*left*) Singapore's petroleum industry is one of its most valuable assets, contributing to nearly 25 percent of all trade. The country has some offshore oil reserves of its own, but is primarily involved in refining. The shipping in the bay is part of the general traffic through Singapore harbor, the largest port in Southeast Asia and second in financial importance only to Rotterdam in the Netherlands.

crumble. World War II and Japanese occupation hastened the process. By the 1940s a new world order had emerged.

Capitalism versus communism

The Southeast Asian countries gained their independence between 1946 and 1958. Decolonization resulted in deep and lasting regional divisions. These became institutionalized in 1967 with the establishment of the Association of Southeast Asian Nations (ASEAN) by Indonesia, Malaysia, the Philippines, Singapore and Thailand (Brunei joined in 1984). The region became increasingly polarized between the pro-Western ASEAN states and the communist states of Indo-China: Kampuchea (Cambodia), Laos and Vietnam. Only Burma (Myanmar) adopted a nonaligned position.

American fears that the entire region would fall to communism, underlaid by a desire to secure the markets and resources of Southeast Asia as a sphere of American economic activity, led to the country's involvement in the protracted Vietnam war. The war exacted terrible social and economic costs on Vietnam. An estimated 2 million people were killed between 1954 and 1974; many more were maimed and made homeless, and about 70 percent of industrial capacity was destroyed.

The communist countries remained almost entirely isolated from the world economy until the late 1980s. Elsewhere in the region, huge amounts of American aid and military expenditure helped to boost the ASEAN economies, particularly the Philippines and Thailand. From the early 1970s, all the ASEAN states embarked on a period of rapid economic growth, characterized by expansion of manufacturing sectors and the emergence of authoritarian, often military, political regimes. Very high levels of military expenditure are still justified in terms of the threat of "communist subversion", though in practice this can mean simply opposition to the government.

GROWTH FALTERS

In the 1980s and 1990s, the southeast Asian countries were among the most dynamic in the world until the region was hit by the financial crisis of 1997–98. Malaysia, Thailand and Vietnam all grew at more than 9 percent in the mid-1990s and other countries were recording growth rates of between 5 and 9 percent. Thailand, Malaysia, Indonesia, South Korea and the Philippines were hardest hit as the values of their currencies plunged on international financial markets but even though other countries suffered much less, the region was expected to experience reduced growth for some time. However, the region has vast potential for further development. It occupies a favorable strategic position, is richly endowed with resources and, with a youthful population of over 531 million, offers a large labor force and extensive market for domestic or imported goods.

The region remains a significant supplier of commodities such as rubber, tin, rice, palm oil and copra to the developed world. Since World War II it has also become a significant producer and processor of oil and natural gas. Japan, for example, is heavily dependent on Indonesian fuels, while Singapore is the region's most important processing and distribution center for petroleum and other primary goods. Since the late 1970s, however, low international commodity prices and the growth of manufacturing exports have greatly reduced the contribution of primary products to the region's export earnings.

Labor-intensive light industries such as electronics and clothing manufacture now provide the region's most valuable exports. All countries actively promoted the expansion of manufacturing industry during the postcolonial period, initially to replace imports with domestic production, later to generate exports.

The foreign factor

Since the 1970s, multinational corporations and foreign capital have flowed into the region, encouraged by the receptive policies of most governments and a more stable political climate. Furthermore, the

Levels of affluence (*right*) This multistorey shopping mall in Kuala Lumpur, Malaysia, is evidence of rapid new economic growth. Although consumer goods are widely available, this a not a spendthrift culture, and people continue to save a high proportion of income.

region offers foreign investors an abundant supply of cheap, well-disciplined and largely nonunionized labor. High profits can be made, especially as the region has shown an ability to sustain prolonged rates of economic growth.

Under pressure from the International Monetary Fund (IMF) and the World Bank Indonesia, Malaysia, the Philippines and Thailand reformed their economies during the 1980s to allow market forces to operate more freely. The reforms – such as lifting trade and investment barriers, and reducing government intervention in the economy – gave a further boost to export manufacturing and direct and indirect foreign investment.

Since the 1980s Thailand and Malaysia – and to a lesser extent Indonesia and the Philippines – have become growing centers for labor-intensive manufacturing, mainly by foreign-owned companies. This reflects the decision by countries such as Japan, South Korea and Taiwan to relocate their labor-intensive manufacturing to other parts of Asia in the face of rising domestic labor costs and concern over industrial pollution. Since 1979 Singapore has deliberately allowed wage levels to rise and encouraged the development of more skilled, capital-intensive manufacturing. Consequently, Singapore, also, is relocating its labor-intensive industries elsewhere in the region, particularly to neighboring Jahore in Malaysia and Bataan in Indonesia, creating a "triangle of growth". These developments have created new divisions of labor within Asia: first, between the more developed economies of east Asia, led by Japan, and the low labor-cost countries of Southeast Asia;

and secondly between Singapore and the rest of Southeast Asia.

Future trends

Southeast Asia has become a Japanese sphere of influence in terms of trade and investment. Japan exports capital and manufactured goods to the region, importing almost exclusively raw materials in return, while Japanese plants in Southeast Asia produce manufactured goods for export to European and American markets. Vietnam showed strong growth in the early 1990s although hampered by the slow pace of structural reform, particularly of the banking system. Thailand's lead in investing in the former Indo-Chinese states was followed by other east Asian countries. Growth in the region was also spurred by investment by Japanese, European and American banks although the build up of foreign debt was one of the underlying causes of the Asian financial crisis of 1997–98. By late 1999, southeast Asia was showing signs of recovery: swift action by the international community in the form of aid packages stabilized the situation as did investment on more openness to trade and on the availability of quality financial information – such reforms, combined with the cheap labor and raw materials available in the region, should see a return to stable growth.

COMMERCE AND THE CHINESE COMMUNITY

The Chinese are Southeast Asia's largest minority: populations range from 77 percent in Singapore, which is effectively a Chinese city, through 26 percent in Malaysia to a regional low of 1.5 percent in the Philippines. Large-scale migration into Nang Yang ("the Southern Ocean") only began during the early 19th century, when migrants from the overcrowded provinces of southern China were attracted by the trade and investment opportunities then opening up in Southeast Asia.

Although most Chinese immigrants remained poor, a significant proportion established themselves in local trading, petty manufacturing and money-lending, acting as middlemen between the colonial powers and the indigenous populations. The Chinese flair for commerce enabled them to amass considerable assets and develop a business network that now dominates the domestic economies. For instance, it was estimated in 1998 that the Chinese, who comprise 4 percent of the population, account for 70 percent of Indonesia's private economic activity. There are similarly high levels of Chinese economic participation in the other countries of the region.

Despite their economic dominance, the Chinese have little political power. Indeed, they have been the object of much resentment and discrimination. Malaysia made a sustained effort to reduce Chinese economic power in the 1970s and 1980s, and the Chinese communities in both Indonesia and Vietnam have been severely persecuted. Nevertheless, Chinese enterprise and capital remain of crucial importance to the economies of Southeast Asia.

The rag-doll trade (*left*) Hand-sewn goods like these soft dolls (made mostly by women) account for a large sector of the Philippine export industry. Women are most likely to be employed in casual or part-time jobs like this one, but the official workforce is mostly male – 63 percent in 1995.

Coconut oil 2.8%
Telecommunications equipment 5.4%
Clothing 5.7%
Food and live animals 6.8%
Consumer goods 11.5%
Machinery and transport equipment 24.4%
Fish 2.1%
Copper 1.4%
electronics 39.9%
Exports US$136.4 bn
Imports US$182.7 bn
machinery and transport equipment 35.8%
Others 28.6%
Fuels 9.3%
Chemicals and related products 7.9%
Food and live animals 6.9%
Iron and steel 4.4%
Crude materials excl fuels 3.7%
Consumer goods 3.4%

The Philippines' balance of merchandise trade Machinery and transport equipment is a significant part of the Philippines' export sectors although it also makes up 24.4 percent of imports. The largest import sector is in electronic goods while consumer goods is the third largest import. The United States continues to be a major trading partner across the region, though in the 1990s Japan was the largest single source of imports.

Trading partners
- Germany
- China
- Hong Kong
- Japan
- North Korea
- Singapore
- Taiwan
- United States
- other countries

Exports
34.9%
4.2%
4.6%
4.6%
6.4%
16.6%
24.1%

Imports
32.4%
2.4%
3.3%
4.3%
5%
6%
6.1%
19.9%
20.6%

LONGSTANDING POVERTY AND NEW WEALTH

Wealth is very unevenly spread both between and within the countries of Southeast Asia. Singapore ranks with many developed countries in terms of per capita income and general standards of living. Malaysia and Thailand have been developing quickly and are now rated as middle-income economies while Vietnam, Laos, Cambodia and Myanmar are among the poorest countries in the world. The gap between Southeast Asia's rich and poor countries has widened considerably over the last two decades.

Apart from Singapore, Malaysia and the Philippines, most of the region's population lives in rural areas and is dependent on agriculture. Although all governments have reiterated their commitment to reducing poverty and regional inequalities over the last 30 years, in practice national development programs have concentrated on achieving accelerated industrial growth in the urban centers. Rural areas have been neglected by comparison, with the result that their large populations are effectively excluded from a share in the economic and social benefits that have accompanied national economic growth.

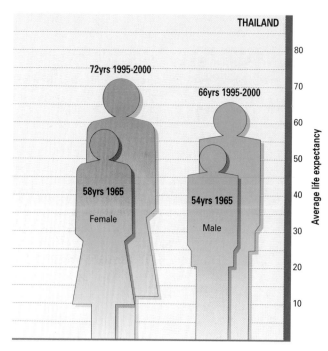

THAILAND

72yrs 1995-2000

66yrs 1995-2000

58yrs 1965

Female

54yrs 1965

Male

Average life expectancy

Bangkok by night (*right*) The glow of English-language neon signs in Thailand's capital reflects the number of foreign visitors: over 7.7 million in 1998, contributing more than $6 billion to the economy. Most are tourists, come to see the beautiful scenery and exotic temples; many are male and are clients of the sex trade, which flourishes in spite of its official nonexistence.

Life expectancy (*left*) Life expectancy in Thailand, at 72 years for women and 68.5 for men, is about average for the region. Laos and Cambodia have the lowest life expectancy in the region, while Singapore (at a combined average for men and women of 77) has the highest. Thailand's birthrate has held fairly steady over the past few decades. In 1997, 25 percent of its inhabitants were under 15, well below the average figure for the region, which is better represented by the Philippines, where 40 percent of the population is under 15.

While the economic differences between rural and urban areas are great, there are even sharper divisions within the cities. Rural poverty is propelling vast numbers of people into a relatively small number of cities: Southeast Asia has some of the highest rates of urban growth in the world. The urban centers have been unable to cope with such rapid population growth; many recent migrants can find neither adequate

work nor shelter and are forced to live in appalling conditions in sprawling squatter settlements on the city fringe. Furthermore, welfare systems are poorly developed and often woefully underfunded. The poverty of large sections of Southeast Asia's urban populations is in sharp contrast to the prosperity of the elite who live and work in the luxurious downtown apartment and office blocks.

Wealth, poverty and ethnicity

Inadequate welfare systems and channeling of government resources into urban-industrial development mean that high levels of poverty and severe regional inequalities persist throughout the region, though trends are far from uniform. In the late 1990s, Laos had an estimated 46 percent of the population living below the poverty line, Vietnam and Cambodia had 37 and 36 percent respectively while Thailand had only 12.6 percent and Malaysia a mere 6.8 percent. Assessment of relative wealth is complicated by marked ethnic differences in levels of income and employment opportunities which may be seriously affected by government policy.

The colonial administration of Malaysia encouraged an ethnic division of labor, whereby the indigenous Malays were

General issue for sale (*left*) Acquired, often illegally, from a nearby United States' military base in the Philippines, equipment from army stores is openly on sale. Trade on the black market is brisk – it is one of the region's fastest ways of making a large profit.

TOURISM AND THE SEX INDUSTRY IN THAILAND

Since the late 1970s tourism has become a major sector of the Thai economy, with tourist revenues generating US $22.5–27 billion annually. The growth of tourism has been helped by Thailand's reputation as an exotic center for the sex industry. Amid the country's scenic and cultural delights, the "red light" districts of Bangkok and coastal resorts such as Pattaya and Phuket are now important tourist attractions.

Apart from the "sex package tours" marketed from Japan, Germany, the Netherlands and the United States, the role of the sex trade in tourism can only be measured indirectly. For example, around two-thirds of tourists are male. Increasing tourist traffic from Singapore and Malaysia comprises predominantly single men.

The number of female prostitutes has also risen from an estimated 400,000 in 1974 to over 800,000 in 1990s. Similarly, in the mid-1990s, several thousand children, chiefly from Myanmar, Laos, Cambodia and China, were estimated to be working in the sex trade. Clients are as likely to be Thai as tourist: it has been estimated that about 95 percent of Thai men use prostitutes at some time in their lives. Households in the poorer rural areas of the north and northeast of the country are becoming increasingly dependent on remittances from prostitutes working in the resorts and cities.

The tourist and sex industries are suffering from international recession and the soaring rate of HIV infection. Since 1989 education campaigns sponsored by the government have tried to alter behavior and promote condom use. However, in the late 1990s, Thailand had the fourth highest number of AIDS cases in the world.

regarded as "natural rice growers", while Chinese and Indian immigrants were seen as labor for the modern industrial and commercial sectors. The ingrained socio-economic divisions that resulted from this policy caused considerable tension, leading eventually to race riots in 1969. The Malay-controlled government then implemented a five-year plan to positively discriminate in favor of the Malay population in employment and higher education and to raise the percentage of Malay-owned businesses from 4 to 30 percent. This created considerable discontent amongst the Chinese community and by 1990, when the policy was relaxed, Malay equity ownership had reached only 18 percent. In 1998, in response to the regional and financial crisis, the racial laws that favored Malaysian businesses were further relaxed but it was also announced that several hundred thousand immigrant workers would be repatriated.

The plight of Vietnam's boat people

Between 1976 and 1990 about 1 million refugees left Vietnam by sea, often packed into tiny fishing vessels and with no certain destination. The vast majority of these refugees were ethnic Chinese desperate to escape from harsh treatment by the Vietnamese government and the deteriorating economic conditions within the country itself.

By mid 1979 about 200,000 refugees had crossed into China, and perhaps the same number had reached Australia, Hong Kong, Taiwan or other countries in Southeast Asia. Thousands more were believed to have perished at sea, some the victims of pirate attacks. The recipient countries, particularly Indonesia and Malaysia, regarded the refugees as security risks and a drain on already scarce resources. These views were reinforced by the belief that the exodus was taking place with the complicity of the Vietnamese government. Commercial boat owners were perhaps the only group ultimately to profit from the exodus by sea. The owners of the Honduran-registered vessel, the "Southern Cross" reputedly made a profit of $485,000 for shipping 560 children and 690 adults from Ho Chi Min City to Indonesia in 1978.

Resettlement and repatriation
The Vietnamese government agreed to halt the exodus after a United Nations' Conference in 1978. Subsequently, the United Nations High Commission for Refugees (UNHCR) sponsored the Orderly Departure Scheme, under which a further 140,000 people had left Vietnam by 1988. Nevertheless, the illegal departures continued. The large numbers of refugees reached crisis levels in several Asian countries. Between 1976 and 1988 (when screening was initiated) more than 100,000 Vietnamese boat people were received by Hong Kong alone, one of the most popular destinations. Apprehended by the authorities close to the shore, many of the new migrants claimed to have crossed hundreds of miles of open sea from Vietnam. However, ocean patrols often assert that they cross China by land, boarding boats near Hong Kong harbor.

Following huge influxes during this generally receptive period, Hong Kong and Western nations, who were becoming increasingly unwilling to resettle refugees, tightened their immigration policies. Since the International Conference on Refugees from Indo-China of 1989, only those who could convince the authorities that they had fled Vietnam to escape persecution were regarded as refugees entitled to be resettled. Others were classified as "economic immigrants' and kept in detention camps until they could be repatriated. Conditions in the camps were harsh and outbreaks of violence became common. In 1989, Vietnam agreed to take back the boat people and promised that they would not be punished for fleeing. However, this presented the Vietnamese government with the social and financial problems of reabsorbing the migrants. Financial help included a $120 million assistance program from the European Community (EC) and cash payments from the United Nations (UN). The UNHCR set up a plan of action through which every asylum seeker was screened individually for refugee status: those who were given refugee status would be resettled in the West while economic migrants would be returned to Vietnam as part of an orderly departure program.

In 1990, the UK government began a repatriation program of boat people from Hong Kong and by the end of 1993 about 31,000 Vietnamese remained in Hong Kong camps and a further 20,000 in Indonesia, Malaysia and other parts of southeast Asia. More boat people were returned over the next few years and in 1996 the UNHCR terminated its financial assistance and Indonesia, Malaysia, the Philippines, Singapore and Thailand closed their camps, the inmates being either voluntarily or forcibly repatriated. In some cases this provoked violent resistance and the Philippines allowed 1,500 boat people to stay permanently. China made it clear to Britain that it wanted the remainder of refugees removed before it took over the territory in 1997 and by the end of that year approximately 2,000 remained. Many of these people were ethnic Chinese whom Vietnam refused to accept and who had also been refused by other countries.

In 2000 Hong Kong closed the last camp and their future was still uncertain.

No refuge A Vietnamese family's hopes of a new life are dashed as Hong Kong police take them into custody after their vessel was intercepted. They would have been detained in a camp and probably sent back to Vietnam by air.

PEOPLES AND CULTURES

PEOPLES OF THE FORESTS, VALLEYS AND ISLANDS · A MIX OF CULTURES
THE OLD AND THE NEW IN CONFLICT

The cultural complexity of Southeast Asia reflects both its fragmented island geography and its central location on ancient trading routes. Since earliest times, the sea has linked even the most distant groups, serving to transmit cultural ideas and behavior within the region – for example, women nearly everywhere play an important role in trade and ritual. Water and forest – the twin characteristics of the environment of Southeast Asia – have strongly influenced human activity: rice cultivation is almost universal and a number of common cultural features have arisen around it. But there is enormous diversity, too. Over the millennia immigrants and traders from outside the region (including most recently European colonialists) have introduced a succession of languages and religious cultures.

COUNTRIES IN THE REGION
Brunei, Cambodia, Indonesia, Laos, Malaysia, Myanmar, Philippines, Singapore, Thailand, Vietnam

POPULATION
Over 175 million	Indonesia
Over 50 million	Thailand, Philippines, Vietnam
10 million–49 million	Myanmar, Malaysia, Cambodia
2 million–10 million	Laos, Singapore
Under 1 million	Brunei

LANGUAGE
Countries with one official language (Bahasa Indonesia) Indonesia; (Bahasa Malaysia) Malaysia; (Burmese) Myanmar; (Khmer) Cambodia; (Lao) Laos; (Thai) Thailand; (Vietnamese) Vietnam

Countries with two official languages (English, Malay) Brunei; (English, Pilipino) Philippines

Country with four official languages (Bahasa Malaysia, Chinese, English, Tamil) Singapore

RELIGION
Country with one major religion (B) Cambodia

Countries with two major religions (B,I) Laos; (B.M) Thailand

Countries with three or more major religions (B,C,T) Vietnam; (B,C,H,M) Indonesia; (B,C,I,M) Myanmar, Brunei; (B,M,P,RC) Philippines; (B,C,H,M,T) Singapore, Malaysia

Key: B–Buddhist, C–Various Christian, H–Hindu, I–Indigenous religions, M–Muslim, P–Protestant, RC–Roman Catholic, T–Taoist

PEOPLES OF THE FORESTS, VALLEYS AND ISLANDS

Until the 18th century Southeast Asia was a region of forests, and in comparison to India and China, its immediate neighbors, it was only relatively lightly populated. Except in a few areas, such as the island of Java and the Red river delta of northern Vietnam, land was abundant, and the earliest groups of people inhabiting the region were able to develop ways of life that took advantage of this fact. They worked with the forest, periodically clearing it for shifting cultivation or living a hunting-gathering existence within it. In the forested uplands of the region, small and dispersed groups of people survive in this way to the present day.

The water of life
Water has been no less important to the patterns of human settlement and culture in the region. An abundant supply of water was necessary for the wet cultivation of rice, the staple crop of Southeast Asia, and it was in the well-watered lowland valleys of the mainland and on the islands of Indonesia that the region's major agrarian kingdoms and civilizations developed. The control of water, both technologically, through sophisticated irrigation schemes, and culturally, through ritual and magic, are common threads that bind together the varied peoples of Southeast Asia. Another habit that links them all together is the use of the *ani ani*, or finger knife, in rice harvesting, which is to be found nearly everywhere in the region.

Water also provided the means by which people could exchange goods and ideas with each other, and with the wider world. The rivers and seaways that permeate Southeast Asia, act as corridors through dense forest and link the distant islands. The region lies on the maritime crossroads between India and China, and many of its early empires – including the Sumatra-based Srivijaya empire (from the 7th to the 14th century), the Majapanit empire centered on Java (from the 13th to the 15th century) and the empire established by the port of Malacca on peninsular Malaysia (from the 15th to the 16th century) – owed their power and prosperity to their ability to control the trade between east and west.

Cultural contacts
Over the last 2,000 years Southeast Asia has witnessed a series of cultural invasions from both east and west. The Chinese influence is strongest in Vietnam, where it can be traced back at least to the 2nd century BC. The Mandarin system of government, the philosophical, political and ethical doctrines of Confucianism – which stress the obligation of respect to elders, social conformity and the importance of ancestors and lineage – as well as the Chinese "religion" of Taoism, which is often regarded as standing in opposition to Confucianism – have all taken deep root here. Over the centuries there has also been considerable migration of Chinese people into the Malay Peninsula and into some of the islands of the region.

In the other direction, traders and migrants from the Indian subcontinent introduced a succession of cultural and religious influences. The earliest of these

Songkran celebrations (*above*) in the Thai city of Chieng-Mai. The Buddhist New Year is greeted by a wave of festivities. Worshippers visit shrines and monasteries, taking food and gifts to the monks.

A cremation in Bali (*right*) Belief in reincarnation is very strong among the people of this small Indonesian island, the last stronghold of Hinduism in the region. Cremations, which liberate the souls of the dead for the onward journey, are performed with elaborate rites.

A floating market in Thailand (*left*) Waterways are a vital element of life in Southeast Asia, often providing the main links between and within communities.

was Hinduism, which is now adhered to only by the people of the Indonesian island of Bali. The missionary nature of Buddhism encouraged its spread into the region from the 3rd century BC onward: it remains the predominant religion of the mainland. From the 13th century AD Arab traders began to extend their activities into Southeast Asia and helped to establish Islam in the Malay Peninsula, on the islands of Indonesia, and on the southern Philippines.

They were followed not much later by European traders – first the Portuguese, and then the British and Dutch. Over the next three or four centuries European influence was transformed into colonial rule – the Portuguese, Dutch and British in Indonesia, Malaysia and Burma, the Spanish and United States in the Philippines, and the French in Indochina. They introduced, along with Christianity, Western-style systems of government and economic structures, and technology.

A MIX OF CULTURES

A number of clear patterns can be distinguished within Southeast Asia's cultural complexity. The traditions of the peoples of the islands are substantially different from those of the mainland, and there are similar distinctions between those of the uplands and the lowlands. In addition, within the region popular animist beliefs exist beside, and mingle with, the world's major religious faiths, and introduced cultural elements confront indigenous ways of life.

The island–mainland division is discernible in the distribution of languages within the region. On most of the islands a range of related Austronesian languages are spoken, which had their common source in a parent language originating in the Pacific region about 5,000 years ago. The mainland languages are much more varied, and their origins – whether from

the Tibetan and Chinese families of languages, or from those of the Pacific and Indian subcontinent – are the subject of dispute. In more modern times, immigrant Chinese have introduced various Chinese languages, while indentured laborers from southern India have added Tamil. European languages, particularly English and French, are spoken among the urban elites.

Religious patterns
The distribution of religions shows the same broad divisions. Across the mainland, the practice of Theravada Buddhism is predominant, though in Vietnam the Mahayana Buddhism of eastern Asia is more common, as well as Taoism and Confucianism, reflecting the country's close cultural links with China. Among the islands, Islam prevails across Indonesia, Brunei, Malaysia and also the southern Philippine island of Mindanao. The Indonesian island of Bali remains the

last stronghold of a once much stronger Hindu tradition, and most people in the Philippines are Roman Catholic – a legacy of Spanish colonial rule.

All these religions were introduced to the region from outside, and this has led some experts to regard Southeast Asia as a mere receptacle for foreign cultural influences. But, in reality, the religions are syncretic: they have been molded to meet the particular needs of their Southeast Asian adherents, and each incorporates a range of traditional animist beliefs in spirits and ancestors who are held to inhabit the natural world. Filipino Christians, for example, wear magic amulets, believe in spirits and perform supposedly Christian rites that have their origins in an animist past.

The Karen hill people of northern Thailand and Burma believe in the ancestral spirit (*bgha*) and life principle (*k'la*), and a multitude of other gods and spirits, but a significant proportion also accept Christian ideas. Living in isolated groups among the dense upland forests, these people had been little affected by the ideas of Buddhism, but Christian missionaries who first began to arrive in the area at the end of the 19th century succeeded in converting the Karen by drawing upon their myths to make comparisons between the Karen religion and Biblical Christianity. The Karen proved receptive to this approach and by 1919 nearly 20 percent of the Burmese Karens had become Christian. Many Christian missionaries continue to proselytize in the marginal areas of Southeast Asia, for example among the Dayaks of eastern Malaysia, the Papuans of Irian Jaya (West Papua) and the hill peoples of Thailand.

Traditional beliefs

Many of the traditional beliefs and practices of rural people persist, reflecting their dependence upon the natural world for survival. Forests, trees and rivers contain spirits, while water is revered and honored. Festivals, magic and ritual ensure the arrival of the monsoon rains,

Lips stained red (*above*) from chewing betel – the dried nut of the areca palm – are a common sight in Southeast Asia. The nut juice is considered an aid to digestion.

The distribution of religions (*below*) on the mainland and in the islands shows very clearly how the region's position and natural resources have made it a magnet over the centuries for successive waves of traders and colonizers from both east and west.

Religions

- Animist
- Christian
- Confucian and Taoist
- Hindu
- Muslim
- Theravada Buddhism

The public face of Islam Two young Malaysian Muslim girls walk home together past a mosque in a busy street in Kuala Lumpur. The *dakwah*, or Islamic revival, has persuaded increasing numbers of women to resume wearing traditional headgear in public.

which mark the beginning of the rice-growing cycle. In rural parts of Thailand, during periods of drought, female cats, held to personify dryness, are carried in procession and drenched while villagers entreat for rain. The rice season is marked by rituals to propitiate the spirits of the soil, and of the rice itself, thus ensuring a good harvest.

Commercialization, consumerism, new technologies and Western cultural values have all impinged upon traditional life in modern Southeast Asia. Even the remote, forested areas have become accessible to the outside world. As a result the cultural diversity existing among small, widely dispersed groups is being eroded. The customs and exotic dress of the hill peoples of northern Thailand and of Borneo may serve as attractions for tourists, but their ways of life – the bases of their particular cultures – are rapidly giving way to change as they are assimilated into a wider national, and even international, culture.

It is in the cities, however, that Western culture, economic activity and political ideology have had the most dramatic impact. It is there, born in the struggle for independence from colonial rule, that nationalist revolutionary movements took root, and the postcolonial transformation of the traditional economy has wrought enormous social change. Large communities of immigrants, such as the Chinese, are concentrated in these crowded urban areas, and slum settlements contain millions of people whose way of life seems far removed from their traditional roots in the countryside – in Bangkok alone there are an estimated 1.2 million such displaced slum dwellers.

Yet, despite the harsh physical alteration of their living conditions, the cultural outlook and values of these people may be substantially unchanged, continuing to influence their lives as they did in the past. Young Buddhist men still strive to enter the monkhood and, in contrast to the urbanized societies of South America, ties between city and countryside remain strong. Rural migrants send their earnings home to their families, and most intend to return to the village, buy some land, and settle down as farmers.

THE WAYANG PUPPET THEATER OF INDONESIA

Wayang is a Javanese word meaning shadows. The earliest record of *Wayang* theater is found in a poem of the 11th century, by which time it was already well established in Java. Since then it has spread to all the other islands of the Indonesian archipelago.

The performers enact dramas by using puppets of leather, cloth and wood, or painted paper, and sometimes even live actors, to cast shadows on a white screen. Performances are usually staged to mark important moments in an individual's life – for example, birthdays, circumcision, marriage – and provide far more than just entertainment: the characters stand as role models and the stories contain ethical lessons and frequently comment on current affairs. Originally the puppets represented ancestral spirits, and the puppeteer was probably a shaman, a traditional healer

and priest. Later, under Indian influence, the epic poems that tell of the Hindu gods and heroes, the *Ramayana* and *Mahabharata*, were incorporated into the repertoire.

The oldest and commonest form of *Wayang* uses two-dimensional, finely carved and painted leather puppets, jointed at the elbows and shoulders and manipulated by horn rods. To enact the entire repertoire of 177 plays, some 200 puppets are used; a single performance may need as many as 60 and last up to nine hours. The puppets are highly stylized and immediately recognizable to the audience – key characters in the drama may be represented by a number of puppets to depict different moods. A coconut oil lamp was used to cast the shadows, but today electric light is employed, which diminishes some of the mystery of the occasion.

THE OLD AND THE NEW IN CONFLICT

Rapid economic and social change of the kind that the countries of Southeast Asia have experienced since 1945 inevitably leads to friction as the lifestyles, cultural values, religious ideals and economic aspirations of different groups of the population come into conflict with one another. The need to build stable nation states in the years after decolonization led many governments to attempt to integrate, by persuasion and sometimes by force, those groups living on the periphery, both in a geographical and in a cultural sense.

Consequently, in Indonesia the forest peoples of Kalimantan (Borneo) and Irian Jaya (West Papua) have been encouraged to abandon their traditional systems of shifting agriculture and to settle, grow rice, learn the national language, and convert to the national religion of Islam: in short, to become wholly "Indonesian". In Kalimantan, for example, traditional practices such as marriage ceremonies are reported to have been banned by the authorities. In resisting cultural imperialism of this kind, groups in Irian Jaya (West Papua) have taken up arms to protect their cultural as well as their political independence. The hill peoples of Myanmar have also resisted the attempts of the lowland-dominated government to assimilate them culturally.

The attraction of the West

There is a wider, but corresponding, conflict between traditional and Western ways of life. Many Southeast Asians feel that in the rush to modernize their economic and social structures they have jeopardized their cultural identity. In material terms, young people in particular are ignoring their own traditions in favor of Western-style houses, food, clothes and art. Throughout the region pizza and burger restaurants are becoming increasingly popular; jeans, T-shirts and suits are replacing the *sarong*, the loose skirt worn by both men and women; and Western fashions are becoming the hallmark of wealth and success.

Many people, especially the older generation, are fearful that a similar but more sinister change is overtaking non-material cultural values. Respect for elders is declining, crime and violence are on the increase, and traditional religious practices are ignored – all changes that are, rightly or wrongly, seen to be characteristic of Western culture. So far had this process gone that the Singapore government, which had done more than any other to promote a Western world view, saw the need, some 25 years after independence, to cultivate a distinctive Singaporean identity among its predominantly Chinese citizens. Accordingly, Confucianist ethics and virtues were stressed, Western individualism frowned upon, and the greater use of Mandarin Chinese encouraged.

Modernization has led many people throughout the region to become more secular in their outlook, provoking a resurgence of various forms of religious fundamentalism in reaction. In Malaysia, the *dakwah*, or Islamic revival, has promoted Islam as a way of life, leading to demands for an Islamic state and Islamic law (*syariah*). In schools and universities girls are encouraged to wear Islamic headgear and are dissuaded from mixing with male classmates.

Winners and losers

In rural areas, the favoring of commercialized farming methods over traditional subsistence systems has had widespread impact on people's lives. Some farmers have had their land repossessed by moneylenders as market forces turned against them, compelling them to become landless wage laborers. Responding to this threat of dispossession, there has been a demand for a return to the traditional village ideals of self-help and self-reliance. The *Wattanatham Chumchon* ideology ("community culture") in Thailand is one such movement that builds on folk culture and local concepts.

The old and the new (*above*) mix in this Penan settlement in Mulu National Park, Sarawak, Borneo. The government has forcibly relocated this community to one small area, and the abandonment of their traditional culture is proving a difficult adjustment.

A PEOPLE DIVIDED BY WAR

Since World War II, ideological division, rooted in the nationalist struggle for independence, has brought terrible conflict, physical devastation and cultural turmoil to the countries of Indochina. On the people of Vietnam, divided by war from 1947 to 1979, the effects have been enormous. The presence of large numbers of United States' forces had great impact on the south: Saigon, the capital, had 56,000 registered prostitutes and countless drug addicts. Since "reunification" in 1975 the government of the Socialist Republic of Vietnam has tried to reform and rehabilitate these people using innovative methods such as acupuncture, self-criticism and re-education: success rates are reported to be high.

In former North Vietnam the effects of the war were equally dramatic. To protect industries and people from the American bombing campaign, perhaps as much as three-quarters of the population of the capital, Hanoi, were evacuated to the countryside: some 750,000 people. The process of socialist development replaced traditional patterns of land ownership and labor, and the war caused major disruption to village life throughout Vietnam.

Years after reunification, the differences between the northern and southern halves of the country are marked. In the south Ho Chi Minh City (formerly Saigon) bustles with life. Young people are relatively Westernized and consumer goods are widely available. In the north, entrepreneurs are few, the bureaucracy more stifling and life is harder. Vietnam still consists of two very different halves – almost two countries.

Two-wheeled traffic (*below*) dominates the streets of Ho Chi Minh City. The bicycle is the favored form of transportation in many Asian countries: the cost of motorized vehicles is prohibitive for most people, though motorbikes are increasing in popularity.

In the cities, competition for economic resources is at the root of conflict between different ethnic groups. Large numbers of Chinese, and to a lesser degree Indian, immigrants not only introduced new cultural traditions but also became prosperous as traders and manufacturers. In Malaysia, resentment by Malays of the economic success of the Chinese community led to antagonism between the two groups, which in 1969 resulted in sectarian riots. The Malay-dominated government introduced positive discrimination to redress the economic balance in favor of the Malays, but in spite of some narrowing of inequalities, considerable enmity remains.

Theravada Buddhism

Although the practice of Buddhism, the religion and philosophy founded by Siddhartha Gautama – the Buddha, or Enlightened One (c. 563–483 BC) – in India in the 5th century BC, had spread to Southeast Asia as early as the 3rd century AD, the school of Buddhism embraced by most Southeast Asians today, Theravada Buddhism, was not introduced until the 12th century by monks from Sri Lanka. It is both a universal and, importantly, a popular religion: it emphasizes the composite nature of all things.

The performance of meditative techniques and rituals as the path to *nirvana*, the state of enlightenment – becoming one with God – that Buddhists aspire to, often appears to conflict with the noisy ceremonies designed to help the dead on their way, and the copious consumption of alcohol that is part of the ordination of the Buddhist monk. However, *nirvana* is a remote goal for Theravada Buddhists. Instead, they mainly concentrate their efforts on living within the law of *Karma*, the reduction of suffering.

An individual's position in society and the path his or her life takes is explained in terms of this law and of the accumulation of merit acquired in the course of innumerable deaths and rebirths. Theravada Buddhists try to perform good deeds and avoid being wicked in this lifetime, not only to live a holy life now, but also to avoid providing a cause for unhappiness in a future life or lives. *Karma* is not fate, as so commonly thought in the West. It is a direct result of, and may be changed by, an individual's actions throughout his life – it involves free will.

A religion for everyday

Theravada Buddhism in Southeast Asia blends quite comfortably a number of elements taken from different Indian religions – Brahmanism and Hinduism – and from animism and ancestor worship. Amulets are worn for protection from harm; spirits and ghosts are appeased; various shrines and natural objects are believed to have supernatural powers, and astrologers are avidly consulted and their instructions followed. These aspects of the religion provide worldly assurance for its adherents and are perceived to be complementary to Karmic law.

In Myanmar, Thailand, Cambodia and

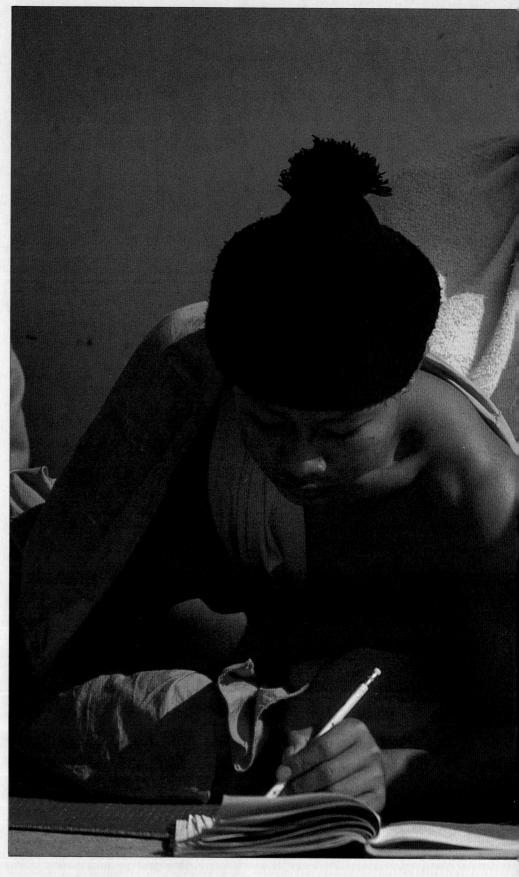

Laos, the countries of Southeast Asia where Buddhism is the dominant faith, almost every village contains a monastery and most young men are expected to become monks at least once in their lives, usually during the three-month Buddhist Rains Retreat, from July to October, but sometimes for considerably longer. This

period of monkhood is invaluable in a number of respects. It enables a man to study Buddhist teachings, to further his general education, to gain merit for his family, particularly his mother, and to prepare for a responsible moral life – in short to become complete and mature. Theravada Buddhist monks live solely on

what is given to them, and they begin each day by walking through the village or town to accept offerings of food – usually from women.

Theravada Buddhism has had to struggle to come to terms with a rapidly changing secular world. Monks have become used to dealing with money and

Novice Theravada Buddhist monks attend class in a monastery school in Tha Ton in northern Thailand. Nearly every Buddhist male spends time as a monk in his early life – considered part of the necessary training for manhood.

many are interested in politics. Some have embraced Marxist ideas, others have become anticommunist. In 1976, the Thai

monk Kittivuddho announced that it was not a wicked act to kill communists – indeed, he stated that it would gain an individual some merit. More commonly, however, monks have become concerned with questions of how to help the poor and disadvantaged, both in a spiritual and in an economic sense.

Peoples of the highlands

When the first Europeans, as late as the 1930s, penetrated the exceptionally mountainous and remote interior of Irian Jaya (West Papua), the western end of the island of New Guinea, now belonging to Indonesia, they found hundreds of small Neolithic ethnic groups, speaking over 1,000 separate languages. Often isolated in small mountain valleys, they had had little contact with anyone but their immediate neighbors, though there must have been links in the past, as pigs were introduced to the region perhaps 10,000 years ago, sweet potatoes 300 years ago, and cowrie shells, used for decoration, would have been obtained by trade with coastal peoples.

These highland peoples are shifting cultivators. Each clan or sub-clan possesses a core area of intensive cultivation, where pigs are raised on sweet potatoes for both ritual slaughter and feasting and for exchange with nearby groups. Around the core, land is cleared and cultivated for two or three years before being abandoned and a new plot started.

Settlements are generally based on patrilineal groups, and men take wives from other clans in exchange for pigs, shells or plumes from birds of paradise. At the center of each settlement stands the men's house, larger than the other dwellings, which is lived in by the married men and initiated youths. It is here that the men's sacred objects are kept and major decisions taken. Men decide when to cultivate new areas, start wars with neighboring groups or conclude them by peace treaty. Women and uninitiated youths live in smaller dwellings, sometimes scattered so as to be close to the garden plots that the women tend. If a settlement's population should become too large for the available land, then a quarrel is taken as a pretext for one or more families to move off and start their own garden.

From the dawn of time Mist rolls gently back from the valley as day breaks over a village in the mountains of Irian Jaya (West Papua).

CITIES

TEMPLE CITIES AND PORTS · CITIES AS MAGNETS · GROWING OUT OF CONTROL

The cities of Southeast Asia are among the most cosmopolitan in the world, containing a rich and complex mix of peoples, cultures, languages and economies that are a consequence both of Southeast Asia's pivotal position between the Pacific and Indian oceans and of the region's long history of international trade and urban culture. The major port cities dominate the settlement pattern. In comparison with other parts of the world, Southeast Asia has a relatively low level of urbanization, but present growth rates are among the highest in the world. Rapid and largely uncontrolled increases in the size of urban centers and their populations are creating problems of congestion, pollution and service provision, all of which are stretching the financial and political capabilities of the countries concerned.

COUNTRIES IN THE REGION

Brunei, Cambodia, Indonesia, Laos, Malaysia, Myanmar, Philippines, Singapore, Thailand, Vietnam

POPULATION

Total population of region (millions)			531.67
	Singapore	Thailand	Indonesia
Population density (persons per sq km)	5,768	116	102
Population change (average annual percent 1960–1990)			
Urban	+1.43%	+2.50%	+4.22%
Rural	0.00%	+0.52%	−0.30%

URBAN POPULATION

As percentage of total population (2000)	100%	22%	41%

TEN LARGEST CITIES

	Country	Population
Jakarta †	Indonesia	10,226,200
Manila †	Philippines	10,032,900
Bangkok †	Thailand	6,416,300
Rangoon †	Myanmar	3,938,900
Singapore †	Singapore	3,637,700
Ho Chi Minh City	Vietnam	3,380,100
Surabaya	Indonesia	2,954,400
Bandung	Indonesia	2,657,600
Medan	Indonesia	2,143,100
Palembang	Indonesia	1,439,900

† denotes capital city

City population figures are for the city proper

TEMPLE CITIES AND PORTS

The environmental and cultural contrasts between the two halves of Southeast Asia – the mainland (Laos, Vietnam, Cambodia, Myanmar, Thailand and the Malay Peninsula) and the islands – help to explain why human settlement developed differently in each. In the mainland, wet rice cultivation in the major lowland areas between mountain chains (the Mekong valley, the central plain of Thailand and the Irrawaddy basin) provided the basis for early settlement. With the development of irrigation techniques came the ability to grow and store enough surplus rice to support substantial nonagricultural populations, giving rise to the first towns. Urban elites gained power over large peasant populations, and so empires developed.

The earliest of these empires was Funan, based in present-day Cambodia. At its height in the 5th century AD its control extended into southern and central Vietnam, central and southern Thailand and over much of the Malay peninsula. The core of this state lay in the area around lake Tonle Sap, and became the focus of the Khmer empire (9th–15th century). Its capital at Angkor is perhaps the most famous of the region's "temple cities", a name reflecting the dominance of religious buildings and palaces in their urban structures. However, these cities were also important administrative and international trading centers, and in many areas of the mainland population densities were once much higher than they are in the present day.

In the islands, agricultural land was much more limited except in the fertile river valleys of Java, and only here did urban centers based on rice surpluses develop. Elsewhere, towns grew up at strategic points on the coast where they could control the seaways between the islands and dominate trade. For example, Srivijaya, with its river port of Palembang, in southern Sumatra rose to spectacular power between the 7th and 13th centuries, based on its command of the searoute between China and India. Palembang was one of the first in a succession of port cities, the most notable of which were Malacca (on the southwest Malay peninsula), Aceh (Sumatra), and the islands of Pinang and Singapore.

These cities were major players in the

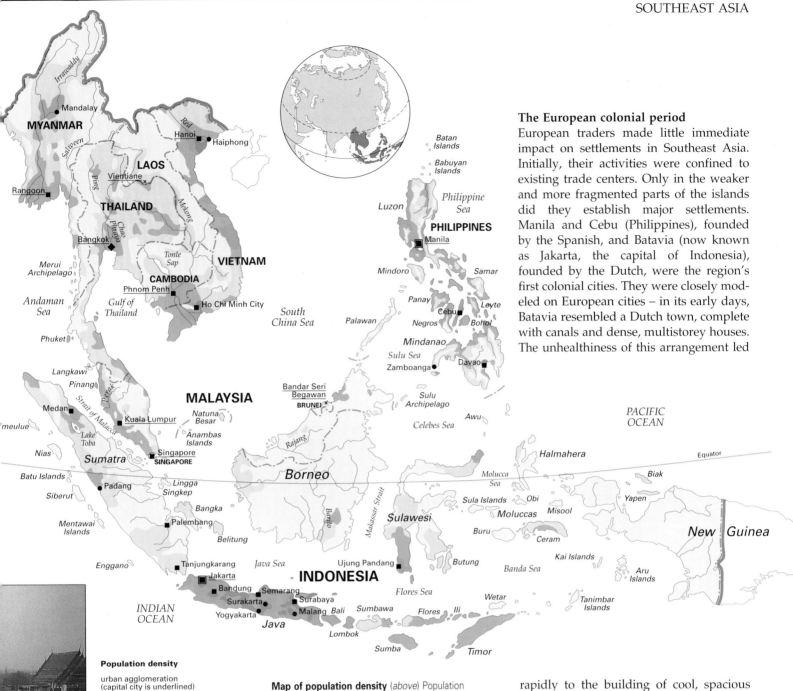

The European colonial period

European traders made little immediate impact on settlements in Southeast Asia. Initially, their activities were confined to existing trade centers. Only in the weaker and more fragmented parts of the islands did they establish major settlements. Manila and Cebu (Philippines), founded by the Spanish, and Batavia (now known as Jakarta, the capital of Indonesia), founded by the Dutch, were the region's first colonial cities. They were closely modeled on European cities – in its early days, Batavia resembled a Dutch town, complete with canals and dense, multistorey houses. The unhealthiness of this arrangement led

Population density

urban agglomeration
(capital city is underlined)
- ■ over 10 000 000
- ◆ 5 000 000–10 000 000
- ■ 1 000 000–4 999 999
- ● 500 000–999 999
- × capital city less than 500 000

persons per square km
- 500
- 200
- 50
- 10

City of temples and trade (left)
Bangkok – Thailand's capital and principal port – owes its origins to a strategic position on the banks of the river Chao Phraya a little distance inland from the Gulf of Thailand. The city was founded in 1782 as the new capital of the kingdom of Siam (renamed Thailand after the peaceful coup of 1939). The temples and royal buildings of the Grand Palace – the original 18th-century walled town – contrast with the bustling port and cosmopolitan commercial districts, and with the areas of overcrowded housing, in today's modern city.

Map of population density (above) Population distribution is extremely uneven. The Indonesian island of Java accounts for over a third of the Southeast Asian population in an area that is just one-thirtieth of the region's total landmass.

increasingly important trade network that connected East Africa with China and supplied the Middle East, the Mediterranean region and Europe with a variety of high-value goods such as silk, spices, drugs and porcelain. By the end of the 15th century perhaps 20 percent of the spice production of Southeast Asia was finding a destination in Europe. On the eve of European contact, the urban centers of Southeast Asia were thriving, cosmopolitan places. At the beginning of the 16th century, Malacca, founded only in 1409, may well have had a population of more than 100,000, and a handful of others probably had between 50,000 to 100,000 inhabitants – this in a period when few European cities had populations of more than 40,000.

rapidly to the building of cool, spacious suburbs that incorporated many features of Javanese layout and house design.

In time, an extensive chain of European-dominated port cities was established, of which Batavia, Bangkok (Thailand), Manila, Rangoon (Myanmar) and Saigon-Cholon (Vietnam; now Ho Chi Minh City) were the most important. All except Bangkok were on existing sites, but extensively remodeled. In Rangoon, the British laid out what was in effect a new city, but planned it round elements of the old settlement.

These cities fulfilled many functions, but their key role was trade. The central areas were therefore dominated by docks, "godowns" (warehouses) and rice and timber processing plants. Large numbers of immigrant laborers, especially from China and India, were attracted to the cities, and particular residential areas and occupations within them became reserved for particular ethnic groups.

CITIES AS MAGNETS

Most people in Southeast Asia are still farmers. Although urban populations are growing extremely rapidly, they are concentrated in a relatively small number of major centers. Rural links are made directly with the major urban centers rather than through a hierarchy of smaller cities and towns – a pattern that is much more typical of the developed world. Agricultural produce is collected and delivered directly to the major markets; goods and services are sent out from the cities to the rural areas without a network of distribution centers in between. This marked "urban primacy" is at its most extreme in Thailand: the capital, Bangkok, is some 25 times the size of the next largest settlement and contains 60 percent of the urban population.

There are many reasons why migration from the rural areas gravitates toward the large cities. Services are generally much more widely available – even squatter settlements on the edge of major centers may be better provided for than small towns. In Bangkok, for example, electricity is available in most of the recognized squatter settlements, and piped water in all. Road and rail links between smaller centers are frequently poor. In many parts of northeast Thailand – which is the source of large numbers of migrants to Bangkok – there are often better bus services and links to the capital than there are to the local provincial center.

Much migration is temporary, often seasonal, and provides much needed additional income for impoverished rural communities. For example, remittances sent back from those working in Bangkok amount to very nearly half of average household incomes in Thailand's rural northeast. Despite the appalling living conditions that are the lot of newly-arrived migrants to the city, even the lowest levels of urban employment are likely to produce a higher income than could be earned in rural areas.

The presence of a group of friends, relatives or fellow villagers in the city acts as a magnet, persuading others from the same family or community to try their luck in the urban environment. Once established, they in their turn attract yet another group of migrants. In this way, "migration chains" are set up, which result in migrants from one particular area

The rural scene The graceful lines of communal longhouses in the village of Toraja in Indonesia are typical of the region's traditional architecture. Villages are becoming increasingly exposed to urban influences through migrants returning from the cities.

becoming settled in a certain part of the city and following similar occupations. As migrants are drawn increasingly from remote areas farther away from the cities, they need the emotional support of people who share the same roots to survive in their new environment, and in this way distinctive cultural and linguistic enclaves are created.

Urban opportunities

Urban growth in Southeast Asia does not appear to be as closely related to industrial development as it was in western countries when they changed from being predominantly agricultural to predominantly urban societies. "Formal" employment opportunities – whether in the manufacturing or service sectors (both of which are expanding rapidly) – are only capable of absorbing a small proportion of the available labor force of migrants to the cities. An increasingly large part of the urban

DE-URBANIZATION IN VIETNAM

Following the end of the Vietnam war in 1975 and the reunification of North and South Vietnam an ambitious program of de-urbanization and rural settlement was announced. In part, this occurred as a response to the over-urbanization of the South – the result of forced and spontaneous migration from the rural areas during the war. Additionally there were ideological, strategic and economic reasons for reducing a largely non-productive urban population, promoting rural settlement and expanding agricultural production. Large areas of land had passed out of cultivation, particularly in the former "rice bowl" districts of the Mekong delta, and the country faced a chronic food shortage.

Between 1976 and 1980 over 1 million people were moved from the urban areas. Many of those that fled the country as refugees during this period did so to avoid forceable resettlement. However, whatever the human cost of these settlement programs, they played a significant part in expanding agricultural production.

The stated aim of the Vietnam government is to keep the size of the southern cities constant by planned resettlement and by restricting urban-rural migration. While these programs have faltered since the early 1980s, a combination of resettlement, limited opportunities in urban areas and severe restrictions on movement to the cities has limited urban growth. Indeed, the population of Ho Chi Minh City fell from 3.4 million in 1979 to 3.1 in 1989.

High contrasts (*above*) Modern skyscrapers – one showing strong Islamic influences – frame the lavish colonial State Secretariat building in central Kuala Lumpur, the capital of Malaysia. Originally a tin-mining camp, it has grown rapidly since independence to become a major commercial and industrial center, though with its share of squatter colonies.

Shacks on the sidewalk (*left*) Recent migrants to Manila erect makeshift shelters wherever they can find space on the city streets. Homelessness is a serious problem in Manila, as it is in most Southeast Asian cities; housebuilding programs are unable to keep pace with explosive population growth caused by migration from rural areas.

population consequently obtains its income and necessities for hiring from the so-called "informal" sector, and is supported by systems of "shared poverty".

This situation explains the proliferation of street vendors, automobile window cleaners, collectors of waste materials, producers of goods on an often tiny scale, and the large number of middlemen handling minute quantities of goods and taking minuscule "cuts" on each transaction. In the past these activities were officially frowned on, and sometimes were even declared illegal. However, colorful street vendors have been found to be a major tourist attraction, and are now mostly tolerated – some authorities have even introduced registration or licensing schemes. Furthermore, by supplying the basic needs of much of the urban population, the informal sector helps to hold wage levels down across the whole workforce, and this is a magnet for foreign investment to the large cities.

Resisting change

All these factors help to reinforce the growth of the major urban centers at the expense of smaller ones. Nearly all the governments of the region have attempted to reverse the trend by implementing policies that will divert migration and encourage a more even distribution of people, development and resources.

Population inbalance is particularly extreme in Indonesia – 60 percent of the people live in Java, which represents only 7 percent of the land area. Attempts to resettle millions of Javanese through land colonization schemes in the outer islands have not met with longterm success and have attracted widespread criticism, since they have displaced indigenous communities and destroyed large areas of forest. Generally, efforts to influence or control urbanizing forces throughout the region are often contradicted by other government policies, and are proving less than effective against the powerful draw of the regional cities.

GROWING OUT OF CONTROL?

The layout of most major towns and cities in Southeast Asia reflects their evolution as trading centers during the colonial period. At this time western administrative and commercial districts, with wide boulevards and grandiose European-style buildings, developed around the central port zone. Beyond were the bungalows and villas of the European residents, each in its own leafy, well-watered garden. The large immigrant populations (predominantly Chinese, and to a lesser extent Indian) lived in separate areas of the city, and these in turn were sharply demarcated from the areas occupied by the indigenous population.

City contrasts

These basic divisions still exist today. The westernized central business district, the ports and industrial areas, the spacious residential suburbs and high-rise luxury apartments contrast sharply with the narrow streets of tenements in the "Chinatowns", where families live above their shops, and with the overcrowded districts of poor housing – lacking drainage or water – where most of the urban population lives.

The city landscape is always varied, juxtapositions often surprising. In many cities, the needs of a growing, comparatively wealthy urban middle class are being met by the development of major shopping and leisure complexes outside the centers. Very often these have been

built in close proximity to, and in sharp contrast with, a traditional street market.

Squatter settlements have sprung up on the edges of all the cities, and uncontrolled urban growth has engulfed villages that have barely been integrated into the urban fabric. It can be difficult to gauge the full extent of squatter settlements. In Bangkok, for example, according to official statistics only 13 percent of the urban population lives in them, but the real figure is much nearer 23 percent.

Life in these settlements is very hard. There is appalling overcrowding and conditions are insanitary. Many houses are little more than makeshift shelters. However, the extent of poverty is far from uniform, and a few households may be comparatively wealthy.

The bustling streets of Hanoi (*left*) attest to the resilience of the Vietnamese people. The centuries-old capital was transformed into a French-inspired city in the colonial period. Heavily bombed in the Vietnam war (1965–75), most of its population was moved to the countryside, and life in the city still remains harsh today.

Central Jakarta (*below*) Western architectural styles are very much in evidence in the modern commercial and business center of Jakarta, Indonesia's capital and largest city. In the surrounding residential areas houses are still commonly constructed of traditional bamboo or wood.

Future prospects

Rapid urban growth, combined with lack of regulations and insufficient funding for urban programs, is already resulting in major problems of congestion and pollution throughout the region. Provision of freshwater supplies, sewerage and drainage, electricity, surfaced roads and transportation are all inadequate to meet present needs, let alone cope with future expansion. But government attempts to limit migration and develop secondary centers and outlying rural areas have so far proved ineffective.

By the year 2000 the populations of Bangkok, Jakarta and Manila had reached 6.4 million, 10.2 million and 10 million respectively. Given the current level of pollution, congestion and deprivation in these centers, and the lack of adequate housing, employment and services, the prospect of a further population explosion is frightening to say the least. Most urban growth in the region appears to be not merely uncontrolled, but considerably out of control.

Following the example of Singapore, which is the most modern and highly managed city in Southeast Asia, national governments in the region have assumed direct control over planning and administration in their capital cities. This has had the effect of turning each capital into a ministate. However, investment for redevelopment has been concentrated in the modern corporate sectors of

the cities. The building of luxury hotels, apartments, office blocks and conference centers can be very successful in attracting further investment from foreign business sources, but it does little to raise the standard of living of the majority of the population.

Investment in low-cost housing, transportation and other urban facilities for the poor has been very much a secondary consideration. In any case, given present rates of growth, most housing programs and schemes to upgrade slums and squatter settlements (which have been launched in all major cities) are only touching the fringes of the problem. In Indonesia the National Urban Development Corporation, for example, constructs between 25,000 and 30,000 low-cost housing units a year, but housing need continues to grow at an estimated 300,000 a year.

THAT SINKING FEELING

Bangkok is situated on the delta of the Chao Phraya river about 40 km (25 mi) from the Gulf of Thailand. It receives about 1,520 mm (60 in) of rain a year, and relies on a system of canals to provide drainage. However, today the city is sinking. A major cause is the excessive pumping out of ground water. The problem has been exacerbated by the filling in of many canals for development and the weight of modern buildings. In the east of the city, the annual rate of subsidence exceeds 10 cm (4 in) and in central areas it varies from 5 cm (2 in) to 10 cm (4 in). In a number of places the city is already below sea level.

Floods are an ever-present risk, and are increasing both in frequency and in severity. Signs of subsidence are widespread: cracks in buildings, holes in roads, fractured pipes and elevated canal bridges. In addition, the depletion of aquifers by overpumping has enabled seawater to penetrate them, allowing the remaining reserves to become contaminated.

Bangkok also suffers some of the worst urban pollution and traffic congestion in the region. These, and the pressing problem of subsidence, can only be dealt with through investment in infrastructure and the imposition of stringent planning controls. However, neither the finance nor the political will necessary for the implementation of such policies are as yet present.

Singapore – a modern city-state

Keeping up appearances An elderly street-cleaner ensures that the sidewalk in Singapore's central business district is cleaned of debris. Government policies have created an urban environment that is attractive to foreign business investors.

Consisting of an island and a number of smaller islets at the southern tip of the Malay Peninsula, Singapore covers an area of 58,000 ha (143,324 acres) and has a population of over 4 million. Yet, since establishing itself as an independent republic in 1965, this tiny city-state has achieved a regional and global significance out of all proportion to its size.

A trading city on Singapore Island flourished in the 13th century but was destroyed by the Javanese in 1356. The island remained uninhabited until the 19th century. Developed as a port within Britain's colonial empire, Singapore acted as an intermediary in the flow of raw materials from the resource-rich countries of Southeast Asia to the industrialized world. Since the mid 1960s, it has successfully expanded its economy from this base into finance and manufacturing, and has transformed its urban fabric.

Today the city-state's economic base is multifaceted. The port, the largest in Southeast Asia, still lies at its heart and it remains a regional and global distribution center for commodities and manufactured goods. The city is also a key player in the financial system of Asia, an oil-refining center and a leading producer of services and manufactured goods. Multinational companies wishing to expand into Southeast Asia have established their regional headquarters in Singapore, and the government – which wants to see the city-state become the economic hub of

Southeast Asia – has used every method in its power to keep and attract further foreign investment.

A miracle by design

The transformation of Singapore has been termed a "miracle by design". There are few aspects of Singaporean life in which the state has not intervened in an effort to create an attractive environment for foreign capital. Since the mid 1960s, there has been a major urban renewal program with heavy investment in power, sewerage, water supply, transport, industrial estates and housing. Slums and squatter settlements have virtually disappeared, and all that remains of the old colorful, if seedy, Chinatown are a few shop-houses and night markets that provide harmless tourist attractions.

These clearances had the double purpose of dispersing concentrated areas of opposition to the ruling government party and providing space for an expanded central business district. The densely packed tenements and shop-houses that characterized central Singapore were replaced with modern shopping, leisure and commercial complexes under the auspices of the Urban Redevelopment Authority. New townships and estates were built on the

peripheries to rehouse the inner-city population. Between 1970 and 1990, the population of the inner city fell by 40 percent while that of the outer areas rose by approximately 60 percent.

The state's major housing and welfare programs have been expensive – in the 1960s they absorbed as much as 58 percent of recurring government expenditure. Singapore's housing provision is outstanding – in 2000, 80 percent of the population lived in public housing – and its people are the best educated and healthiest in Southeast Asia. Singapore is by far the least congested and least polluted city in the region. This has proved undeniably attractive to multinational companies and international investors. It has been achieved, however, by exerting a degree of government control over political, economic and social affairs that many find unacceptably high.

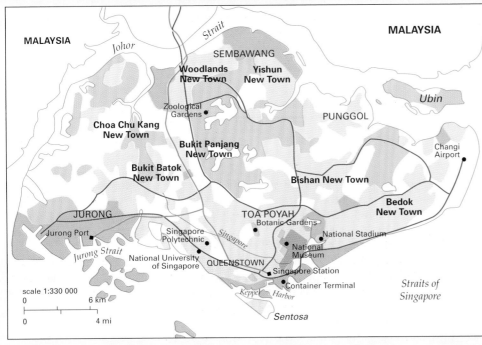

Singapore skyline (*above*) The impressive view of highrise headquarters of multinational corporations bears witness to Singapore's phenomenal economic development since independence in 1965. Singapore commands a prime position on the region's oceanic trading routes; its port is one of the largest in the world. Rapid economic growth has been accompanied by a major program of urban clearance and redevelopment.

Island site (*left*) The island of Singapore is at the southern extremity of the Malay Peninsula. The business and financial districts are close to the ports and industrial areas; the new towns house people whose homes were cleared during the redevelopment of the city center.

Land use

- important site
- — major road
- ◆— major railroad (with terminus)
- central business district
- industrial
- residential
- parks and forest
- other

GOVERNMENT

NEW STATES IN TURMOIL · MANY PEOPLES, MANY REGIMES·
CONFRONTATION IN SOUTHEAST ASIA

Three major civilizations – Buddhist, Confucian and Islamic – had shaped the cultural and political development of Southeast Asia long before the arrival of colonizers from Europe from the 16th century onward. Of the present-day states of the region, only Thailand remained free of European control. A Dutch commercial empire was based on the East Indies (Indonesia); British rule extended over Burma (Myanmar), the Malay peninsula and northern Borneo; the French established a colonial empire in Indochina (Cambodia, Laos and Vietnam); and in 1898 the United States acquired the Philippines from Spain. During World War II the entire region came under Japanese rule. It was after 1945 that its present political structure began to take shape – giving rise to civil war and extreme political instability.

COUNTRIES IN THE REGION

Brunei, Cambodia, Indonesia, Laos, Malaysia, Myanmar Philippines, Singapore, Thailand, Vietnam

Disputed borders Cambodia/Thailand, Cambodia/Vietnam, Indonesia/Malaysia, Vietnam/China

STYLES OF GOVERNMENT

Republics Cambodia, Indonesia, Laos, Myanmar, Philippines, Singapore, Vietnam

Monarchies Brunei, Cambodia, Malaysia, Thailand

Federal state Malaysia

Multi-party states Cambodia, Indonesia, Malaysia, Philippines, Singapore, Thailand

One-party states Brunei, Myanmar, Laos, Vietnam

Military influence Indonesia, Myanmar, Thailand

CONFLICTS (since 1945)

Coups Burma 1962, 1992; Cambodia 1970, 1975; Indonesia 1965; Laos 1975; Thailand 1947, 1973, 1991

Revolution Philippines 1986, 2001

Civil wars Burma 1948–51; Cambodia 1970–75, 1978–91; Indonesia (East Timor) 1976–; Laos 1953–73

Independence wars Indonesia/Netherlands 1945–49; Malaysia/UK 1948–60; North Vietnam/France 1946–54

Interstate conflicts North Vietnam/South Vietnam/USA 1957–75; Cambodia/Vietnam 1978–79; Vietnam/China 1979

MEMBERSHIP OF INTERNATIONAL ORGANIZATIONS

Association of Southeast Asian Nations (ASEAN) Brunei, Indonesia, Laos, Malaysia, Myanmar, Philippines, Singapore, Thailand, Vietnam

Colombo Plan members Cambodia, Indonesia, Laos, Malaysia, Myanmar, Philippines, Singapore, Thailand

Organization of Petroleum Exporting Countries (OPEC) Indonesia

---

NEW STATES IN TURMOIL

In the postwar period Southeast Asia was the setting for a series of violent struggles instigated by communist-aligned guerrilla movements. These groups, whose origins lay in their common resistance to the Japanese, directed their activities after 1945 toward preventing a resumption of colonial rule. The first state to declare its independence was Indonesia, in 1945, though it took another four years for the Dutch to agree to a negotiated withdrawal. The Philippines became fully self-governing in 1946, and Burma gained its independence in the aftermath of the British withdrawal from India (1948). By the end of the next decade, troubled and violent years, colonial power had ceased everywhere in the region. The nationalist struggle, especially in Indochina, had far-reaching consequences.

The "domino theory"

Western observers, especially in the United States, persisted in regarding nationalist guerrilla movements as part of a concerted Soviet- and Chinese-led effort to subvert and control the region – a belief that gave rise to the "domino theory". This held that once one country fell to communist insurgency, its neighbors would also succumb, like a collapsing line of dominoes. The theory was fatally flawed, however, because it overlooked sharply defined ethnic and linguistic divisions between the different groups of insurgents, which frequently gave rise to conflict between them. It also failed to take note of the varied nature of the societies they were operating in.

In Malaya, for example, the "emergency" that began in 1948 was essentially the result of activity by communist groups that sprang from the minority Chinese community. The British strove to control them by a combination of military force with large-scale population resettlement that cut off the guerrillas from their support villages.

In Indochina, on the other hand, the communist Vietminh movement led by Ho Chi Minh (1890–1969) was deeply rooted in the nationalist resistance to the colonial order. By 1954 sustained guerrilla warfare brought about the withdrawal of the French, following their defeat at Dien Bien Phu. This left Vietnam divided at the 17th parallel of latitude, with a com-munist government in the north, centered on Hanoi, and a weak government in the south, supported by the United States.

Communist guerrilla activity in the south, led by the National Liberation Front, or Viet Cong, was supported by North Vietnam and China. It was seen by the United States as part of a much bigger plan for the advance of communism. Military involvement by the United States escalated throughout the 1960s: at its height 1.25 million American and South Vietnamese troops were being deployed in the war.

This ferocious application of military might failed to eradicate the guerrillas. Politicians in the United States lost the will to sustain the struggle, but a ceasefire agreement, negotiated in 1973, was breached by the North Vietnamese.

With the final withdrawal of United States troops in 1975, North Vietnam invaded and overran the south. Its capital, Saigon, was renamed Ho Chi Minh City, and in July 1976 the Socialist Republic of Vietnam was proclaimed.

In the same year the Vietnamese-backed Pathet Lao seized power in Laos, and the communist Khmer Rouge took control of Cambodia. In 1978 Vietnam invaded Cambodia, which had become increasingly hostile to it, and toppled the genocidal Khmer Rouge regime. The years of turmoil in Indochina led to the flight of over a million

A city destroyed Saigon, the South Vietnamese capital, in ruins after the final bombing offensive before it was taken by North Vietnam's armies on 30 April 1975. The former colonial capital had been laid out like a French town, with broad tree-lined boulevards and pavement cafés. Before the outbreak of war it had been a thriving center of trade. It had been the scene of a four-week battle in 1968.

Colonialism in retreat French wounded are evacuated by helicopter from the battlefield of Dien Bien Phu. Defeat at the hands of the Vietminh communist rebels dealt a devastating blow to French national pride, precipitating their withdrawal from their colonies in Indochina.

A diverse region Conflict has centered most tragically on Indochina, where the post-colonial communist nationalist movements were met by Western intervention, culminating in the Vietnam war. Elsewhere ethnic and religious diversity has proved an obstacle to national unity, and border disputes are frequent.

refugees from Cambodia, Laos and Vietnam and, in Cambodia alone, to more than a million deaths between 1975 and 1978.

Other causes of unrest

Outstanding territorial claims in the region gave rise to frequent clashes between states in the post-colonial period. Indonesia successfully annexed West Irian (formerly Dutch New Guinea) and Portuguese Timor, although unrest continued in both; however, it failed to make good its claim to Sarawak and Sabah from Malaysia. There were border disputes between Thailand and Cambodia. Cambodia has a longstanding claim to Cochin China in the southern tip of the Indochina peninsula, now part of Vietnam. The Spratly and Paracel islands in the South China Sea are also the subject of contested claims.

The government of Myanmar is controlled by ethnic Burmese from the lowland river valleys. It has never successfully incorporated the Kachin, Shan and Karen minorities of the border areas.

Likewise, the stability of the region's island states has been threatened by ethnic, linguistic and religious tensions. In Indonesia there were several rebellions in the outer islands against the largely Javanese-dominated central government. There is a strong independence movement among Muslims on Mindanao, in the south of the Philippines. The demographic profile of Malaysia's population continues to present a challenge to national integrity – 55 percent of Malaysians are Muslim Malays; the rest are ethnic Chinese and Indians. Malays still dominate the government, while the Chinese are the driving force behind the economy.

Southeast Asia since 1945

→ state boundary
✳ conflict
● civil unrest
— Vietnam boundary 1954
1958 date of independence

former colonial power
☐ France
☐ Netherlands
☐ Portugal
☐ United Kingdom
☐ United States

INDIA
since 1948
CHINA
1979
MYANMAR **1948**
1948
1975
TAIWAN
Irrawaddy
LAOS **1953**
● Hanoi
1948
Vientiane ●
Hainan
Rangoon ■
THAILAND
1975
Paracel Islands
Luzon
since 1946
Bangkok ■ 1976
1976
VIETNAM **1954**
Manila ■
PHILIPPINES **1946**
1970–75, 1979–91
1978
South China Sea
CAMBODIA **1953**
Phnom Penh
● Ho Chi Minh City
PACIFIC OCEAN
COCHIN CHINA
Palawan
Spratly Islands
Mindanao
since 1946
Malay Peninsula
MALAYSIA **1958**
Bandar Seri Begawan
SABAH
Celebes Sea
New Guinea
Kuala Lumpur ■
BRUNEI **1984**
1977–79
Singapore ● SINGAPORE **1965**
SARAWAK
Western New Guinea annexed by Indonesia 1963
Sumatra
Borneo
Sulawesi
Java Sea
INDONESIA **1945**
INDIAN OCEAN
■ Jakarta
1998
Java
Flores Sea
Flores
1977
East Timor annexed by Indonesia 1976
Sumba
Timor

MANY PEOPLES, MANY REGIMES

Democratic institutions play an important part in some Southeast Asian states, but there are other political systems – single-party hegemony, military dictatorship, autocratic monarchy – that also figure prominently. Diversity is the rule rather than the exception, and there is a wide range of ideologies, from Marxism to absolutist Islamic monarchy.

By the early 1990s Vietnam was one of a handful of countries in the world where the Communist Party remained in firm control; the impoverished, land-locked state of Laos was still dependent on Vietnam. Cambodia became a constitutional monarchy during the 1990s holding its first free, multiparty elections in 1993.

The power of the military

The parliamentary democracy established in Burma on independence was toppled in 1962 by a military coup. It remains military in character; a civilian constitution was introduced in 1975 and legislative elections were held in 1990 but the ruling military council refused to recognize the result. Many of the elected representatives were subsequently imprisoned or forced to flee. Aung San Suu Kyi, the leading opposition figure, has remained under house arrest and the military regime has been condemned for human rights abuses.

Under General Suharto, the army in Indonesia performed a more sophisticated role within a system that incorporated political parties, periodic elections and elements of a capitalist economy.

Since 1971 elections to the Indonesian national parliament had been contested by a number of political parties, though in such a way as to ensure a majority for Golkar, the regime's former ruling party. In 1999, multiparty politics were introduced and in elections later that year an independent legislative was elected including representatives from 21 parties. With the fall of Suharto in May 1998, a drive began to reduce the power of the military through democratic elections and a ban on serving officers holding civilian positions of power.

The extent to which the power of the military could genuinely be restricted remained to be seen. Separatist violence in Aceh and Irian Jaya (West Papua) ensured that the government remained dependent on the military in the short term.

Although the Buddhist religious leaders and the hereditary monarch, who is formal head of state, have a significant political role in Thailand, the army has a long tradition of intervening in government. A period of "open politics" between 1973 and 1976 ended with a military coup. Although elections were later reinstated and a civilian government formed in 1983, martial law was maintained. Elected coalition governments have prevailed apart from during 1991 when the government was toppled in a bloodless coup. A new, reformist constitution was promulgated in 1997 and was followed by much-disputed elections in 2000.

Gloria Arroyo's first day in the Malacanang Palace Arroyo became the Philippines' 14th president in 2001, succeeding Joseph Estrada who was forced to relinquish power following a "people's revolution", protesting against his corrupt government.

An unusual federal arrangement Malaysia is a federation of 13 states, each with its own constitution, head of state and elected assembly. Nine retain their traditional rulers, the sultans. The constitution provides for these to elect one of their number to be supreme head of the federation for a term of five years, with powers similar to those of the British monarch. Effective power rests with the prime minister and cabinet drawn from the majority party or coalition in the house of representatives (Dewan Rakyar) of the two-chamber federal parliament, which is elected every five years by popular vote.

Students protesting in Jakarta, Indonesia, try to make their voices heard in a country which is barely coping with religious and separatist struggles, endemic political corruption and an economy which is at an all-time low.

ELECTORATE

elects — Cabinet — Prime minister

House of representatives

Senate

Federal level

Parliament — elects 32 members

Supreme head of the federation

Each assembly elects 2 members

13 state assemblies — appoints — Cabinet — Prime minister

elects

State level

Nine hereditary rulers of Malay states

The legacy of British rule

With the exception of Brunei, an absolutist Islamic monarchy ruled by Sultan Hassanal Bolkiah, the constitutions of the former British colonies in Southeast Asia preserved elements of the British style of parliamentary government.

The most important political party in Malaysia is the United Malays' National Organization (UMNO). It was formed in 1946 to fight against colonial rule, and came to lead the multiparty National Front coalition, which ruled all federal and most state administrations after 1974.

Singapore, an independent republic since it left the Malaysian federation in 1965, also adopted British parliamentary institutions. The dominant party since 1959 has been the People's Action Party (PAP) led by Lee Kuan Yew. Strong social and political controls asserted by the government have constrained the activities of opposition parties.

On gaining independence in 1946 the Philippines adopted the political institutions of the former ruling power, the United States. These have never worked well in a peasant society still dominated by a relatively small number of wealthy families. A period of martial law (1972–81) weakened these institutions still further.

President Corazón (Cory) Aquino replaced Ferdinand Marcos' personal dictatorship in 1986 with a more conciliatory style of government. In 1992 Mrs. Aquino endorsed her former defense minister Fidel Ramos for the presidency and he won the election to succeed her. Ramos was succeeded in 1998 by Joseph Estrada who was forced to resign by a "people's revolution" in 2001. Vice-president Gloria Arroyo was sworn in as the 14th president.

CONFRONTATION IN SOUTHEAST ASIA

With the exception of Myanmar, which maintains a policy of strict nonalignment and is closed to foreigners (though a recipient of Japanese and other international aid), the states of Southeast Asia divide into two main groups. On the one hand are the formerly Soviet-aligned states of Indochina, and on the other the island states of the Pacific. These remain to a greater or lesser degree within the United States' orbit of influence.

Following the North Vietnamese take-over of the south, Chinese and Vietnamese interests in Southeast Asia came into ever-increasing conflict. China

developed a close relationship with the Khmer Rouge regime in Cambodia; its claim to exclusive control of the Paracel and Spratly islands in the South China Sea was vigorously contested by Vietnam. A series of border clashes with the Khmer Rouge led Vietnam to seek closer ties with the Soviet Union. These were strengthened when Vietnam invaded Cambodia to expel the Khmer Rouge in 1978. The following year China led a raid into Vietnam in retaliation.

The government of Hun Sen that replaced the Khmer Rouge in Cambodia was installed and kept in place with massive Vietnamese support. After 1975, when it helped the communist Pathet Lao to seize power in Laos, Vietnam maintained a considerable influence there as

well, leading to fears of further Vietnamese expansion in the region.

By the late 1980s Soviet President Mikhail Gorbachev's reshaping of the Soviet Union's foreign policy objectives had brought a substantial reduction of military and economic aid to Vietnam. As a result, its troops were gradually withdrawn from Cambodia between 1987 and 1989. All-party peace agreements in Paris in 1991 saw the abandonment of communism in Cambodia, and later Vietnam resolved its differences with China.

Regional cooperation
Political cooperation to withstand Marxist influence in the region became an objective of the states that belonged to the Association of Southeast Asian Nations

Soviet-made tanks in Ho Chi Minh City The Soviet Union's support for Vietnam after the takeover of the south exacerbated existing bad relations with China, particularly after the Soviet Union also provided massive aid to Vietnam to maintain Hun Sen's puppet government in Cambodia.

The victims of war Refugees from the turmoil in Indochina have sometimes had to endure years of detention in conditions that can be appalling. Over 125,000 Cambodians fled from the fighting between Khmer Rouge guerrillas and the invading Vietnamese army in 1978–79 to camps like this one on the Thai border.

(ASEAN): Indonesia, Malaysia, the Philippines, Singapore and Thailand and, after 1984, Brunei. Vietnam, Laos, Myanmar and Cambodia joined in the 1990s. ASEAN, established in 1967, was originally intended to foster social, cultural and economic relations between its members. Moves toward economic integration did not develop significantly, though member states did act together in some international trade negotiations. The organization had greater success in achieving concerted political action. After Vietnam's invasion of Cambodia, ASEAN (together with China and the United States) provided political and economic aid to Khmer Rouge groups on the Thai border.

Despite these common efforts, there were clear differences in the foreign policies and the international relations separately pursued by the ASEAN states. After a brief flirtation with China in the early 1960s, Indonesia was careful to follow a course of nonalignment. Thailand and the Philippines were original signatories to the Manila Pact of 1954, which inaugurated the Southeast Asia Treaty Organization (SEATO). This was established by Western powers, including Britain, France, Pakistan and the United States, after the Korean war (1950–53) to resist possible communist aggression in the southern hemisphere. After 1971 the security of both Malaysia and Singapore was underwritten by the Five-Power Defense Arrangement with Australia, Britain and New Zealand. Brunei retained a special defensive relationship with Britain.

By the end of the century, the United States' reappraisal of its international security role seemed likely to lead to realignments within the region. In 1991 the Philippines' senate voted to urge the withdrawal of all United States' forces, and did not renew the lease of Subic Bay naval base. The ASEAN states were set to gain greater prosperity within the expanding Pacific economy.

THE FLOOD OF REFUGEES

In 1989 the number of people displaced from their country of birth by war, famine, political upheaval, repression and persecution reached more than 14 million worldwide. While greater movements of people have taken place elsewhere – more than 7 million have been displaced in Africa alone – the desperate plight of refugees caught up in the catastrophe of the Vietnam war and other conflicts in Indochina caused worldwide concern. The problem of resettlement of such vast numbers continued to demand a concerted political response, including the determination to tackle the root causes of displacement, which the developed world seemed unable to find.

In the decade after the end of the Vietnam war more than 1.6 million people fled the country, many of them taking to the seas in tiny fishing boats. One million of these began the painful process of rebuilding their lives in another country. Others did not have the chance. In the late 1980s thousands of Vietnamese refugees remained in camps throughout Southeast Asia, and the unstemmed flight of further numbers was placing enormous pressure on desperately meager resources. Western governments were unwilling to resettle Southeast Asians without clear proof of persecution, and the refugees faced forced repatriation or lengthy detention.

The tragedy of Cambodia

The area now known as Cambodia was occupied between the 6th and 15th centuries by the Khmer empire, a civilization that left the temple complex of Angkor Wat as its most durable legacy. On its break-up its territories were fought over for the next four centuries by the armies of Thailand and Vietnam, until it was brought under French control in the mid-19th century.

Cambodia became an independent state in 1953, following the collapse of French colonial power in Indochina. It was ruled by Norodom Sihanouk, first as king and then, after his abdication in 1955, as prime minister. He endeavored to remain neutral throughout the Vietnam war, maneuvering a course between the United States and the communist powers, until he was overthrown in 1970 by a military revolt while he was absent from the country on a trip to Moscow; a pro-US government, led by Marshal Lon Nol, was installed. Sihanouk formed a government in exile, which allied itself with the Cambodian communist movement (the Khmer Rouge), backed by Vietnam and China. The Lon Nol government became increasingly dependent on US military aid to fight the guerrillas and maintain its tenuous authority. Intensive US bombing of the countryside shattered the already fragile economy, and drove many people into the already overcrowded cities or into the ranks of the guerrillas.

In April 1975 Lon Nol's government fell and the Khmer Rouge occupied the capital, Phnom Penh. It looked as if the whole of Indochina would come under allied Marxist rule, but once in power the Khmer Rouge become dominated by a clique of intellectuals who had been students together in France. The most notorious of them, Pol Pot and Ieng Sary, had already begun to purge the movement of pro-Vietnamese elements, and they now ruthlessly suppressed and removed all other factions and groups within the Khmer Rouge. Sihanouk, though at first titular head of state, was imprisoned in his residence in the capital, and many of his family were killed.

The "killing fields" of Pol Pot

The regime emptied the cities, setting their populations to work on massive agricultural programs. Between 1975 and 1978 more than a million Cambodians died, either as a result of forced labor or in purges aimed at destroying the educated class of society, which it was feared might form a center of opposition to the regime. In the countryside mass graves ("killing fields") are testimony to the brutality of Pol Pot's regime.

Not content with remaking Cambodian society, the Khmer Rouge also sought to restore the ancient glory of the Khmer people through the recovery of territory lost to Vietnam in the 18th and 19th cen-turies. Border incursions provoked tension between the two countries, and the Pol Pot regime developed close links with China as the Vietnamese drew nearer to the Soviet Union.

In December 1978 Vietnam invaded Cambodia and replaced the Khmer Rouge with a client government led by Hun Sen. Thousands of refugees fled to the Thai border. Armed by China and aided by the

Sihanouk – an indefatigable politician As king of Cambodia Norodom Sihanouk, born in 1922, declared his country's independence from France. Overthrown in 1970, he allied himself with the Khmer Rouge and was reappointed head of state in 1975, until Pol Pot turned against him. He later formed an uneasy coalition with the Khmer Rouge and one other resistance group against the Vietnamese occupation.

ASEAN states and the United States, the remnants of the Khmer Rouge mounted attacks against the new regime.

Hun Sen's regime made only slow progress in recovery and reconstruction. The cost of supporting the regime placed an enormous strain on Vietnam's economy, and in 1988–89, with the encouragement of the Soviet Union, it began to withdraw its troops from Cambodia. A UN peace plan was signed in 1991 and UN-supervised elections in May 1993 resulted in the formation of a coalition government headed by the nationalist FUNCINPEC and the Cambodian People's Party (PCC). Prince Sihanouk returned to reclaim his crown but peace was marred by the guerilla activities of the Khmer Rouge, who continued fighting until 1998. The process of bringing to trial those who had committed human rights abuses under the Pol Pot regime slowly took shape during the late 1990s.

Testimony to horror A mass grave in one of the killing fields of Cambodia. Many victims of Pol Pot's regime died as a result of famine and disease; others were murdered in mass purges of "intellectuals".

A brutal regime A propaganda poster erected by the pro-Vietnamese government displays the stark brutalities of Pol Pot's drive to create a self-reliant peasant society.

ENVIRONMENTAL ISSUES

THE ACCELERATING PACE OF CHANGE · THE ENVIRONMENT AT RISK · DEVISING STRATEGIES FOR THE FUTURE

The environment of Southeast Asia is under great pressure from population increase and rapid economic growth. Air and water quality have deteriorated as a result of urban expansion, industrialization forest fires and the intensive use of fertilizers to increase food production. Plantations of rubber and oil palm have replaced large areas of the indigenous rainforest; elsewhere it is rapidly being cleared for commercial logging and farming. Deforestation increases water runoff, leading to erosion, loss of soil nutrients and silted rivers, but so far schemes to control the scale of timber extraction and encourage replanting have met with only limited success. The forest and mangroves of Vietnam and neighboring countries in Indochina suffered widespread damage during the Vietnam war (1961–75) and later political upheavals.

COUNTRIES IN THE REGION

Brunei (B), Cambodia (C), Indonesia (I), Laos (L), Malaysia (Ma), Myanmar (My), Philippines (P), Singapore (S), Thailand (T), Vietnam (V)

POPULATION AND WEALTH

	Highest	Middle	Lowest
Population (millions)	224.784 (I)	41.734 (My)	0.336 (B)
Population increase (annual growth rate, % 1990–95)	2.6% (L)	1.4% (S)	0.9% (T)
Energy use (kg per year per person of oil equivalent)	7,843 (S)	2,310 (Ma)	296 (My)
Purchasing power parity (Int$/per year)	25,772 (S)	6,790 (T)	1,255 (L)

ENVIRONMENTAL INDICATORS

CO$_2$ emissions ('000 tonnes/year)	296,132 (I)	106,604 (Ma)	308 (L)
Car ownership (% of pop.)	49%(B)	14%(Ma)	<1%(My)
Proportion of territory protected, including marine areas (%)	21% (B)	12% (L)	0.3% (My)
Forests as a % of original forest	65% (C)	30% (L)	3% (S)
Artificial fertilizer use (kg/ha/year)	3,287 (S)	158 (Ma)	2 (My)
Access to safe drinking water (% population; rural/urban)	100%/100% (S)	73%/88% (T)	12%/20% (C)

MAJOR ENVIRONMENTAL PROBLEMS AND SOURCES

Air pollution: urban high; high greenhouse gas emissions
Marine/coastal pollution: medium; *sources*: industry, agriculture, sewage, oil, foresty, fish farming
Land degradation: *types*: soil erosion, deforestation, habitat destruction; *causes*: agriculture, industry, population pressure
Resource issues: fuelwood shortage; inadequate drinking water and sanitation
Population issues: population explosion; urban overcrowding; inadequate health facilities
Major events: Burkit Suharto (1982–83), fire in coal seams and peat; Bangkok (1991), chemical explosion and fire; Indonesia forest fires (1997); flooding Mekong (2000); Manila garbage slide (2000)

THE ACCELERATING PACE OF CHANGE

The earliest, and greatest, changes to the environment of much of Southeast Asia came about with the domestication of rice between 9,000 and 5,000 years ago. Plains and river deltas were covered in complex wet-rice irrigation systems and mountain foothills were transformed by elaborate hillside terraces to grow rice. Only the region's extensive forested uplands and swampy, mangrove-fringed coasts were unaltered by farming.

The exploitation of the region's rich resources during the period of European colonialism brought further significant changes. The coastal deltas of the Irrawaddy in Myanmar and the Mekong in Vietnam were extensively cleared and drained to increase the area of land that could be used for growing profitable cash crops. Plantations growing rubber trees, introduced from South America, and other commercial crops such as oil palm replaced large areas of the original forest in Malaysia, Indonesia and southern Vietnam. Mining also had a widespread impact on the environment. Chinese miners had first extracted tin from the river gravels of Perak and Selangor in western Malaysia by hand, but their efforts were intensified by the introduction of dredgers and other European mining techniques, which have left many deep scars on the landscape.

Modern pressures

In recent times, population increase has put enormous strain on land and resources. The so-called "Green Revolution", which combined the planting of improved rice varieties with increased irrigation, fertilizers and pesticides, has had considerable success in raising food production to meet the growing demand. However, it has also had considerable impact on the ecology of lowland farming areas and on traditional land-use patterns.

Much of the region's primary forest has been depleted. Many areas have been categorized as belonging to the state, thereby opening the way for governments to lease the timber rights to private companies. The indigenous forest peoples have been dispossessed and widespread ecological damage resulted from the scramble for wealth on this new frontier. Where largescale clearance has taken place for settlement, tenacious grasses (*Imperata cylindrica*) may become established. These are hard to eradicate,

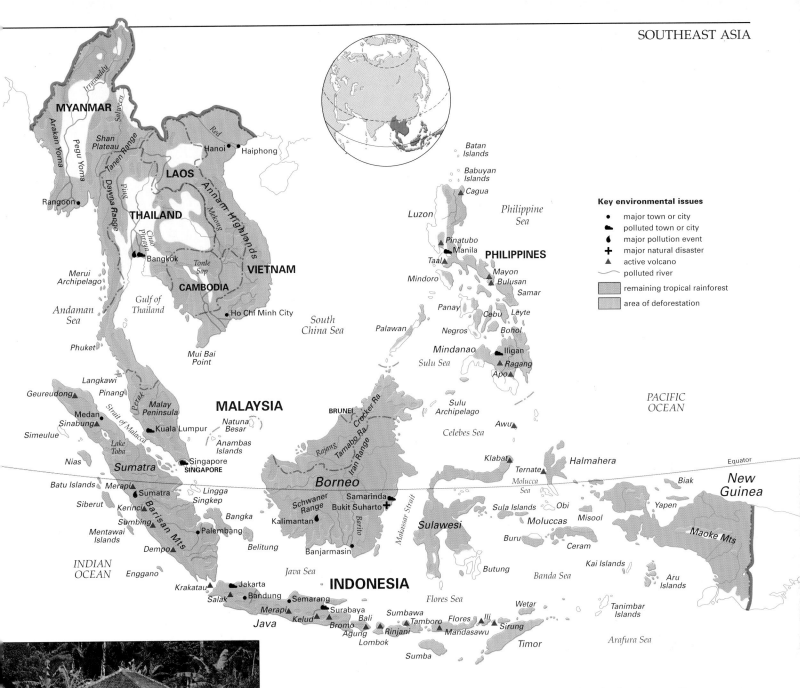

Key environmental issues

- • major town or city
- ◖ polluted town or city
- ◗ major pollution event
- ✚ major natural disaster
- ▲ active volcano
- 〜 polluted river
- ▦ remaining tropical rainforest
- ▦ area of deforestation

Map of environmental problems (*above*) Southeast Asia's forests are being cleared at an alarming rate both for timber and to grow food for the region's rapidly expanding population. Erosion and soil degradation are the inevitable result.

Buried by mud (*left*) A village and its crops in Java have been struck by a landslide caused by a flash flood. Intensive logging increases the risks of landslides by leaving the soils on stripped slopes vulnerable to slippage after seasonal heavy rains.

making reforestation difficult. If soils are left bare after plowing, severe erosion is likely to follow. A pattern of droughts and flash floods – with high risk to human life – replaces the thorough absorption and slow release of rainfall in the forests.

The roads cut by the loggers allow settlers to move in who often introduce farming methods and crops that are inappropriate for the fragile forest soils. Some of these new settlers are government sponsored. Indonesia has initiated several largescale resettlement schemes in the less populated islands to relieve population pressure in Java and Bali. Elsewhere, for example in Thailand and the Philippines, land hunger has fueled the migration of the rural poor into previously forested upland areas.

Rapid industrialization and growth of urban populations have brought serious problems of air and water pollution to the cities. More recently, developing industries have begun to move into the countryside to tap the large pool of unemployed rural labor, taking their pollution with them. In southern Thailand and on the west coast of peninsular Malaysia agricultural land is being turned into housing estates for workers; and the roads are constantly choked with trucks transporting industrial raw materials and finished goods. Coastal mangrove swamps – breeding grounds for fish and other aquatic life – are at risk from urban pollution, as well as from tourism and commercial prawn and shrimp farming.

THE ENVIRONMENT AT RISK

International environmentalists have identified the destruction of Southeast Asia's rainforests as a major contributor to global warming, caused by the buildup of carbon dioxide (CO_2) in the atmosphere. Tracts of forest act as a "sink" for CO_2, which is lost through largescale clearance; in addition, the burning that often accompanies clearing adds to carbon emissions, as does the breakdown of organic matter in the soil after clearance. In 1997 forest fires burned for several months in Sumatra and Kalimantan, Indonesia. They released an estimated 180 million tonnes of CO_2 into the atmosphere. Methane, produced by decomposing vegetation in wetlands and paddy fields and as a byproduct of digestion by ruminant animals such as cattle, is also a significant "greenhouse gas" – but is a less emotive issue than deforestation.

Although countries in the region are sensitive to their environmental image, they nevertheless defend their right to exploit their forests. However, logging companies interested in quick profits violate many of the rules drawn up for the proper management of forest and soil resources, and many ignore their obligation to replant. Logging increases the intensity of forest fires by leaving flammable detritus on the forest floor, and roads cut through the forest funnel the flames. A conflagration that destroyed 4.2 million ha (10 million acres) on the island of Borneo in 1982–83 spread in this way.

The threat to the rice supply
It is increasingly recognized that the success of the Green Revolution in boosting

Smokey Mountain (*right*) – a giant garbage heap in Manila – provides a living for hundreds of people. Regardless of the threats to health, many live in shacks built into the heap, which is continuously smoking due to the buildup of gases.

Deforestation of watersheds (*below*) Forest clearance has a far-reaching impact on river drainage systems. The forest acts as a sponge – once removed, less rain soaks into the ground and surface runoff increases, washing soils into the rivers.

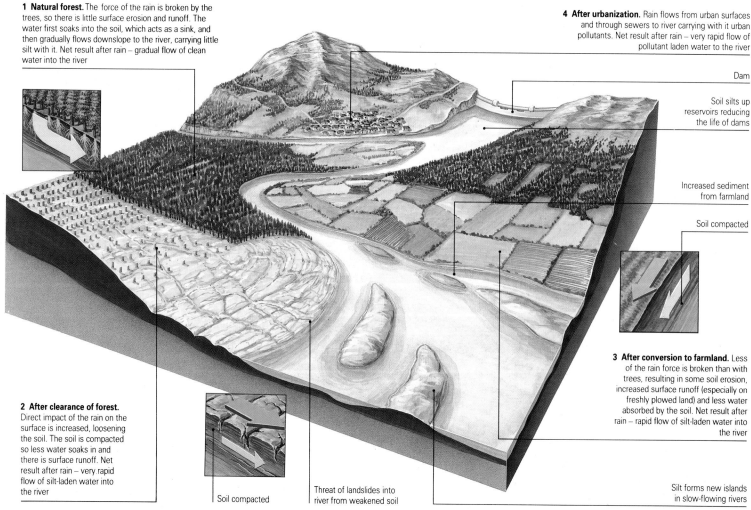

1 Natural forest. The force of the rain is broken by the trees, so there is little surface erosion and runoff. The water first soaks into the soil, which acts as a sink, and then gradually flows downslope to the river, carrying little silt with it. Net result after rain – gradual flow of clean water into the river

4 After urbanization. Rain flows from urban surfaces and through sewers to river carrying with it urban pollutants. Net result after rain – very rapid flow of pollutant laden water to the river

Dam

Soil silts up reservoirs reducing the life of dams

Increased sediment from farmland

Soil compacted

3 After conversion to farmland. Less of the rain force is broken than with trees, resulting in some soil erosion, increased surface runoff (especially on freshly plowed land) and less water absorbed by the soil. Net result after rain – rapid flow of silt-laden water into the river

2 After clearance of forest. Direct impact of the rain on the surface is increased, loosening the soil. The soil is compacted so less water soaks in and there is surface runoff. Net result after rain – very rapid flow of silt-laden water into the river

Soil compacted

Threat of landslides into river from weakened soil

Silt forms new islands in slow-flowing rivers

insect predators of the planthopper while it was safely maturing inside the rice stalk. A ban on many types of insecticide was imposed in Indonesia as attempts were made to find other measures of controlling the problem. The most successful method has been the use of a hormone that prevents the planthopper developing to sexual maturity.

Water and air pollution

Agricultural chemicals drain into water courses – one of many sources of pollution that affect water quality throughout the region. The Chao Phraya river in Thailand, which flows through the capital city of Bangkok, graphically illustrates some of the difficulties of providing clean water. Both sewage and domestic garbage are dumped directly in the river, along with industrial effluents. Bangkok contains at least 50,000 factories, too many for the city's hardpressed officials to monitor any failure to observe the regulations for treating waste water.

The Chao Phraya has consequently become an open sewer. The main offtake for Bangkok's water supply, 90 km (56 mi) from the mouth, is heavily polluted, with levels of health-threatening bacteria well above the limit set for drinking water, necessitating the addition of large quantities of chlorine to make it safe. The situation in the lower reaches is still worse. With an oxygen level of zero, the fish and shrimps that were still common in the estuarine waters only 10 years ago have entirely disappeared.

Rapid economic growth has meant that this pattern is repeated throughout the region. In Indonesia, the water supplies of Jakarta and Surabaya on Java are badly polluted with industrial waste, and are likely to deteriorate still further unless strong corrective measures are taken. Air pollution in the region has also increased due to a rapid growth in industrialization and urbanization with a resulting increase in energy consumption. Energy use doubled in the region between 1975 and 1995 as did carbon dioxide emissions. The use of poor quality fuel and the raging forest fires have also added to the deteriorating air quality. The region generally experiences low wind conditions, so pollutants are not readily dispersed. The number of vehicles is also increasing. The Singapore government has attempted to cut traffic levels by imposing heavy taxes on private cars and by constructing a subway system.

grain yields in the region's rice-growing lowlands has had unforeseen ecological consequences. A few new high-cropping rice varieties have displaced thousands of local strains. In Indonesia, it has been estimated that 1,500 rice varieties have been lost since 1975. Traditionally, farmers rotated the varieties they sowed on their plots, thereby reducing susceptibility to attack from disease and pests. Reliance on the new varieties, and the increasing practice of growing the same crop year after year, has heightened the need for nonspecific insecticides and pesticides. There has been a significant loss of genetic diversity in the region's staple food supply.

Some of the consequences have been worrying. Within seven years of the new varieties being introduced into Java, Indonesia's main rice-growing area, rice crops were devastated by a once minor pest, the brown planthopper. It was eventually realized that spraying the rice plants with insecticides destroyed the

FORESTS UP IN SMOKE

In 1997 forest fires, started in Kalimantan and Sumatra to clear ground for agricultural development, burned out of control for several months. Fires are the cheapest and often only available way for smallholders to clear ground for plantation and wildfires are a regular occurrence in the forests. However, in 1997 the situation was exacerbated by the climatic effects of El Niño and the period of drought in East Kalimantan which began in June of that year and lasted until April 1998 (some rain did fall during December 1997).

The fires destroyed about 1 million ha (2.4 million acres) of tropical forest and created a massive smoke haze which increased air pollution levels in the region significantly and released an estimated 180 million tonnes of carbon dioxide into the atmosphere. The smoke haze spread for more than 3,200 km (1,984 mi) over six Southeast Asian countries and even reached as far as Darwin, Australia. It affected about 70 million people, disrupted shipping and aviation, and even forced the closure of international airports. In the cities nearest the fires the Air Pollution Index, which measures levels of sulfur dioxide, nitrogen dioxide, carbon monoxide, ozone and dust particles, rose to critically high levels. This inevitably caused respiratory and other health problems; it has been estimated that the levels of pollution were equivalent to smoking 80 cigarettes a day and the death rate increased by several hundred people a day across the area of the smoke haze. The economic losses and ecological destruction have caused long-lasting damage to the whole of the region.

DEVISING STRATEGIES FOR THE FUTURE

Southeast Asian governments are under mounting pressure to safeguard the longterm future of their natural resources and environment. At the same time, they need to develop their economic and industrial base to support their growing populations. Development targets often take priority over conservation goals. Southeast Asia's timber trade is unsustainable; it has been estimated that, at current rates of logging, the reserves will last for no more than 40 years.

Southeast Asia's most urgent environmental requirement is to halt the present high rate of deforestation and restore the balance of forest loss. In countries such as Thailand, Vietnam and the Philippines, which have lost 78, 83 and 94 percent of their tree cover respectively, replanting is the only viable way to restore the forests. However, Indonesia and eastern Malaysia (Sarawak and Sabah on Borneo) are "forest rich" – despite the high rate of felling, the size of their indigenous forests is such that almost two-thirds of their land area remains forested. Theoretically, they should be able to rely on natural regeneration to stabilize their forest resources, but natural regeneration is slow and difficult to achieve.

Regrowing a flood barrier (*above*) Mangrove trees are being replanted under a new program in Java. Mangroves thrive in tidal waters and nurture a variety of plant and marine life. The roots accumulate soil and provide a crucial barrier in flood-prone coastal regions.

Commercial planting – pros and cons

The wood-processing industries are central to the economies of Indonesia, Malaysia, Thailand and the Philippines. Thailand is already having to import timber, as does peninsular Malaysia and the Philippines. The communist countries of Vietnam and Cambodia make heavy use of timber reserves for fuelwood. In every country in the region, therefore, there is a powerful need to maintain high levels of timber supply. Most reforestation schemes consist of largescale planting of introduced species such as *Acacia mangium* or, in drier areas, *Eucalyptus camaldulensis*, which are fast-growing and higher yielding than teak and other varieties of indigenous hardwoods.

It is argued that these plantations take pressure off the remaining areas of natural forest. But the introduced trees deprive the already poor forest soils of nutrients, and their susceptibility to pests and diseases means that their longterm sustainability is far from certain. While they provide dense cover, concentration on a single species means that the complex ecosystems of the natural forest are being destroyed.

Plantation schemes also have considerable social costs. In 1985, the government of Thailand set itself the target of restoring tree cover to 40 percent of the country. This was to be achieved through an extensive program of eucalyptus planting, known as the "Green Isan" project. However, in this ambitious scheme, the interests of the local forest communities were left entirely out of the reckoning, resulting in frequent conflicts between villagers and the plantation companies. Since the plantations encroached on communal forests, many villagers were displaced from their land. Large numbers settled illegally on other degraded areas of land within the forest reserves. Others have added their numbers to the stream of migrants that flock to the cities, particularly Bangkok.

A more positive approach has been adopted in the Philippines, where local farmers in an area surrounding a pulp processing mill have been given 10 ha (25 acres) of land. On 2 ha (5 acres) they grow food crops, and on the rest they raise quick-growing pulpwood trees. Because they are assured of an income through supplying the pulp to the mill and have comparative security of tenure, the scheme has won popular acceptance.

Pineapple and coconut (*left*) thrive in each other's company in the Philippines. The trees stabilize the soil in which the profitable crops are grown. Mixed land use is an increasingly common solution to balancing economic and ecological priorities.

Action for change

Environmental legislation in the region has not always been implemented, thanks to the weakness of institutions, such as government environment ministries, which are often underfunded and understaffed. Sometimes, it has taken an environmental disaster to bring about action. Following disastrous flash floods in Thailand in 1988, exacerbated by soil erosion caused by deforestation, the government imposed a total ban on logging. And yet smallscale illegal logging still occurs. Public participation in environmental management has been encouraged in some countries, notably Thailand, and non-governmental organizations (NGOs) have begun to emerge as important campaigners for the environment.

In the Philippines, an altogether more radical approach has been taken to environmental activism, with tree spiking (driving large nails into the trunks of trees, which makes it highly dangerous to cut them down with a chainsaw) becoming a common method of curbing the activities of the loggers. The 8th National Economic and Social Development Plan (1997–2001) of the Philippines places strong emphasis on sustainable forest management. Similarly, ASEAN (Association of Southeast Asian Nations) has adopted a Strategic Plan of Action for the Environment, which recognizes environmental protection as essential to the longterm future of the region.

EDUCATION SAVES THE CORAL REEFS

The coral reef around Bolinao in the northern Philippines is important as a spawning ground for 90 percent of the area's fish; it is also home to over 350 species of marine animals and plants. Fishing is the mainstay of local economy with over 50,000 people and about one-third of the villages of Bolinao municipality making a living from it. In 1993, a Taiwanese business consortium announced plans to build the world's largest cement factory on the coastline where it could quarry the limestone in the reef. About two-thirds of the local coral reefs had already been destroyed by dynamite and cyanide fishing and the over-exploitation of species such as sea urchins. A highly polluting cement industry was seen as the death knell for this vulnerable ecosystem with potential environmental damage from air pollution, dust, oil pollution and destruction of parts of the reef to widen the shipping channel.

The Marine Science Institute at the University of the Philippines undertook research on the threats to the reef and launched a local education campaign to teach the community about the richness and importance of the marine ecosystem. This spurred local citizens to take stock of their coastal resources and their importance to a sustainable local economy. They mounted a successful campaign against the cement factory plans and in 1996 the government denied the planning application. Since then the citizens and local environmental groups have worked together to develop a coastal resource management plan which allows the community to participate in decision-making about their marine areas. This grassroots approach has been a major success with a large degree of public acceptance of the coastal development plans. It has also provided a model for other communities and organizations in the Philippines.

The rainforest controversy

Southeast Asia's tropical rainforests are being felled at an unsustainable rate. Between 1976 and 1980, 1.5 million ha (3.7 million acres) of forest were being cut down every year; by 1986–90 this rate had more than doubled to 3.4 million ha (8.4 million acres) a year; by 1990 and 1995 the rate fell to 1.8 million ha (4.4 million acres). The region's forests are severely depleted and as long as conflicting economic interests continue to tussle for control over forest and land resources, sustainable management schemes have little chance of success.

The governments in the region generally divide the forests into three separate categories for management. Protected areas are set aside for the purposes of species conservation and watershed protection. Timber harvesting is carried out within productive areas of the forest. Finally, converted areas of forest land are set aside for farming, resettlement or industrial development. The most difficult problem is to prevent migrant settlers crossing the unmarked boundaries into the permanent forested areas. Only in peninsular Malaysia – where most of the rural population have been absorbed into urban industries or settled in agricultural schemes – is this avoided.

Timber harvesting should not result in deforestation. Most governments have established selective logging policies to ensure that only mature trees and certain varieties are taken. Seedlings and saplings must be replanted to allow the forest to regenerate. However, logging concessions are commonly let out to subcontractors who ignore the environmental protection laws to extract quick profits. There are too few forestry officials to police distant concessions, and very often the offenders have moved on before they can be caught; sometimes officials are bribed to turn a blind eye to violations.

The past practice in Myanmar and Thailand of using manual labor and elephants to harvest the forest caused little disturbance. But today the heavy machinery used may damage up to half the remaining trees, so the forest will not have regenerated when the next harvest is due. Elephants were still used in the teak forests of Myanmar until very recently, but since 1989 the government has been selling logging concessions to Thai firms no longer able to operate in their own country because of the ban on logging. Their heavy machinery has devastated forests in the borderlands of Myanmar, and they ignore the traditional obligation to replant.

Deep in the rainforest (*right*), a truck removes illegally cut trees. Patrolling for smallscale operations is difficult in remote areas where the forest is still abundant. Low-lying forests have been decimated and loggers are moving to higher altitudes.

"Don't build your home with ours" (*below*) The Penan people of Sarawak's forest have become passionate campaigners to stop largescale logging, which threatens their livelihoods. Control of resources is the central issue.

Both Malaysia and Indonesia have provided sponsorship for urgently needed largescale resettlement schemes on forest land. Such programs alleviate rural poverty and (in the case of Indonesia) also relieve population pressure in Java and Bali, which are both very densely populated. However, they have also attracted international criticism. In the past, farmers were encouraged to grow food crops, particularly rice, that were unsuited to the forest soils. Recently there has been a switch to tree-crop schemes, which are ecologically sounder but much more expensive to establish.

Clash of cultures

These resettlement schemes are also criticized for their negative impact on the forest peoples. Over hundreds of years, forest-dwellers in Southeast Asia have evolved systems for farming the forest and extracting its products without upsetting the ecological balance. In parts of West Kalimantan (the southern half of Borneo, belonging to Indonesia), centuries-old agroforestry systems have established managed forests of useful trees whose produce is gathered: tengkawang nuts and fruits such as durian and rambutan. Elsewhere in Kalimantan thorny rattan vines, used to make furniture and mats, are planted on cleared forest plots, to be harvested seven years or more later from the forest regrowth.

Yet the indigenous peoples' knowledge of the forest's ecology has been ignored by government departments responsible for forest management. Officials frequently attempted to attribute blame to indigenous people for the destruction of the forests. Sarawak has been the scene of particularly violent confrontations between indigenous peoples and loggers. In the most famous of these, a small group of hunter-gatherers, the Penan, who claimed the loggers were damaging their wild food and water supplies, blocked the paths of timber industry bulldozers. The Penan's campaign has received international support with one of their leaders even addressing the UN General Assembly in 1992. In 1999, two Penan communities won a court case against a logging company who had been illegally cutting the forest; the company was told to leave the area and to compensate the Penan. Governments in the region, sometimes under international pressure, have begun to acknowledge the rights of some indigenous people and their role in managing forests sustainably.

GLOSSARY

Acid rain Rain or any other form of PRECIPITATION that has become more acid by absorbing waste gases (for example, sulfur dioxide and nitrogen oxides) discharged into the ATMOSPHERE.

Acid soil Soil that has a pH of less than 7; it is often PEATY.

Added value A higher price fetched by an article or RESOURCE after it has been processed, such as crude oil after refining.

Agricultural economy An economy where most people work as cultivators or PASTORALISTS.

AIDS Acquired Immune Deficiency Syndrome, a disease that damages the body's immune system, making people more susceptible to disease. Human Immunodeficiency Virus (HIV) is one of the viruses that can lead to AIDS.

Air pollution The presence of gases and suspended particles in the air in high enough concentrations to harm humans, other animals, vegetation or materials. Human activity is the source of most pollution.

Alkaline soil Soil that has a pH of more than 7; chalk or limestone soils.

Alpine (1) A treeless ENVIRONMENT found on a mountain above the tree line but beneath the limit of permanent snow. (2) A plant that is adapted to grow in the TUNDRA-like environment of mountain areas.

Amphibian An animal that lives on land but whose life cycle requires some time in water.

Apartheid A way of organizing society to keep different racial groups apart. Introduced in South Africa by the National Party after 1948 as a means of ensuring continued white political dominance, it was dismantled in the 1990s.

Aquifer An underground layer of permeable rock, sand or gravel that absorbs and holds GROUNDWATER.

Arctic The northern POLAR region. In biological terms it also refers to the northern region of the globe where the mean temperature of the warmest month does not exceed 10°C (50°F).

Arid (climate) Dry and usually hot. Arid areas generally have less than 250 mm (10 inches) of rain a year.

Atmosphere The gaseous layer surrounding the Earth. It consists of nitrogen (78 percent), oxygen (21 percent), argon (1 percent), tiny amounts of carbon dioxide, neon, ozone, hydrogen and krypton, and varying amounts of water vapor.

Atoll A circular chain of CORAL reefs enclosing a lagoon. Atolls form as coral reefs fringing a volcanic island; as sea levels rise or the island sinks a lagoon is formed.

Autonomy The condition of being self-governing, usually granted to a subdivision of a larger STATE or to a territory belonging to it.

Balance of payments A statement of a country's transactions with all other countries over a given period.

Balance of power A theory of political stability based upon an even distribution of power among the leading STATES.

Basalt A fine-grained IGNEOUS ROCK. It has a dark color and contains little silica. Ninety percent of lavas are basaltic.

Bible The book of scriptures of CHRISTIANITY and JUDAISM. The Jewish Bible contains many books in common with the Christian version describing historical events and prophetic teachings, but the latter also includes accounts of the life and teachings of Jesus Christ.

Biodegradable (of a substance) easily broken down into simpler substances by bacteria or other decomposers. Products made of organic materials such as paper, woolens, leather and wood are biodegradable; many plastics are not.

Biodiversity The number of different species of plants and animals found in a given area. In general, the greater the number of species, the more stable and robust the ECOSYSTEM is.

Biomass The total mass of all the living organisms in a defined area or ECOSYSTEM.

Biosphere The thin layer of the Earth that contains all living organisms and the ENVIRONMENT that supports them.

Biotechnology Technology applied to biological processes, including genetic engineering, the manipulation of the genetic makeup of living organisms.

Birthrate The number of births expressed as a proportion of a population. Usually given as the annual number of live births per 1,000 population (also known as the crude birth rate).

Black economy The sector of the economy that avoids paying tax.

Bloc A group of countries closely bound by economic and/or political ties.

Boreal Typical of the northern climates lying between the ARCTIC and latitude 50°N, characterized by long cold winters and short summers. Vegetation in these regions is dominated by BOREAL FOREST.

Boreal forest The name given to the CONIFEROUS FORESTS or TAIGA of the northern hemisphere.

Brown coal A peat-like material, also known as lignite, which has a lower energy value than more mature forms of coal.

Buddhism A religion founded in the 6th and 5th centuries BC and based on the teachings of Siddhartha Gautama; it is widely observed in southern and southeast Asia.

Bureaucracy The body of STATE officials that carry out the day-to-day running of government. It may also refer to a system of a ministration marked by the inflexible application of rules.

Capital Machinery, investment funds or an employment relationship involving waged labor.

Capitalism A political and economic system based on the production of goods and services for profitable exchange in which labor is bought and sold for wages. Capitalist economies can be more or less regulated by governments. In a capitalist mixed economy the government owns some of the country's utilities and industries and also acts as a major employer.

Cash crop A crop grown for sale rather than for SUBSISTENCE.

Caste A system of rigid hereditary social divisions, normally associated with the Hindu caste system in India, where an individual is born into the caste of his or her parents, must marry within it, and cannot leave it.

Caucasian (1) A racial classification based on white or light skin color. (2) An inhabitant of the Caucasus region or the Indo-European language of this people.

Cereal A cultivated grass that has been bred selectively to produce high yields of edible grain for consumption by humans and livestock. The most important are wheat (*Triticum* sp.), rice (*Oryza sativa*) and maize (*Zea mays*).

CFCs (chlorofluorocarbons) Organic compounds made up of atoms of carbon, chlorine and fluorine. Gaseous CFCs used as aerosol propellants, refrigerant gases and solvent cleaners are known to cause depletion of the OZONE LAYER.

Christianity A religion based on the teachings of Jesus Christ and originating in the 1st century AD from JUDAISM; its main beliefs are found in the BIBLE. The Roman Catholic, Orthodox and Protestant churches are its major branches.

CITES (Convention on International Trade in Endangered Species) An international agreement signed by over 90 countries since 1973. SPECIES (FAUNA and FLORA) placed in Appendix I are considered to be in danger of EXTINCTION, and trade is prohibited without an export permit. Signatory countries must supply data to the World Conservation Union, which monitors IMPORTS and EXPORTS. Appendix II species may be threatened with extinction if trade is unregulated.

City-state An independent STATE consisting of a single city and the surrounding countryside needed to support it. Singapore is an example of a modern city-state.

Class (1) A group of people sharing a common economic position, for example large landowners, waged laborers or owners of small businesses. (2) (in zoology and botany) A rank in the taxonomic hierarchy coming between phylum and order. *See* CLASSIFICATION.

Classification A system of arranging the different types of living organisms according to the degree of similarity of their inherited characteristics. The classification system enables organisms to be identified and may also reveal the relationships between different groups. The internationally accepted classification hierarchy groups organisms first into divisions, then phyla, CLASSES, orders, FAMILIES, GENERA, SPECIES and SUBSPECIES.

Collectivization The organization of an economy (typically communist) by collective control through agencies of the state. *See* COMMUNISM.

Colonialism The political practice of occupying a foreign country for settlement and economic exploitation.

Colony A territory under the sovereignty of a foreign power.

COMECON The Council for Mutual Economic Assistance, formed in 1947 as an organization to further trade and economic cooperation between communist countries. It had 10 members before its collapse in 1989: the Soviet Union, Bulgaria, Czechoslovakia, Hungary, Poland, Romania, East Germany, Mongolia, Cuba, and Vietnam.

Commonwealth A loose association of STATES that were members of the former British EMPIRE, with the British monarch at its head.

Communism A social and economic system based on the communal ownership of property. It usually refers to the state-controlled social and economic systems in the former Soviet Union and Soviet-bloc countries and in the People's Republic of China. *See* SOCIALISM.

Coniferous forest A forest of mainly coniferous, or cone-bearing trees, frequently with evergreen needle-shaped leaves and found principally in the TEMPERATE ZONES and BOREAL regions.

Conservation The use, management and protection of NATURAL RESOURCES so that they are not degraded, depleted or wasted. *See also* SUSTAINABILITY.

Constitution The written statement of laws that defines the way in which a country is governed.

Consumer goods Goods that are acquired for immediate use, such as foodstuffs, radios, televisions and washing machines.

Continental climate The type of climate associated with the interior of continents. It is characterized by wide daily and seasonal ranges of temperature, especially outside the TROPICS, and by low rainfall.

Continental drift The theory that today's continents, formed by the breakup of prehistoric supercontinents, have slowly drifted to their present positions. The theory was first proposed by Alfred Wegener in 1912.

Continental shelf An extension of a continent, forming a shallow, sloping shelf covered by sea.

Coral A group of animals related to sea anemones and living in warm seas. Individuals, called polyps, combine to form a COLONY.

Culture (1) The beliefs, customs and social relations of a people. (2) The assumptions that a people make in interpreting their world.

Cyclone A center of low atmospheric pressure. Tropical cyclones are known as HURRICANES or typhoons.

Dead lake (or Dead river) An area of water in which dissolved oxygen levels have fallen as a result of acidification, overgrowth of plants or high levels of pollution, to the extent that few or no living things are able to survive.

Debt The financial obligations owed by a country to the rest of the world, usually repayable in US dollars. Total external debt includes public, publicly guaranteed, and private long-term debt.

Decolonization The transfer of government from a colonial power to the people of the COLONY at the time of political independence.

Deforestation The felling of trees and clearing of forested land to be put to other uses.

Delta A large accumulation of sediment, often fan-shaped, deposited where a river enters the sea or a lake.

Democracy A form of government in which policy is made by the people (direct democracy) or on their behalf (indirect democracy). Indirect democracy usually takes the form of competition among political parties at elections.

Desert A very ARID area with less than 25 cm (10 in) rainfall a year. In hot deserts the rate of evaporation is greater than the rate of PRECIPITATION, and there is little vegetation.

Desertification The creation of desert-like conditions usually caused by a combination of overgrazing, soil EROSION, prolonged DROUGHT and climate change.

Devaluation A deliberate reduction by a government in the exchange value of its own currency in gold, or in relation to the value of another currency.

Developed country Any country with high standards of living and a sophisticated economy, in contrast to DEVELOPING COUNTRIES. Various indicators are used to measure a country's wealth and material well-being: the GROSS NATIONAL PRODUCT, the PER CAPITA consumption of energy, the number of doctors per head of population and the average life expectancy, for example.

Developing country Any country that is characterized by low standards of living and a SUBSISTENCE economy. Sometimes called THIRD WORLD countries, they include most of Africa, Asia and Central and South America.

Dictator A leader who concentrates the power of the STATE in his or her own hands.

Divide see WATERSHED.

Dominant species The most numerous or prevailing SPECIES in a community of plants or animals.

Dormancy A period during which the metabolic activity of a plant or animal is reduced to such an extent that it can withstand difficult environmental conditions such as cold or DROUGHT.

Drought An extended period in which rainfall is substantially lower than average and the water supply is insufficient to meet demand.

EC *See* EUROPEAN COMMUNITY.

Ecology (1) The study of the interactions of living organisms with each other and with their ENVIRONMENT. (2) The study of the structure and functions of nature.

Ecosystem A community of plants and animals and the ENVIRONMENT in which they live and react with each other.

Effluent Any liquid waste discharged into the ENVIRONMENT as a byproduct of industry, agriculture or sewage treatment.

Emission A substance discharged into the air in the form of gases and suspended particles, from automobile engines and industrial smokestacks, for example.

Empire (1) A political organization of STATES and territories in which one dominates the rest. (2) The territory that constitutes such a group of states.

Endangered species A SPECIES whose population has dropped to such low levels that its continued survival is threatened.

Endemic species A SPECIES that is native to one specific area, and is therefore often said to be characteristic of that area.

Environment (1) The external conditions – climate, geology and other living things – that influence the life of individual organisms or ECOSYSTEMS. (2) The surroundings in which animals and plants live and interact.

Erosion The process by which exposed land surfaces are broken down into smaller particles or worn away by water, wind or ice.

Ethnic group A group of people sharing a social identity or **culture** based on language, religion, customs and/or common descent or kinship.

Euro The common currency of the EUROPEAN UNION, introduced in 1999. The euro operates at a fixed rate alongside the national currencies of member states until 2002, when it will supersede them. To enter the euro trading zone countries needed to meet financial convergence criteria set out in the Maastricht Treaty of 1992. Eleven countries did so: Austria, Belgium, Finland, France, Germany, Ireland, Italy, Luxembourg, the Netherlands, Portugal and Spain. Membership in the euro zone involves ceding control of monetary policy to the European Central Bank, which some countries – notably Britain – remain reluctant to do.

European Community (EC) An alliance of western European nations formed to agree common policies on trade, aid, agriculture and economics. The founder members in 1957 were France, West Germany, Belgium, Holland, Luxembourg and Italy. Britain, Ireland and Denmark joined in 1973, Greece in 1981 and

Spain and Portugal in 1986. East Germany became a member when it was reunited with West Germany in 1990. It became the EUROPEAN UNION with the Maastricht Treaty of 1992.

European Union (EU) The former EUROPEAN COMMUNITY, created by the Maastricht Treaty, which was signed in 1992 and implemented from 1993. The treaty gave the European parliament wider powers, setting the agenda for achieving full monetary and political union. Austria, Finland and Sweden joined the EU in 1995.

Evolution The process by which SPECIES develop their appearance, form and behavior through the process of NATURAL SELECTION, and by which new species or varieties are formed.

Exotic (animal or plant) Not native to an area but established after being introduced from elsewhere, often for commercial or decorative use.

Exports Goods and services sold to other countries, bringing in foreign exchange.

Extinction The loss of a local population of a articular SPECIES or even the entire species. It may be natural or be caused by human activity.

Family A taxonomic term for a group of related plants or animals. For example, the family Felidae (cat family) includes the lion, the tiger and all the smaller cats. Most families contain several GENERA, and families are grouped together into orders. *See* CLASSIFICATION.

Famine An acute shortage of food leading to widespread malnutrition and starvation.

Fault A fracture or crack in the Earth along which there has been movement of the rock masses.

Fauna The general term for the animals that live in a particular region.

Feudalism (1) A type of society in which landlords collect dues from the agricultural producers in return for military protection. (2) A hierarchical society of mutual obligations that preceded CAPITALISM in Europe.

First World A term sometimes used to describe the advanced industrial or DEVELOPED COUNTRIES.

Fjord A steep-sided inlet formed when the sea floods and covers a glaciated U-shaped valley. *See* GLACIATION.

Flora The plant life of a particular region.

Fossil fuel Any fuel, such as coal, oil and NATURAL GAS, formed beneath the Earth's surface under conditions of heat and pressure from organisms that died millions of years ago.

Free trade A system of international trade in which goods and services are exchanged without TARIFFS, QUOTAS or other restrictions.

GATT The General Agreement on Tariffs and Trade, a treaty that governs world imports and exports. Its aim is to promote FREE TRADE, but many countries impose TARIFF barriers to favor their own industries and agricultural produce.

GDP *See* GROSS DOMESTIC PRODUCT.

Genus (pl. genera) A level of biological CLASSIFICATION of organisms in which closely related SPECIES are grouped. For example, dogs, wolves, jackals and coyotes are all grouped together in the genus *Canis*.

Ghetto A slum area in a city that is occupied by an ETHNIC minority. The word originally referred to the area of medieval European cities to which Jews were restricted by law.

Glaciation The process of GLACIER and ice sheet growth, and their effect on the landscape.

Glacier A mass of ice formed by the compaction

and freezing of snow and which shows evidence of past or present movement.

Global warming The increase in the average temperature of the Earth that is believed to be caused by the GREENHOUSE EFFECT.

GNP *See* GROSS NATIONAL PRODUCT.

Greenhouse effect The effect of certain gases in the ATMOSPHERE, such as carbon dioxide and METHANE, in absorbing solar heat radiated back from the surface of the Earth and preventing its escape into space. Without these gases the Earth would be too cold for living things, but the burning of FOSSIL FUELS for industry and transportation has caused atmospheric levels of these gases to increase, and this is believed to be a cause of GLOBAL WARMING.

Green Revolution The introduction of high-yielding varieties of seeds (especially rice and wheat) and modern agricultural techniques to increase agricultural production in DEVELOPING COUNTRIES. It began in the early 1960s.

Gross Domestic Product (GDP) The total value of a country's annual output of goods and services, with allowances being made for depreciation. Growth in GDP is usually expressed in constant prices to offset the effects of inflation. GDP is a useful guide to the level of economic activity in a country.

Gross National Product (GNP) A country's GROSS DOMESTIC PRODUCT plus income from abroad.

Groundwater Water that has percolated into the ground from the Earth's surface, filling pores, cracks and fissures. An impermeable layer of rock prevents it from moving deeper so that the lower levels become saturate . The upper limit of saturation is known as the WATER TABLE.

Growing season The period of the year when the average temperature is high enough for plants to grow. It is longest at low altitudes and latitudes. Most plants can grow when the temperature exceeds 5°C (42°F).

Habitat The external ENVIRONMENT to which an animal or plant is adapted and in which it prefers to live, usually defined in terms of vegetation, climate or altitude – eg grassland habitat.

Hard currency A currency used by international traders because they think it is safe from DEVALUATION.

Hinduism A body of religious practices, originating in India in the 2nd millennium BC, that emphasizes ways of living rather than ways of thought. Its beliefs and practices are based on the Vedas and other scriptures and are closely intertwined with the culture of India's people.

HIV (Human Immunodeficiency Virus) *See* AIDS.

Hunter-gatherers People who obtain their food requirements by hunting wild animals and gathering the berries and fruits from wild plants.

Hurricane A tropical CYCLONE, usually found in the Caribbean and western North Atlantic.

Hybrid An animal or plant that is the offspring of two genetically different individuals. Hybrid crops are often grown because they give higher yields and are more resistant to disease.

Ice age A long period of geological time in which the temperature of the Earth falls, and snow and ice sheets are present throughout the year in mid and high latitudes.

Igneous rock Rock formed when magma (molten material in the Earth's crust) cools and solidifies.

Imperialism The process whereby one country forces its rule on another country, frequently in order to establish an EMPIRE.

Imports Goods and services purchased from other countries.

Import substitution industry Any industry that has been set up (mainly in DEVELOPING COUNTRIES) to manufacture products that used to be imported. Import substitution industries are normally simple ones with an immediate local market, such as the manufacture of cigarettes, soap and textiles. They are protected during their start-up phase by high TARIFFS on foreign rivals.

Indigenous peoples The original inhabitants of a region, generally leading a traditional way of life.

Inflation The general rise in prices when the supply of money and credit in an economy is increasing faster than the availability of goods and services.

Islam A religion based on the revelations of God to the prophet Muhammed in the 7th century AD, which are contained in the Qu'ran. Islam is widely practiced throughout North Africa, the Indian subcontinent, the Middle East and parts of Southeast Asia.

Judaism A religion founded in 2000 BC among the ancient Hebrews and practiced by Jews; its main beliefs are contained in the BIBLE.

Labor force The economically active population of a country or region, including the armed forces and the unemployed. Full-time homemakers and unpaid caregivers are not included.

Leaching The process by which water washes nutrients and minerals downward from one layer of soil to another, or into streams.

Legislature The branch of government responsible for enacting laws.

Mammal A vertebrate animal of the CLASS Mammalia, with a four-chambered heart, fur or hair, and mammae (nipples) for feeding its young on milk. Except for monotremes, mammals do not lay eggs but give birth to live young.

Mangrove A dense forest of shrubs and trees growing on tidal coastal mudflats and estuaries throughout the tropics.

Maquis The typical vegetation of the Mediterranean coast, consisting of aromatic shrubs, laurel, myrtle, rock rose, broom and small trees such as olive, fig and holm oak.

Maritime climate A generally moist climate close to the sea, whose slow cooling and heating reduces variations in temperature.

Market economy An economy in which most activities are transacted by private individuals and firms in largely unregulated markets.

Marxism The system of thought derived from the 19th-century political theorist Karl Marx, in which politics is interpreted as a struggle between economic CLASSES. It promotes communal ownership of property when it is practiced, so is popularly known as COMMUNISM.

Methane A gas produced by decomposing organic matter that burns without releasing pollutants and can be used as an energy source. Excessive methane production from vast amounts of animal manure is believed to contribute to the GREENHOUSE EFFECT.

Migrant workers Part of the LABOR FORCE which has come from another region or country, looking for temporary employment.

Monetarism An economic philosophy that sees INFLATION as the main menace to economic growth and proposes a direct relationship between the rate of growth of the money supply of a country and its subsequent rate of inflation.

Monsoon (1) The wind systems in the TROPICS that reverse their direction according to the seasons. (2) The rain caused by these winds.

Montane The zone at middle altitudes on the slopes of mountains, below the ALPINE zone.

NAFTA The North American Free Trade Agreement, signed by Canada, Mexico and the United States, and implemented on 1 January 1994, lowering trade barriers between them, though many in the US and Canada feared the massive loss of jobs to less expensive Mexico.

Nation A community that believes it consists of a single people, based upon historical and cultural criteria and sharing a common territory. Sometimes used interchangeably with STATE.

Nationalism An ideology that assumes all NATIONS should have their own STATE, a NATION-STATE, in their own territory, the national homeland.

Nation-state A STATE in which the inhabitants all belong to one NATION. Most states claim to be nation-states; in practice almost all of them include minority groups.

Natural gas A FOSSIL FUEL in the form of a flammable gas that occurs naturally in the Earth. It is often found with deposits of petroleum.

Natural resources REOURCES created by the Earth's natural processes including mineral deposits, FOSSIL FUELS, soil, air, water, plants and animals. Most natural resources are harvested by people for use in agriculture, industry and economic activities.

Natural selection The process by which organisms not well suited to their ENVIRONMENT are eliminated by predation, parasitism, competition, etc, and those that are well suited survive, breed and pass on their genes.

Nomad A member of a (usually pastoral) people that moves seasonally from one place to another in search of food, water or pasture for their animals. *See* PASTORALIST.

Nonrenewable resource A NATURAL RESOURCE that is present in the Earth's makeup in finite amounts (coal, oil etc) and cannot be replaced once reserves are exhausted.

OECD (Organization for Economic Cooperation and Development) An international organization set up in 1961 to promote the economic growth of its (now 24) member countries.

One-party system A political system in which there is no competition to the government PARTY at elections (eg communist and military regimes) and all but the government party is banned.

OPEC The Organization of Petroleum Exporting Countries, an 11-member cartel that is able to exercise a degree of control over the price of oil.

Ozone layer A band of enriched oxygen or ozone found in the upper ATMOSPHERE. It absorbs harmful ultraviolet radiation from the Sun. The heat this creates provides a cap for the Earth's weather systems.

Pangea The supercontinent that was composed of all the present-day continents and therefore included both Gondwanaland and Laurasia. It existed between 250 and 200 million years ago. *See also* CONTINENTAL DRIFT.

Parliamentary democracy A political system in which the LEGISLATURE (parliament) is elected by all the adult members of the population and the government is formed by the PARTY that commands a majority in the parliament.

Party An organized group seeking political power to implement an agreed set of policies.

Pastoralism A way of life based on tending herds

of animals such as sheep, cattle, goats or camels; often NOMADIC, it involves moving the herds as the seasons change.

Peat Soil formed by an accumulation of plant material incompletely decomposed due to low temperature and lack of oxygen, usually as a result of waterlogging.

Per capita Per head of population.

Permafrost Soil and rock that remains permanently frozen, typically in the POLAR REGIONS. A layer of soil at the surface may melt in summer, but refreezes in colder conditions.

Pesticide Any chemical substance used to control the pests that can damage crops, such as insects and rodents. Often used as a general term for herbicides, insecticides and fungicides.

pH A measurement on the scale 0–14 of the acidity or alkalinity of a substance.

Plateau A large area of level, elevated land. When bordered by steep slopes it is called a tableland.

Polar regions The regions that lie within the lines of latitude known as the ARCTIC and Antarctic circles, respectively 66°32′ north and south of the Equator. At this latitude the sun does not set in midsummer nor rise in midwinter.

Polder An area of level land at or below sea level obtained by land reclamation. It is normally used for agriculture.

Poverty line A measure of deprivation that varies from country to country. In low-income economies a certain percentage of the population lacks sufficient food and shelter. In the industrial world people are considered to be poor if they earn less than 60 percent of the average wage.

PPP Purchasing power parity – a way of measuring income or GDP for different countries based on standardized dollar values, rather than the conventional method of converting different currencies according to official exchange rates. By taking away the currency exchange factor, PPP is less prone to fluctuations that may distort the comparisons between countries.

Prairie The flat grassland in the interior of North America between 30°N and 55°N, much of which has been plowed and is used to grow CEREALS.

Precipitation Moisture that reaches the Earth from the ATMOSPHERE, including mist, dew, rain, sleet, snow and hail.

Predator An animal that feeds on another animal (the PREY).

President A head of state, elected in some countries directly by the voters and in others by members of the LEGISLATURE. In some political systems the president is chief executive, in others the office is largely ceremonial.

Prey An animal that a PREDATOR hunts and kills for food.

Productivity (1) A measure of economic output in relation to the quantity of economic inputs (labor, machines, land, etc) needed for production. (2) The amount of weight (or energy) gained by an individual, a SPECIES or an ECOSYSTEM per unit of area per unit of time.

Quota A limit imposed on the amount of a product that can be imported in a given time.

Radioactivity The emission of alpha-, beta- and gamma particles from atomic nuclei. This is greatest when the atom is split, as in a nuclear reactor. Prolonged exposure to radioactive material can cause damage to living tissue, leading to cancers and ultimately death.

Rainforest Forest in which there is abundant rainfall all year long – in tropical as well as TEMPERATE ZONES. Rainforests probably contain half of all the Earth's plant and animal species.

Refuge A place where a SPECIES of plant or animal has survived after formerly occupying a much larger area.

Resource Any material, source of information or skill that is of economic value to industry and business.

Runoff Water produced by rainfall or melting snow that flows across the land surface into streams and rivers.

Salinization The accumulation of soluble salts near or at the surface of soil in an ARID climate. Salinization can also occur when water used for irrigation evaporates; the land becomes so salty that it is worthless for cultivation.

Savanna A HABITAT of open grassland with scattered trees in tropical and subtropical areas. There is a marked dry season and too little rain to support large areas of forest.

Second World A term sometimes used to describe the DEVELOPED socialist countries (including the former Soviet Union and former Soviet bloc).

Semiarid land Any area between an ARID DESERT and a more fertile region where there is sufficient moisture to support a little more vegetation than can survive in a desert. Also called semidesert.

Separatism A political movement in a STATE that supports the secession of a particular minority group, within a defined territory, from that state.

Service industries Industries that supply services to customers or to other sectors of the economy: typically banking, transport, insurance, education, healthcare, retailing and distribution.

Shanty town An area of very poor housing consisting of ramshackle huts and other simple dwellings often made from waste materials and with inadequate services.

Shifting cultivation A method of farming prevalent in tropical areas in which a piece of land is cleared and cultivated until its fertility is diminished. The farmer then abandons the land, which restores itself naturally.

Slash-and-burn farming A method of farming in tropical areas in which the vegetation cover is cut and burned to fertilize the land before crops are planted. Often a feature of SHIFTING CULTIVATION.

Socialism An economic system and political ideology based upon the principle of equality between people, the redistribution of wealth and property, and equal access to benefits such as healthcare and education.

Solar energy The radiant energy, produced by the Sun, that powers all the Earth's processes. It can be captured and used to provide domestic heating or converted to produce electrical energy.

Specialization (in natural history) The evolutionary development of a SPECIES, leading to narrow limits of tolerance and a restricted role (or niche) in the community.

Species The basic unit of CLASSIFICATION of plants and animals. Species are grouped into GENERA and variations may be categorized into SUBSPECIES in descending order of hierarchy.

State The primary political unit of the modern world, usually defined by its possession of sovereignty over a territory and its people.

Steppe An open grassy plain with few trees or shrubs, characterized by low andsporadic rainfall, with fluctuating temperatures during the year.

Subsistence A term applied to systems in which producers can supply their own needs for food, shelter, etc but have little or no surplus to trade.

Subspecies A rank in the CLASSIFICATION of plants and animals between SPECIES and variety. It often denotes a geographical variation of a species.

Subtropical The climate zone between the TROPICS and TEMPERATE ZONES. There are marked seasonal changes of temperature but it is never very cold.

Succession The development and maturation of an ECOSYSTEM, through changes in the types and abundance of SPECIES.

Sustainability The concept of using the Earth's NATURAL RESOURCES to improve people's lives without diminishing the ability of the Earth to support life today and in the future.

Taiga The CONIFEROUS FOREST and PEAT landbelt that stretches around the world in the northern hemisphere, south of the TUNDRA and north of the DECIDUOUS forests and grasslands.

Tariff A tax on imported goods or services.

Taxonomy The scientific CLASSIFICATION of organisms.

Temperate zone Any one of the climatic zones in mid latitudes, with a mild climate. They cover areas between the warm TROPICS and cold POLAR REGIONS.

Terrestrial (of a plant, animal etc) spending its entire life cycle on the land.

Third World A term first used to refer to ex-COLONIES that were neither fully capitalist (FIRST WORLD) nor fully socialist (SECOND WORLD). Now used to refer to the poorer, less industrialized countries of the developing world.

Tribe A group of people united by a common language, religion, customs and/or descent and kinship; often used to describe the social groups of peoples who have no developed STATE or government and whose social organization is based on ancestry and extended family systems.

Tropics The area of the Earth lying between the Tropic of Cancer (23°30′ N) and the Tropic of Capricorn (23°30′ S).

Tundra The level, treeless land lying in the very cold northern regions of Europe, Asia and North America, where winters are long and cold and the ground beneath the surface is permanently frozen. See also PERMAFROST.

Urbanization (1) The process by which city populations grow as the rural population diminishes. (2) City formation and growth.

Water table The uppermost level of underground rock that is permanently saturated with GROUNDWATER.

Watershed The boundary line dividing two river systems. It is also known as a water-parting or divide, particularly in the United States, where the word watershed refers to a river basin (the area drained by a river and its tributaries).

Welfare state A social and economic system based on STATE provision of healthcare, pensions and unemployment insurance. These services are financed by contributions from the working population, and access is intended to be available to all, free of charge.

Wetland A HABITAT that is waterlogged all or enough of the time to support vegetation adapted to these conditions.

INDEX

Page numbers in **bold** refer to extended treatment of topic; in *italics* to caption, maps or tables

Acknowledgments

CONTRIBUTORS

General Advisory Editor
Professor Peter Haggett, University of Bristol, UK

COUNTRY PROFILES

Advisory Editor
Dr Victor R. Savage, National University of Singapore, Singapore

Writers
Asgard Publishing Services:
Philip Gardner
Allan Scott
Michael Scott Rohan
Andrew Shackleton
John and Barbara Baines
Ann Furtado

REGIONAL PROFILES

Advisory Editors

Professor Ken J. Gregory, Goldsmith's College, London, UK
Physical Geography

Robert Burton, Huntingdon, UK
Habitats and their Conservation, Animal Life

Professor D.M. Moore, University of Reading, UK
Plant Life

Dr John Tarrant, University of East Anglia, UK
Agriculture

Dr Ian Hamilton, London School of Economics, UK
Industry

Dr Stuart Corbridge, University of Cambridge, UK
Economy

Dr Alisdair Rogers, University of Oxford, UK
Peoples and Cultures

Professor John Rennie Short, Syracuse University, USA
Cities

Dr Peter Taylor, University of Newcastle upon Tyne, UK
Government

Dr Michael Williams, University of Oxford, UK
Environmental Issues

Writers

Professor Ian Douglas, University of Manchester, UK
Physical Geography

Dr Kathy MacKinnon, Environmental Management Development in Indonesia, Kalimantan Selatan, Indonesia
Habitats and their Conservation

Drs Wim J.M. Verheugt, Beuningen, The Netherlands
Animal Life

Dr T.C. Whitmore, University of Cambridge, UK   *Plant Life*

Dr Jonathan Rigg, School of Oriental and African Studies, University of London, UK
Agriculture, Peoples and Cultures

Dr Stewart Richards, University of British Columbia, Canada
Industry

Professor Christopher Dixon, London Guildhall University, UK   *Economy, Cities*

Dr James Cotton, National University of Singapore, Singapore
Government

Dr Lesley Potter, University of Adelaide, Australia
Environmental Issues

Updated edition:

Editorial Director: Graham Bateman
Project Manager: Lauren Bourque
Cartography Manager: Richard Watts
Cartography Editor: Tim Williams
Editorial Assistant: Rita Demetriou
Picture Manager: Claire Turner
Picture Research: Alison Floyd
Design: Martin Anderson
Typesetting: Brian Blackmore
Production: Clive Sparling, Nicolette Colborne

Further Reading

Aitken, S.R. and Leigh, C.H. *Vanishing Rain Forests: the Ecological Transition in Malaysia* (Clarendon Press, Oxford, 1992)

Atkinson, J.M. and Errington, S. (eds.) *Power and Difference: Gender in Island Southeast Asia* (Stanford University Press, Palo Alto, California, 1990)

Dauvergne, Peter *Shadows in the Forest: Japan and the Politics of Timber in Southeast Asia* (MIT Press, Cambridge, MA, 1997)

Dixon, C., Agnew, J., Lee, R., Gregory, D. and Taylor, P. (eds.) *South East Asia in the World-Economy: A Regional Geography* (Cambridge University Press,Cambridge, 1994)

Forbes, D.K *Asian Metropolis: Urbanisation and the South-East Asian City* (Oxford University Press, Oxford, 1996)

Forshee, J., Fink, C. and Cate, S. *Converging Interests: Traders, Travelers and Tourists in Southeast Asia* (University of California: Center for Southeast Asian Studies, Berkeley, 1999)

Hall, R. and Linington, S. *Biogeography and Geological Evolution of Southeast Asia* (Balogh Scientific Books, Champaign, Illinois, 1998)

Kummer, D.M. *Deforestation in the Postwar Philippines* (University of California Press, Berkeley, 1991)

Rigg, J. *Southeast Asia: a Region in Transition* (Unwin Hyman, London, 1991)

Thurston, H.D. *Slash/Mulch Systems: Sustainable Agriculture in the Tropics* (Westview Press, Boulder, Colorado, 1997)

Weightman, B. *Dragons and Tigers: A Geography of South, East and Southeast Asia* (Wiley, John & Sons, Toronto, 2001)

Whitmore, T.C. *Wallace's Line and Plate Tectonics* (Clarendon, Oxford, 1981)

Useful websites:
www.cia.gov/cia/publications/factbook
www.hurricane.com
www.globalissues.org
www.whyfiles.news.wisc.edu

www.virtualhouse.org
www.census.gov/statab
www.igc.org
www.worldwatch.org